How JavaScript Works

How JavaScript Works

Douglas Crockford

virgule
solidus

Front Matter

Did I hear you right, did I hear you sayin'
that you're gonna make a copy of a game
without payin'? Come on, guys, I thought
you knew better. Don't copy that floppy.
MC Double Def DP

How JavaScript Works
Douglas Crockford

Copyright ©2018 Douglas Crockford

ISBN-13 978-1-94-981500-9 Paperback.
ISBN-13 978-1-94-981501-6 Hardcover.
ISBN-13 978-1-94-981502-3 EPUB.

The publisher offers excellent discounts on this book when ordered in quantity for bulk purchases or special sales which may include customized covers. For more information, please contact sales@virgule-solidus.com.

QA76.73.J39
005.2762

Chapter List

Raindrops on roses and whiskers on kittens.
Not Maria Augusta von Trapp

```
[
    {"number": 0, "chapter": "Read Me First!"},
    {"number": 1, "chapter": "How Names Work"},
    {"number": 2, "chapter": "How Numbers Work"},
    {"number": 3, "chapter": "How Big Integers Work"},
    {"number": 4, "chapter": "How Big Floating Point Works"},
    {"number": 5, "chapter": "How Big Rationals Work"},
    {"number": 6, "chapter": "How Booleans Work"},
    {"number": 7, "chapter": "How Arrays Works"},
    {"number": 8, "chapter": "How Objects Work"},
    {"number": 9, "chapter": "How Strings Work"},
    {"number": 10, "chapter": "How Bottom Values Work"},
    {"number": 11, "chapter": "How Statements Work"},
    {"number": 12, "chapter": "How Functions Work"},
    {"number": 13, "chapter": "How Generators Work"},
    {"number": 14, "chapter": "How Exceptions Work"},
    {"number": 15, "chapter": "How Programs Work"},
    {"number": 16, "chapter": "How this Works"},
    {"number": 17, "chapter": "How Classfree Works"},
    {"number": 18, "chapter": "How Tail Calls Work"},
    {"number": 19, "chapter": "How Purity Works"},
    {"number": 20, "chapter": "How Eventual Programming Works"},
    {"number": 21, "chapter": "How Date Works"},
    {"number": 22, "chapter": "How JSON Works"},
    {"number": 23, "chapter": "How Testing Works"},
    {"number": 24, "chapter": "How Optimizing Works"},
    {"number": 25, "chapter": "How Transpiling Works"},
    {"number": 26, "chapter": "How Tokenizing Works"},
    {"number": 27, "chapter": "How Parsing Works"},
    {"number": 28, "chapter": "How Code Generation Works"},
    {"number": 29, "chapter": "How Runtimes Work"},
    {"number": 30, "chapter": "How Wat! Works"},
    {"number": 31, "chapter": "How This Book Works"}
]
```

Chapter 0

Read Me First!

○ ○ ○ ○ ○

> Few images invoke the mysteries and
> ultimate certainties of a sequence of random
> events as well as that of the proverbial
> monkey at a typewriter.
> *George Marsaglia*

JavaScript is not very pretty, but it works.

This book is for people who have had some experience with JavaScript, and want to have a better, deeper understanding of how it works and how to use it well. It is also for experienced programmers who are looking to understand the workings of another language.

This book is not for beginners. I hope to someday write a book for beginners. This is not that book. This is not a light book. If you skim it, you will likely get nothing from it.

This book is not about JavaScript engines or virtual machines. It is about the language itself and the things every programmer should know about it. This book is a radical reappraisal of JavaScript, how it works, how it could be made better, and how it can be better used. It is about how to think about JavaScript and how to think *in* JavaScript. I am going to pretend that the current version of the language is the only version. I am not going to waste your time by showing how things worked in ES1 or ES3 or ES5. That does not matter. The focus is on how JavaScript works for us now.

This book is not comprehensive. There are large, complex chunks of the language that will be dismissed without a word. If I fail to mention your most favorite feature, that is most likely because that feature is crap. I will not be paying much attention to syntax. I am assuming that you already know how to write an `if` statement. If you need assistance with those sorts of details, ask JSLint. `jslint.com`

There are some useful parts of the language that I will spend little time on, such as most of the methods in the primordial prototypes. There are excellent online reference materials for that. My favorite resource is Mozilla Foundation.
`developer.mozilla.org/en-US/docs/Web/JavaScript/Reference`

An important goal in programming language design is to produce a clean, logical language that composes well and is free of weird corner cases. JavaScript came nowhere close to meeting that goal. It gets worse with each revision as more features are agglutinated. The language is full of weird corner and edge cases. This book illuminates only a few of those corners, just to show that there are monsters there. Stay away from the corners and edges. Do not go into the dark. Stay in the part of the language that is simple and clean. Everything you need to write good programs is there.

Ten years ago I wrote a cranky little pamphlet about JavaScript. The premise was unusual, that whilst JavaScript was obviously a mess, there was buried deep inside of it a very good language. By avoiding the bad parts, you could write good programs.

This was quite at odds with the opinion of some programming experts that mastery can only be demonstrated by exploiting all of a language's features. They believed strongly, without any need of proof, that features exist for the demonstration of mastery, so there are no bad features.

That opinion still seems to dominate even though it is deeply wrong. True mastery is shown by writing good programs that are readable, maintainable, and free of error. If you ever feel the need to show off, try doing that. Being a humble programmer, I am always looking at myself and my work, seeking to improve my skills. I have learned the hard way that optimizing for feature exploitation is counterproductive.

This is my most powerful tool for improving a programming language:

> If a feature is sometimes useful and sometimes dangerous and if there is a better option then always use the better option.

So armed, I am always looking to make the language I use smaller and better, to avoid if I can the features that are more likely to create bugs. I am still refining my ideas about what is good practice and what is not. This book represents my latest thinking about JavaScript. I am able to write about JavaScript's good parts only because JavaScript has good parts. Compared to a decade ago, I think less of the language is good, but I think that good part is better.

JavaScript has become the most important programming language in the world. That is at least partly my fault. Sorry. The issuing of new editions of the ECMAScript standard has not repaired JavaScript's deep problems, and sometimes creates new problems. A standards committee has limited power to repair a language. They have almost limitless power to grow the language, increasing its complexity and weirdness. They also have the power to not make things worse, but where is the fun in that?

Aging programming languages suffer from a bad plastic surgery addiction. They are desperately injecting new features in the fevered hope of remaining popular, or at least fashionable. Feature bloat is as big and as deep of a problem as code bloat. I think that we should instead praise JavaScript's inner beauty.

I also recommend that you get the ECMAScript standard. It can be tough reading, but it is free. `www.ecma-international.org/publications/standards/Ecma-262.htm`

Reading the ECMAScript standard literally changed my life. Like most people, I started writing JavaScript without first bothering to learn it well. I found the language to be faulty, confusing, and irritating. It wasn't until I got around to reading the ECMAScript standard for myself that I discovered JavaScript's brilliance.

Heresy

This book about a programming language will make some people angry. I am a harbinger of the next paradigm, and that is threatening to the keepers of the old paradigm. I am used to this. I was attacked when I discovered that JavaScript has good parts, which turned out to be the first important discovery of the 21st century. I was attacked when I discovered JSON, which is now the world's best loved data interchange format.

Communities form around shared beliefs, and communities can provide benefits to their members even when those beliefs are wrong. Communities can feel threatened when those beliefs are questioned. I am a heretic. I value the pursuit of truth over the benefits of community. That is offensive to some people.

I am just a programmer who is trying to figure out the best way to write programs. I might be wrong, but I am working really hard to get it right. Many of the patterns of thought in our profession were cemented in the FORTRAN era. I think it is time that we move beyond that. Change is hard, even in the most innovative of professions.

If you are offended by heresy, then put this book back on the shelf and walk away.

Code

All of the code in this book is in the Public Domain. You are free to use it for any purpose, but please do not use it for evil. Try to do some good with it if that is at all possible.

I strongly recommend that you do not copy and paste code that you do not understand, even mine. This seems to have become a standard practice, but it is dangerous and reckless. It is not nearly as stupid as installing packages that you haven't even looked at, but it is still really bad. Given the current state of the art, the most important security filter is your brain. Use it. This is important.

I make no claim that the programs presented in this book are perfect. I do claim that the programs I am writing now are better than what I was writing ten years ago. I work hard at trying to get better at this. I am hoping that I live long enough to finally get it right. I hope that you do, too. In the meantime, erratums for this book can be found at the book's website. In Latin, the plural of **erratum** is **errata** as is done with second declension neuter nouns in the nominative case. But I am writing in Modern English, and in Modern English we should be forming plural nouns by appending -**s**, or in cases of excess sibilance, -**es**. So, yes, **erratums**. Given a choice between progress and tradition, I am going with progress informed by the lessons of history. That is how things are made better. howjavascriptworks.com/erratums

Please report my many blunders to erratum@howjavascriptworks.com.

Next

This book is about JavaScript, but I sometimes talk about *The Next Language*, the language that will replace JavaScript. I have to believe that there will be a language after JavaScript, because if JavaScript is the last language, that would be really sad. We must find a way to the next language, if only for our kids. They deserve a better legacy than JavaScript.

I believe that children are our future. And also robots.

The next paradigm will be globally distributed, secure, eventual programming. The Internet demands this. Nearly all of our current programming languages, including JavaScript, are still firmly rooted in the old paradigm of local, insecure, sequential programming. I see JavaScript as a transitional language. Adoption of the best practices in JavaScript will be good preparation for understanding the next paradigm.

English

The word for 1 is misspelled. I use the corrected spelling **wun**. The pronunciation of *one* does not conform to any of the standard or special rules of English pronunciation. And having the word for 1 start with the letter that looks like 0 is a bug.

The spelling of **wun** is unfamiliar to you so it might *feel* wrong. I am doing this intentionally to give you practice with the idea that a bad feeling about something unfamiliar is not proof that it is wrong.

This is how spelling reform happens. For example, some cat decides that it really would be better if *through* were spelled *thru* because it does not make sense that half of the letters in a popular word be silent, being wildly inefficient and putting an unnecessary burden on students of the language. Spelling reform is a struggle between tradition and reason, and sometimes, reason wins. I feel the same way about programming languages. So if *wun* makes more sense to you than *one*, then please join me in the effort.

When normal people talk about ranges, like *1 to 10*, the range is understood to end with *10*. But programmers often mean *to* to exclude the *10*. This confusion is due to the common programming practice of numbering from *0* instead of *1*. So I use **to** to mean what programmers usually mean by **to**, and **thru** to mean what normal people mean by **to**. So *0 to 3* mean the range including *0 1 2* whilst *0 thru 3* mean the range including *0 1 2 3*. **To** implies < *less than* and **thru** implies <= *less than or equal*.

And whilst on the subject of **whilst**, in this book about programming, **while** is used for discussion of iteration. When discussing concurrency or simultaneity I use **whilst** which I take to mean *while at the same time*.

Both **cannot** and **can not** are acceptable spellings, but **cannot** is much more popular. **Hasnot** is not acceptable whilst **has not** is. And **willnot** is not acceptable whilst **will not** is. That is why I can not use **cannot**. But if I am in a great hurry, I can still **can't**.

To my many friends for whom English is not your first language: Welcome. Thank you for reading my book. Perhaps unfairly, English has become the language of the Internet and of Software Development. Your ability to read the primary document-ation directly is an important and valuable skill. I deeply respect that.

Examples

I use regular expressions. Unfortunately, regular expressions are extremely cryptic and confusing. I will attempt to mitigate that a bit by pumping lots of whitespace into them. JavaScript does not allow that whitespace, so when you see

```
const number_pattern = /
    ^
    ( -? \d+ )
    (?: \. ( \d* ) )?
    (?:
        [ e E ]
        ( [ + \- ]? \d+ )
    )?
    $
/;
```

be aware that it should be written all smushed together as

```
const number_pattern = /^(-?\d+)(?:\.(\d*))?(?:[eE]([+\-]?\d+))?$/;
```

I do not want to subject you to such unprintable ugliness, so I insert the whitespace.

In many of the chapters I will show examples of JavaScript expressions. I do that by using a special expression statement that ends not with a ; *semicolon* but instead with // *slash slash* followed by the result of the expression.

```
// An example of examples

3 + 4 === 7                                    // true
NaN === NaN                                    // false
typeof NaN                                     // "number"
typeof null                                    // "object"
0.1 + 0.2 === 0.3                              // false
3472073 ** 7 + 4627011 ** 7 === 4710868 ** 7   // true
```

Before the end, all will be explained.

Chapter 1

How Names Work

○ ○ ○ ○ ●

You know my name.
John Lennon and
Paul McCartney

JavaScript wants you to give names (or identifiers) to your variables, properties, and sometimes, functions. JavaScript puts no limit on the length of variables names, so be generous. As much as possible, let your programs tell their own stories. Do not use cryptic names.

I was first taught programming by mathematicians and then I went to work for a company that made computers that were programmed in BASIC. At that time, BASIC variable names were a single uppercase letter and an optional digit, like A1. I developed a very bad habit of using wun letter variable names. Decades later, I am still struggling with that. Wunce something wrong gets into your head, it can be really hard to fix it. We should never stop trying to get smarter. Mathematicians like notations that are cryptic and terse. We have learned the very hard way that programming should strive to be literate and self explanatory. Programming is not mathematics. It is a different sort of art.

Start all of your names with a letter, and end them with a letter. JavaScript allows names to start with _ *underbar* or $ *dollar sign* or to end with _ *underbar* or $ *dollar sign* or a digit. JavaScript allows a lot of things that you really should not do. These tricks should be reserved for code generators and macro processors. Humans should do better.

A beginning or ending _ *underbar* is sometimes intended to indicate a public property or a global variable that would have been private if the program had been written correctly. So, a dangling _ *underbar* is a flag indicating that the coder is incompetent.

The $ *dollar sign* was added to the language for use by code generators, transpilers, and macro processors, so that they could generate names that were guaranteed to not collide with yours. If you are not a program, leave the $ *dollar sign* alone.

A trailing digit in a name is usually an indication that the programmer failed to give enough thought to the name.

I give my *ordinal* variables names like `thing_nr`. I give my *cardinal* variables names like `nr_things`.

It is good to have names containing multiple words, but there is little agreement on how to do that since spaces are not allowed inside of names. There is wun school that insists on the use of camel case, where the first letter of words are capitalized to indicate the word boundaries. There is another school that insists that _ *underbar* should be used in place of space to show the word boundaries. There is a third school that just runs all the words together, losing the word boundaries. The schools are unable to agree on the best practice. This argument has been going on for years and years and does not appear to be approaching any kind of consensus. That is because all of the schools are wrong.

The correct answer is to use spaces to separate the words. Programming languages currently do not allow this because compilers in the 1950s had to run in a very small number of kilowords, and spaces in names were considered an unaffordable luxury. FORTRAN actually pulled it off, allowing names to contain spaces, but later languages did not follow that good example, even though later languages (including JavaScript) followed FORTRAN's very bad examples of using = *equal sign* as the assignment operator and requiring (*left paren* and) *right paren* around the condition of an IF instead of requiring { *left brace* and } *right brace* around the consequence.

I am hoping that the next language does the right thing and allows names to contain spaces to improve readability. We measure memory in gigabytes, so language designers are now free to invent better languages. Until then, use _ *underbar* in multiword names. That will be the easiest transition to the next language.

All names in JavaScript should start with a lowercase letter. This is because of a problem with JavaScript's new operator. If a function invocation is prefixed with new, then the function is called as a constructor, otherwise the function is called as a function. The functionality of constructors and functions can be quite different. Errors can result from calling a constructor the wrong way. Making this more confusing, constructors and functions look exactly the same, so there is no automatic way to detect problems due to a missing or superfluous new. So we have a convention: *All constructor functions should start with an uppercase letter and nothing else should ever start with an uppercase letter.* That gives us a visual indication that could help to identify an error.

My solution to this problem is more reliable: never use new. That eliminates the need to have names that start with an uppercase letter. I still recommend avoiding initial caps in this language because there are an awful lot of awful programs out there that still use new, increasing daily.

Reserved Words

This is JavaScript's reserved word list:

```
arguments await break case catch class const continue debugger default delete
do else enum eval export extends false finally for function if implements
import in Infinity instanceof interface let NaN new null package private
protected public return static super switch this throw true try typeof
undefined var void while with yield
```

Memorize that list. It is important. None of those words should be used as variable names or parameter names. JavaScript's rules about reserved words are surprisingly complex, so there might be some exceptional cases where a few of those words can be used. But even in those weird cases, don't.

The use of reserved words is another misfeature that has its roots in the memory shortages of the 1950s and 1960s. Having reserved words in a language could make things easier for a compiler, allowing it to save a few bytes. Moore's Law has obliterated those shortages, but that constrained mode of thinking persists. Reserved words are obviously a bad thing for programmers. Have you memorized the reserved word list yet? There might be a word that perfectly describes your variable, but it has already been allocated to a lousy feature that you never use, or that might not ever be implemented. Reserved words are also bad for language designers because the brittle reserved word strategy makes it very difficult to add new features to a popular language in a clean, straightforward way. I am hoping that the next language does not stoop to using reserved words.

## Chapter 2

How Numbers Work

○ ○ ○ ● ○

> Look up the number.
> *John Lennon and Paul McCartney*

Computers are machines that manipulate numbers. That is fundamentally all that computers can do. They seem to do that really well. We can map other kinds of information onto numbers. Computers now mediate virtually all human activity.

JavaScript's numbers were inspired by the real numbers, but they are not real numbers. Many of our mathematical understandings and intuitions can be applied to JavaScript numbers, but not completely or consistently. In order to write good programs in JavaScript, we must understand how its numbers work.

JavaScript has a single number type called `number`. It was borrowed from the *IEEE Standard for Floating-Point Arithmetic (IEEE 754)* which was initally developed for Intel's iAPX-432 processor. The 432 contained many brilliant ideas, way too many. The 432's architecture became so complex that it failed to achieve its goals. They lost sight of the best idea, simplicity. Many good ideas died with the 432. The 432's floating-point unit was salvaged and sold as the 8087, a math co-processor for the 8086. It became standard equipment on Pentium and AMD64 chips.

JavaScript is often criticized for having only wun number type, but this is actually wun of its greatest strengths. Programmers are more productive if they do not have to waste time selecting from a confusion of similar types with the risk of obscure failures from choosing the wrong wun. Type conversion errors are avoided. The overflow errors caused by the `int` types are avoided. JavaScript integers are far more reliable than Java ints because overflow can not occur.

```
JavaScript:  2147483647 + 1    //  2147483648   exactly right
Java:        2147483647 + 1    // -2147483648   maximally wrong
```

How can we have confidence in the correctness of programs that are built on a number system that can go wildly wrong at any time without warning? The `int` types do not prevent errors, they cause them.

The idea behind floating point is a simple wun: Represent a number as two numbers. The first number (sometimes called the coefficient, significand, fraction, or mantissa) contains the digits. The second number (called the exponent) identifies where the decimal point (or binary point) should be inserted in the first number. Implementations of floating point can be quite complex. The complexity comes from the need to make the best use of the limited number of bits in a fixed format.

JavaScript does not use the entire IEEE 754 standard. It uses a subset of the subset that Java uses. JavaScript's `number` is very closely related to Java's `double`. It is a 64 bit binary floating point type. A number contains a sign bit, 11 exponent bits, and 53 significand bits. Some clever encoding allows those 65 bits to be packed into a 64 bit word.

IEEE 754, like many floating point systems before it, chose a system with a basis of 2. The first number is split into two parts—the sign and the significand. The sign is placed in the most significant of the 64 bits. It is 1 if the number is negative. The significand is placed in the least significant bits. It normally represents a binary fraction in the range

`0.5 <= ` *significand* ` < 1.0`

In that form, the most significant bit is always a 1. Since that bit is always a 1, it does not need to be stored in the number. This yields the bonus bit.

The second number is the exponent. It fills the space between the sign and the significand. The value of a number would be

sign ∗ *significand* ∗ `(2 ** ` *exponent* `)`

but there are other complications. The exponent is represented as a biased signed magnitude integer. This allows comparisons to be made pretending that the number is a 64 bit integer. That could provide a significant performance benefit, which was important fifty years ago. The exponent can also encode `NaN` and `Infinity` and the subnormals, a special form for representing very small numbers and zero.

Zero

There is no zero but zero. In a correct system, there is only wun zero. The IEEE 754 standard contains two zeros: `0` and `-0`. JavaScript bravely works hard to hide this abomination from you, and nearly always succeeds. You can safely ignore the existence of `-0` except in these cases:

```
(1 / 0) === (1 / -0)                          // false
Object.is(0, -0)                              // false
```

I do not recommend that you ever divide anything by zero. I do not recommend that you ever use `Object.is()`.

Number Literals

There are 18437736874454810627 immutable number objects built into JavaScript, each uniquely representing a number. A number literal produces a reference to the number object that most closely matches the value of the literal. Sometimes it will be exact. In some cases it can be off by as much as 9.979201547673599058281863565184e+291.

A number literal for an integer is simply a sequence of decimal digits. It is also possible to form literals for integers in different bases by use of a radix prefix. All of these literals produce references to `2018`:

```
binary:      0b11111100010
octal:       0o3742
decimal:     2018.00
hexadecimal: 0x7E2
```

JavaScript allows the radix specifier letter to be in uppercase, but putting uppercase letter O in a number literal is certain to cause confusion.

Decimal number literals may contain a decimal point. Very large or very small numbers may be compactly written with e, which multiplies the number by a power of ten. So, `6.022140857747475e23` is short for `(6.022140857747475 * (10 ** 23))` and `6.626070040818182e-34` is short for `(6.626070040818182 * (10 ** -34))`.

`Infinity` is a value that represents all numbers that are too large to be represented. Do not confuse `Infinity` with ∞. In mathematics, ∞ is not a value. It is a metaphor.

`NaN` is a special value that represents numbers that are not numbers. `NaN` stands for *Not a Number*, which is confusing because the `typeof` operator correctly reports that the type of `NaN` is `"number"`.

`NaN` can be the result of a failed string to number conversion. Instead of an exception being raised or the program halting, the `NaN` value is given. The arithmetic operators produce `NaN` when `NaN` is wun of their inputs.

The worst thing about `NaN` is that `NaN` is not equal to itself. This is an IEEE 754 abomination that JavaScript does not hide. The test for `NaN` is different than the test for equality for all other number values. This can be a hazard when writing tests. If the expected value is `NaN`, then the test always fails, even when the actual value is `NaN`. To test if a *value* is `NaN` or not `NaN`, use `Number.isNaN(`*value*`)`. `Number.isFinite(`*value*`)` returns `false` if *value* is `NaN` or `Infinity` or `-Infinity`.

Number

`Number` (not `number`, the initial uppercase `N` is significant) is a function that can make numbers. Numbers in JavaScript are immutable objects. The `typeof` operator returns `"number"` (the initial lowercase `n` is significant) when given a number. You should never use the `new` prefix with the `Number` function. It does not do what you might think it should do.

```
const good_example = Number("432");
const bad_example = new Number("432");
typeof good_example                            // "number"
typeof bad_example                             // "object"
good_example === bad_example                   // false
```

`Number` is also a container of some constants. These constants can provide insight into the workings of numbers.

`Number.EPSILON` is exactly `2.220446049250313080847263336181640625e-16`. It is the smallest positive number that, when added to 1, produces a sum that is larger than 1. Adding any positive number that is less than `Number.EPSILON` to 1 produces a sum that is exactly 1. It should seem absurd that adding a number that is not 0 to 1 yields 1. This is not due to a bug or design error in JavaScript. All fixed size floating point systems have such weirdness, including IEEE 754. It is a reasonable tradeoff.

`Number.MAX_SAFE_INTEGER` is exactly `9007199254740991`, or about 9 quadrillion in the modern illion idiom. JavaScript does not have or need an integer type because its number type can exactly represent all of the integers up to `Number.MAX_SAFE_INTEGER`. JavaScript has 54 bit signed integers within its number type.

Adding 1 to an integer that is larger than `Number.MAX_SAFE_INTEGER` has the same effect as adding 0 to that large number. JavaScript is capable of exact integer arithmetic so long as all of the values and results and intermediate results are integers that lie between `-Number.MAX_SAFE_INTEGER` and `Number.MAX_SAFE_INTEGER`. Within that range, conventional mathematical reasoning can hold. The Associative Law and Distributed Law are in effect. Outside of that range, things are more chaotic. For example, the order in which you add a sequence of numbers can change the sum. So, `((0.1 + 0.2) + 0.3)` produces a larger result than `(0.1 + (0.2 + 0.3))`. `Number.isSafeInteger(`*number*`)` returns `true` if the *number* is in the safe range.

`Number.isInteger(`*number*`)` returns `true` if the *number* is an integer in the safe range or if it is above the safe range. All numbers greater than `Number.MAX_SAFE_INTEGER` are considered to be integers. Some of them are exactly correct. Most of them are not.

`Number.MAX_VALUE` contains the largest number that JavaScript can represent. It is exactly `Number.MAX_SAFE_INTEGER * 2 ** 971` or

```
179769313486231570814527423731704356798070567525844996598917476803157260780028538
760589558632766878171540458953514382464234321326889464182768467546703537516986049
9910576551282076624549009038932894407586850845513394230458323690322294816580855933
21233482747978262041447231687381771809192999881250404026184124858368
```

which is 1 followed by 308 digits. Most of that is phantom significance. These numbers can provide 15.9 digits of significance. The trailing 292 digits are an illusion caused by base 2 beating against base 10.

Adding any positive safe integer to `Number.MAX_VALUE` produces a sum that is also `Number.MAX_VALUE`. It is likely that if a program produces a result that is `Number.MAX_VALUE` then the program is in error. Any result that exceeds `Number.MAX_SAFE_INTEGER` is suspect. The IEEE 754 standard promises the potential of enormous range, but without extraordinary care, it is more likely to lead to mistakes.

`Number.MIN_VALUE` is the smallest number that can be represented that is larger than zero. It is exactly equal to `2 ** -1074` or

```
4.940656458412465441765687928682213723650598026143247644255856825006755072702087
5186529983636163599237979656469544571773092665671035593979639877479601078187812630
0713190311404527845817167848982103688718636056998730723050006387409153564984387
312473397273169615140031715385398074126238565591171026658556686768187039560310624
9319452715914924553293054565444011274801297099995419319894090804165633245247571
47869014726780159355238611550134803526493472019379026810710749170333222684475333
5720832431936092382893458368060106011506169809753078342277318329247904982524730
7763759272478746560847782037344696995336470179726777175851256605511991315048911014
51037862738167250955837389733598993664809941164205702637090279242767544565229008
753868250641971826553344726562625e-324
```

All positive numbers that are smaller than `Number.MIN_VALUE` are indistinguishable from zero. Note that the significand of `Number.MIN_VALUE` contains only a single bit in the least significant position. That lonely bit produces a lot of phantom significance.

`Number.prototype` is an object that all numbers inherit from. `Number.prototype` contains a set of methods. Unfortunately, it is not a very useful set of methods.

Operators

Prefix operators:

+	to number	The **+** *plus sign* prefix operator converts its operand into a number. If the conversion fails, then it produces `NaN`. The `Number` function is preferred because it is more explicit.
−	negate	The **−** *minus sign* prefix operator changes the sign of its operand. Number literals in JavaScript do not have signs. In expressions like (`-1`), the **−** *minus sign* is an operator, not part of the number literal.
`typeof`	type of	If the operand is a number, then it produces the string `"number"`, even if the operand is `NaN`.

Infix operators:

+ *plus sign*	addition	Unfortunately, the **+** *plus sign* operator is also used by strings to do concatenation. This overloading creates a hazard. If either operand is a string, it converts the other operand to a string and concatenates them. Unfortunately, there is no other way in this language to do addition, so you must be careful. The `Number` function can be helpful in assuring that the operands to the **+** *plus sign* infix operator are in fact numbers so that addition will be performed.
− *minus sign*	subtraction	
* *asterisk*	multiplication	
/ *slash*	division	This is not an integer division. If you divide an integer by another integer, you might get a fractional result: `5 / 2` yields `2.5`, not `2`.
% *percent*	remainder	JavaScript does not have a modulo operator. Instead it has a remainder operator. I think modulo is the more useful. The result of remainder takes its sign from the dividend. The result of modulo takes its sign from the divisor. `-5 % 2` is `-1`.
** *asterisk asterisk*	exponentiation	JavaScript adopted FORTRAN's double asterisk to give the language a quaint, old timey look.

Bitwise Operators

JavaScript has a set of bitwise operators similar to those found in C and other languages. They all operate on JavaScript numbers by converting them to signed 32 bit ints, performing the bitwise operation, and then converting back to JavaScript numbers. It would have been better if they acted on 54 bit safe integers, but they do not, so the 22 high order bits can be lost without warning.

In some languages, a shift might be used instead of a multiply or divide, or a bitwise *and* might be used as a modulo operator. If you do that in this language, you may be discarding the 22 most significant bits. In some cases you can get away with that. In some cases you can not.

This is why the bitwise operators are used less often in JavaScript than in other languages. But even when they are not used, they are a syntactic hazard. **&** *ampersand* and | *vertical bar* could be confused with **&&** *ampersand ampersand* and || *vertical bar vertical bar*. **<<** *less than less than* and **>>** *greater than greater than* could be confused with **<** *less than* and **>** *greater than*. It is not obvious to me why **>>** *greater than greater than* is the right shift that does sign extension and **>>>** *greater than greater than greater than* is not. In C, sign extension was determined by the type. In Java, sign extension was determined by the operator. JavaScript copied Java's bad choice. Be careful out there.

The only bitwise unary operator is ~ *tilde*, bitwise not.

The bitwise binary operators:

& *ampersand*	bitwise and
| *vertical bar*	bitwise or
^ *circumflex*	bitwise exclusive or
<< *less than less than*	left shift
>>> *greater than greater than greater than*	right shift
>> *greater than greater than*	right shift sign extended

The Math Object

The `Math` object contains an important set of functions that should have been built into `Number`. This is another example of Java being a bad influence.

In addition to the trigonometric and logarithmic functions, it contains practical functions that should have been provided as operators.

`Math.floor` and `Math.trunc` both produce an integer from a number. `Math.floor` gives the smaller integer, and `Math.trunc` gives the integer closer to zero. Which wun you use depends on what you want to happen to negative numbers.

```
Math.floor(-2.5) // -3
Math.trunc(-2.5) // -2
```

`Math.min` and `Math.max` return the smallest or the largest of the arguments.

`Math.random` returns a number between 0 and 1. It is suitable for games, but not for cryptographic applications or casino games.

The Monster

JavaScript does not provide tools for deconstructing a number into its components, but we can easily write such a tool in JavaScript. We can then see a number's true nature.

I am going to be using a coefficient instead of a significand because I want to work entirely in integer space where things can be clear and exact. The fractional significand requires much more explanation.

```
function deconstruct(number) {
```

This function deconstructs a number, reducing it to its components: a sign, an integer coefficient, and an exponent, such that

number = sign * coefficient * (2 ** exponent)

```
    let sign = 1;
    let coefficient = number;
    let exponent = 0;
```

Remove the sign from the coefficient.

```
    if (coefficient < 0) {
        coefficient = -coefficient;
        sign = -1;
    }

    if (Number.isFinite(number) && number !== 0) {
```

Reduce the coefficient: We can obtain the exponent by dividing the number by two until it goes to zero. We add the number of divisions to -1128, which is the exponent of Number.MIN_VALUE minus the number of bits in the significand minus the bonus bit.

```
        exponent = -1128;
        let reduction = coefficient;
        while (reduction !== 0) {
```

This loop is guaranteed to reach zero. Each division will decrement the exponent of the reduction. When the exponent is so small that it can not be decremented, then the internal subnormal significand will be shifted right instead. Ultimately, all of the bits will be shifted out.

```
            exponent += 1;
            reduction /= 2;
        }
```

Reduce the exponent: When the exponent is zero, the number can be viewed as an integer. If the exponent is not zero, then adjust to correct the coefficient.

```
        reduction = exponent;
        while (reduction > 0) {
            coefficient /= 2;
            reduction -= 1;
        }
        while (reduction < 0) {
            coefficient *= 2;
            reduction += 1;
        }
    }
```

Return an object containing the three components and the original number.

```
    return {
        sign,
        coefficient,
        exponent,
        number
    };
}
```

Now that we are equipped, we can look directly at the beast.

When we deconstruct `Number.MAX_SAFE_INTEGER`, we get

```
{
    "sign": 1,
    "coefficient": 9007199254740991,
    "exponent": 0,
    "number": 9007199254740991
}
```

`Number.MAX_SAFE_INTEGER` is the largest number that fits in a signed 54 bit integer.

When we deconstruct 1, we get

```
{
    "sign": 1,
    "coefficient": 9007199254740992,
    "exponent": -53,
    "number": 1
}
```

Notice that `1 * 9007199254740992 * (2 ** -53)` is 1.

Now let's try a tricky wun: `0.1`. A tenth. A dime.

```
{
    "sign": 1,
    "coefficient": 7205759403792794,
    "exponent": -56,
    "number": 0.1
}
```

When you do the math, `1 * 7205759403792794 * 2 ** -56` is not `0.1`. It is exactly `0.1000000000000000055511151231257827021181583404541015625`.

It is well known that JavaScript is bad at handling decimal fractions, particularly money. When you enter `0.1` or most other decimal fractions into your program, JavaScript is unable to accurately represent that value, so it *aliases*, substituting a value that it can represent.

When you type a decimal point into your program, or read in a data value with a decimal point, it is likely that you are introducing a small error into your program. Sometimes the errors are so small that they are not noticed. Sometimes the errors cancel each other out, but sometimes the errors accumulate.

When we deconstruct `0.3`, we get a different result than when we deconstruct `0.1 + 0.2`.

```
{
    "sign": 1,
    "coefficient": 5404319552844595,
    "exponent": -54,
    "number": 0.3
}

{
    "sign": 1,
    "coefficient": 5404319552844596,
    "exponent": -54,
    "number": 0.30000000000000004
}
```

Note that neither `0.299999999999999988897769753748434595763683319091796875` nor `0.3000000000000000444089209850062616169452667236328125` is actually equal to `0.3`.

Let's look at wun more example. When we deconstruct `100 / 3`, we get

```
{
    "sign": 1,
    "coefficient": 9382499223688534,
    "exponent": -48,
    "number": 33.333333333333336
}
```

Notice that JavaScript says that the number is `33.333333333333336`. The final `6` is an indication that JavaScript is unable to understand the correct answer, or even a reasonable answer. But the truth is much worse. JavaScript actually thinks the answer is exactly `33.33333333333333570180911920033395290374755859375`.

Floating point systems come with functions that convert between the internal binary representation and the external decimal representation that humans insist on using. Those functions are designed to hide the truth to the extent that it is possible to hide it. There is real concern that if we were forced to constantly experience the truth of IEEE 754, we would rebel and demand something more suitable. And on a practical basis, we don't want to see that noise in our results, and we don't want to show that noise to our clients. It would make us look incompetent. It is easier if we all pretend that everything is fine.

The first users of binary floating point were mathematicians and scientists. The mathematicians understood well that computers, being finite devices, can not exactly represent the real numbers, so they relied on numerical analysis techniques to tease useful results from finite systems. The scientists were doing work on experimental data, which is noisy, so the inexactness of binary floating point was not a significant problem. But early business users rejected binary floating point because their customers, and the law, demand exact decimal values. When you are counting money, you are legally required to get the right sum.

That was over a half century ago. Since then, we seem to have forgotten about the tradeoffs that come with binary floating point. We should have moved onto something better by now. It is inexcusable that in the 21th century, we can not reliably add `0.1` to `0.2` to get `0.3`. I am hopeful that the language that replaces JavaScript will possess a single number type that can exactly express the decimal fractions. Such a system still can not exactly represent the real numbers. No finite system can. But it could exactly represent the numbers that are most important to humanity: the numbers that are made of decimal digits.

In the meantime, try to work as much as possible in the safe integer range. I recommend converting all money values into cents, where they can be exactly processed as integers. The danger in that approach is in the interaction with code or systems that do not also do that. Such interface errors could produce results that are a hundred times too large or too small. That would be very bad indeed. Perhaps inflation will save us here by making cents too worthless to bother with.

When you do work outside of the safe integer set, numbers containing a . *decimal point* or an e *decimal exponent* might not be exactly the truth. Adding numbers of similar magnitudes produces less error than adding numbers of different magnitudes. That is why totalling of subtotals is more accurate than totalling of individual values.

## Chapter 3

How Big Integers Work

○ ○ ○ ● ●

> He say five, I say six. He say eight, I say nine. He say ten, I say eleven. I no stop for nothing. I bid 'em up. I go higher, higher, higher.
>
> *Chico Marx*

Wun of the popular complaints about JavaScript is that it does not have 64 bit ints. An `int64` type could hold exact integers as large as `9223372036854775807`, which is three digits more than you can get with JavaScript numbers with their paltry `Number.MAX_SAFE_INTEGER` of `9007199254740991`.

There are problems with the idea that we should just inject a new number type. This appears to not be a problem at all. Other languages have multiple number types. Why shouldn't JavaScript be more like the other languages?

When you have a language with wun number type, adding another is an act of violence. There is a big loss of simplicity and a large new potential for bug formation. Every type declaration and every type conversion is a potential error.

There is also the question: Is 64 bits enough? Perhaps we should be looking at 72 bits, or 96 bits, or 128 bits, or 256 bits. Whatever number you choose, there is an equally good argument that the number should be even higher.

I think it was a mistake to add big integers to the language. It should instead be a library. Most users of the language do not need them, and they do not solve the biggest problem that the current numbers have. With a little programming, there is no need to mutilate the language. We can do exact integer arithmetic in any bit allocation just with JavaScript the way it is. There are many ways to do it. The implementation I am presenting here was not optimized for speed or smallness, but was instead optimized for explainability. I want to present a complete library, but not consume too many pages in presenting it.

I am going to keep big integers in arrays. Arrays are a good choice because they can come in any size. (Strings could also be a good choice, where each character is treated as an unsigned 16 bit integer.) Each element of the array contains a number that holds some of the big integer's bits. An important design question is *How many bits per element?* The largest possible answer is 53, the size of a positive safe integer. The language provides motivation to make it 32 or less because that allows use of the bitwise operators. If our word size is larger than 32 bits, then the bitwise operators can not be used and the implementation gets more complicated.

But even 32 is too large if we consider the needs of multiplication and division. In implementing big integer multiplication and division, we want to make use of JavaScript's multiplication operator, which is only accurate to 53 bits. That means that our word size should be no more than half that. I chose 24 bits. I could have gone with 26, but I like 24 because it is rounder. (My first program ran on a Control Data Corporation 3150, a 24 bit mainframe.) We call these 24 bit units **megadigits** because they can represent over a million times the number of values that an ordinary digit can represent.

I chose a signed magnitude representation. The zeroth element of the array contains the sign of the number, either `"+"` or `"-"`. The wunth element contains the least significant megadigits. The last element contains the most significant megadigits. So 9000000000000000000 would look like this:

```
["+", 8650752, 7098594, 31974]
```

That is not very pretty, but it works because

```
9000000000000000000 = 8650752 + ((7098594 + (31974 * 16777216)) * 16777216)
```

I made constants and functions to make it easier to get to the internal features of the big integer.

```
const radix = 16777216;
const radix_squared = radix * radix;
const log2_radix = 24;
const plus = "+";
const minus = "-";
const sign = 0;
const least = 1;

function last(array) {
    return array[array.length - 1];
}

function next_to_last(array) {
    return array[array.length - 2];
}
```

We make some constants. We don't really need these, but they make the code read a little better.

```
const zero = Object.freeze([plus]);
const wun = Object.freeze([plus, 1]);
const two = Object.freeze([plus, 2]);
const ten = Object.freeze([plus, 10]);
const negative_wun = Object.freeze([minus, 1]);
```

We need predicate functions to detect big integers and negative big integers.

```
function is_big_integer(big) {
    return Array.isArray(big) && (big[sign] === plus || big[sign] === minus);
}

function is_negative(big) {
    return Array.isArray(big) && big[sign] === minus;
}
```

```
function is_positive(big) {
    return Array.isArray(big) && big[sign] === plus;
}

function is_zero(big) {
    return !Array.isArray(big) || big.length < 2;
}
```

The mint function removes the last words from the array if they are zero. It substitutes wun of the constants if there is a match. If there is not a match, it freezes the array. An implementation could claim to be faster in some cases if it allows modification of the arrays, but it would also be less pure and likely to be buggier. Our big integers are immutable, just as JavaScript's numbers are.

```
function mint(proto_big_integer) {
```

Mint a big integer number from a proto big integer. Delete leading zero megadigits. Substitute a popular constant if possible.

```
    while (last(proto_big_integer) === 0) {
        proto_big_integer.length -= 1;
    }
    if (proto_big_integer.length <= 1) {
        return zero;
    }
    if (proto_big_integer[sign] === plus) {
        if (proto_big_integer.length === 2) {
            if (proto_big_integer[least] === 1) {
                return wun;
            }
            if (proto_big_integer[least] === 2) {
                return two;
            }
            if (proto_big_integer[least] === 10) {
                return ten;
            }
        }
    } else if (proto_big_integer.length === 2) {
        if (proto_big_integer[least] === 1) {
            return negative_wun;
        }
    }
    return Object.freeze(proto_big_integer);
}
```

Our first practical functions are negation, absolute value, and sign extraction.

```
function neg(big) {
    if (is_zero(big)) {
        return zero;
    }
    let negation = big.slice();
    negation[sign] = (
        is_negative(big)
        ? plus
        : minus
    );
    return mint(negation);
```

```
    }

    function abs(big) {
        return (
            is_zero(big)
            ? zero
            : (
                is_negative(big)
                ? neg(big)
                : big
            )
        );
    }

    function signum(big) {
        return (
            is_zero(big)
            ? zero
            : (
                is_negative(big)
                ? negative_wun
                : wun
            )
        );
    }
```

The `eq` function determines if two big integers contain the same bits.

```
    function eq(comparahend, comparator) {
        return comparahend === comparator || (
            comparahend.length === comparator.length
            && comparahend.every(function (element, element_nr) {
                return element === comparator[element_nr];
            })
        );
    }
```

The `abs_lt` function determines if the absolute value of a big integer is less than the absolute value of another big integer. The `lt` function determines if the signed value of a big integer is less than the signed value of another. These functions must work a little harder if the two big integers have the same length. They could work less hard if there were a version of `reduce` that could go in reverse and also quit early.

```
    function abs_lt(comparahend, comparator) {
        return (
```

Ignoring the sign, the number with more megadigits is the larger. If the two numbers contain the same number of megadigits, then we must examine each pair.

```
            comparahend.length === comparator.length
            ? comparahend.reduce(
                function (reduction, element, element_nr) {
                    if (element_nr !== sign) {
                        const other = comparator[element_nr];
                        if (element !== other) {
                            return element < other;
                        }
                    }
                    return reduction;
```

```
            },
            false
        )
        : comparahend.length < comparator.length
    );
}

function lt(comparahend, comparator) {
    return (
        comparahend[sign] !== comparator[sign]
        ? is_negative(comparahend)
        : (
            is_negative(comparahend)
            ? abs_lt(comparator, comparahend)
            : abs_lt(comparahend, comparator)
        )
    );
}
```

When you have **lt**, you can easily make the other comparisons by complementing and swapping:

```
function ge(a, b) {
    return !lt(a, b);
}

function gt(a, b) {
    return lt(b, a);
}

function le(a, b) {
    return !lt(b, a);
}
```

Now we make the bitwise functions. Each of our big integers contains bits. We assume that signs are not relevent for bitwise operations, so signs are ignored on input, and "+" on output.

Our first bitwise functions are and, or, and xor. The and function wants to process the shorter array. The and function does not care about the excess words in the longer array. The excess words are anded with zero and disappear. The or and xor functions want to work on the longer array.

```
function and(a, b) {
```

Make **a** the shorter array.

```
    if (a.length > b.length) {
        [a, b] = [b, a];
    }
    return mint(a.map(function (element, element_nr) {
        return (
            element_nr === sign
            ? plus
            : element & b[element_nr]
        );
    }));
```

```
    }

    function or(a, b) {
```

Make a the longer array.

```
        if (a.length < b.length) {
            [a, b] = [b, a];
        }
        return mint(a.map(function (element, element_nr) {
            return (
                element_nr === sign
                ? plus
                : element | (b[element_nr] || 0)
            );
        }));
    }

    function xor(a, b) {
```

Make a the longer array.

```
        if (a.length < b.length) {
            [a, b] = [b, a];
        }
        return mint(a.map(function (element, element_nr) {
            return (
                element_nr === sign
                ? plus
                : element ^ (b[element_nr] || 0)
            );
        }));
    }
```

Some of our functions take a small integer as an argument. The int function makes it easy to handle both numbers and big integers.

```
    function int(big) {
        let result;
        if (typeof big === "number") {
            if (Number.isSafeInteger(big)) {
                return big;
            }
        } else if (is_big_integer(big)) {
            if (big.length < 2) {
                return 0;
            }
            if (big.length === 2) {
                return (
                    is_negative(big)
                    ? -big[least]
                    : big[least]
                );
            }
            if (big.length === 3) {
                result = big[least + 1] * radix + big[least];
                return (
                    is_negative(big)
                    ? -result
```

```
                  : result
            );
        }
        if (big.length === 4) {
            result = (
                big[least + 2] * radix_squared
                + big[least + 1] * radix
                + big[least]
            );
            if (Number.isSafeInteger(result)) {
                return (
                    is_negative(big)
                    ? -result
                    : result
                );
            }
        }
    }
  }
}
```

The shift_down function downsizes numbers by deleting the least significant bits. This can make the big integer smaller. It is like dividing by a power of two. This operation is usually known as *right shift* (>>>) which is confusing because it uses the *greater than* symbol to make numbers smaller. The numbering of bits is a completely arbitrary thing, so the notion that bits grow from right to left is confusing. We are making values from arrays, which are generally thought to grow from left to right, so we grow from right to left and left to right at the same time. Also, some writing systems are left to right, and others are right to left, so the naturality of left and right are not universal. The *Endian Problem* has its roots in this confusion. Shifting right and left is less precise than downsizing and upsizing.

If the shift count is a multiple of 24, then shifting is easy. Otherwise, we need to realign all of the bits.

```
function shift_down(big, places) {
    if (is_zero(big)) {
        return zero;
    }
    places = int(places);
    if (Number.isSafeInteger(places)) {
        if (places === 0) {
            return abs(big);
        }
        if (places < 0) {
            return shift_up(big, -places);
        }
        let skip = Math.floor(places / log2_radix);
        places -= skip * log2_radix;
        if (skip + 1 >= big.length) {
            return zero;
        }
        big = (
            skip > 0
            ? mint(zero.concat(big.slice(skip + 1)))
            : big
        );
        if (places === 0) {
```

```
            return big;
        }
        return mint(big.map(function (element, element_nr) {
            if (element_nr === sign) {
                return plus;
            }
            return ((radix - 1) & (
                (element >> places)
                | ((big[element_nr + 1] || 0) << (log2_radix - places))
            ));
        }));
    }
}
```

The `shift_up` function upsizes numbers by inserting zeros at the least significant end. It is like multiplying by a power of two. This can make the big integer larger. In most systems, bits may be lost when they are shifted past the capacity of numbers, but in this system, capacity is unlimited so no bits are lost.

```
function shift_up(big, places) {
    if (is_zero(big)) {
        return zero;
    }
    places = int(places);
    if (Number.isSafeInteger(places)) {
        if (places === 0) {
            return abs(big);
        }
        if (places < 0) {
            return shift_down(big, -places);
        }
        let blanks = Math.floor(places / log2_radix);
        let result = new Array(blanks + 1).fill(0);
        result[sign] = plus;
        places -= blanks * log2_radix;
        if (places === 0) {
            return mint(result.concat(big.slice(least)));
        }
        let carry = big.reduce(function (accumulator, element, element_nr) {
            if (element_nr === sign) {
                return 0;
            }
            result.push(((element << places) | accumulator) & (radix - 1));
            return element >> (log2_radix - places);
        }, 0);
        if (carry > 0) {
            result.push(carry);
        }
        return mint(result);
    }
}
```

We would like to have a `not` function that complements all of the bits, but we have no limit on the number of bits, so it isn't clear how many bits should be flipped. So we have a `mask` function that makes a big integer of some specific number of 1 bits. We can then use `mask` and `xor` to make `not`, but `not` must be told the size of the bit field.

```
function mask(nr_bits) {
```

Make a string of 1 bits.

```
    nr_bits = int(nr_bits);
    if (nr_bits !== undefined && nr_bits >= 0) {
        let mega = Math.floor(nr_bits / log2_radix);
        let result = new Array(mega + 1).fill(radix - 1);
        result[sign] = plus;
        let leftover = nr_bits - (mega * log2_radix);
        if (leftover > 0) {
            result.push((1 << leftover) - 1);
        }
        return mint(result);
    }
}

function not(a, nr_bits) {
    return xor(a, mask(nr_bits));
}
```

The `random` function makes a big random integer. It takes the number of bits to generate, and an optional random generator function that returns a number between 0 and 1. If you do not pass in a random generator function, it uses `Math.random`, which is fine for most purposes, but not for cryptographic applications.

```
function random(nr_bits, random = Math.random) {
```

Make a string of random bits. If you are concerned with security, you can pass in a stronger random number generator.

First make a string of 1 bits.

```
    const wuns = mask(nr_bits);
    if (wuns !== undefined) {
```

For each megadigit, get a random number between 0.0 and 1.0. Take some upper bits and some lower bits and xor them together. Then and it to the megadigit and put it into the new number.

```
        return mint(wuns.map(function (element, element_nr) {
            if (element_nr === sign) {
                return plus;
            }
            const bits = random();
            return ((bits * radix_squared) ^ (bits * radix)) & element;
        }));
    }
}
```

We do addition the same way you did in school, except we are using radix 16777216 instead of radix 10. We use closure to make the carry available to the adder.

```
function add(augend, addend) {
    if (is_zero(augend)) {
        return addend;
    }
    if (is_zero(addend)) {
        return augend;
    }
```

If the signs are different, then turn this into a subtraction problem.

```
        if (augend[sign] !== addend[sign]) {
            return sub(augend, neg(addend));
        }
```

The signs are the same. Add all the bits, giving the result the same sign. We can add numbers of different lengths. We give .map the longer wun, and use the || operator to replace nonexistant elements with zeros.

```
        if (augend.length < addend.length) {
            [addend, augend] = [augend, addend];
        }
        let carry = 0;
        let result = augend.map(function (element, element_nr) {
            if (element_nr !== sign) {
                element += (addend[element_nr] || 0) + carry;
                if (element >= radix) {
                    carry = 1;
                    element -= radix;
                } else {
                    carry = 0;
                }
            }
            return element;
        });
```

If the number overflowed, then append another element to contain the carry.

```
        if (carry > 0) {
            result.push(carry);
        }
        return mint(result);
    }
```

Subtraction is similarly straight forward.

```
    function sub(minuend, subtrahend) {
        if (is_zero(subtrahend)) {
            return minuend;
        }
        if (is_zero(minuend)) {
            return neg(subtrahend);
        }
        let minuend_sign = minuend[sign];
```

If the signs are different, turn this into an addition problem.

```
        if (minuend_sign !== subtrahend[sign]) {
            return add(minuend, neg(subtrahend));
        }
```

Subtract the smaller from the larger.

```
        if (abs_lt(minuend, subtrahend)) {
            [subtrahend, minuend] = [minuend, subtrahend];
            minuend_sign = (
                minuend_sign === minus
                ? plus
                : minus
            );
        }
        let borrow = 0;
```

```
        return mint(minuend.map(function (element, element_nr) {
            if (element_nr === sign) {
                return minuend_sign;
            }
            let diff = element - ((subtrahend[element_nr] || 0) + borrow);
            if (diff < 0) {
                diff += 16777216;
                borrow = 1;
            } else {
                borrow = 0;
            }
            return diff;
        }));
    }
```

Multiplication is slightly more complicated. We use nested `forEach` functions because we must multiply every element of `multiplicand` with every element of `multiplier`. Each of those products can be 48 bits, but an element can only hold 24 bits, so the overflow must be carried.

```
    function mul(multiplicand, multiplier) {
        if (is_zero(multiplicand) || is_zero(multiplier)) {
            return zero;
        }
```

The sign of the result will be positive if the signs match.

```
        let result = [
            multiplicand[sign] === multiplier[sign]
            ? plus
            : minus
        ];
```

Multiply each element of `multiplicand` by each element of `multiplier`, propagating the carry.

```
        multiplicand.forEach(function (
            multiplicand_element,
            multiplicand_element_nr
        ) {
            if (multiplicand_element_nr !== sign) {
                let carry = 0;
                multiplier.forEach(function (
                    multiplier_element,
                    multiplier_element_nr
                ) {
                    if (multiplier_element_nr !== sign) {
                        let at = (
                            multiplicand_element_nr + multiplier_element_nr - 1
                        );
                        let product = (
                            (multiplicand_element * multiplier_element)
                            + (result[at] || 0)
                            + carry
                        );
                        result[at] = product & 16777215;
                        carry = Math.floor(product / radix);
                    }
                });
```

```
            if (carry > 0) {
                result[multiplicand_element_nr + multiplier.length - 1] = carry;
            }
        }
    });
    return mint(result);
}
```

The `divrem` function performs division, returning both the quotient and the remainder. For convenience, we also provide a `div` function that returns only the quotient.

```
function divrem(dividend, divisor) {
    if (is_zero(dividend) || abs_lt(dividend, divisor)) {
        return [zero, dividend];
    }
    if (is_zero(divisor)) {
        return undefined;
    }
```

Make the operands positive.

```
    let quotient_is_negative = dividend[sign] !== divisor[sign];
    let remainder_is_negative = dividend[sign] === minus;
    let remainder = dividend;
    dividend = abs(dividend);
    divisor = abs(divisor);
```

We do long division just like you did in school. We estimate the next digit of the quotient. We subtract the divisor times that estimate from the dividend, and then we go again. We are using base 16777216 instead of base 10, and we are being more systematic in predicting the next digit of the quotient.

In order to improve our predictions, we first mint the divisor. We shift it left until its most significant bit is 1. We also shift the dividend by the same amount. See Algorithm 4.3.1D in The Art of Computer Programming.

To determine the shift count, we find the number of leading zero bits. The `clz32` function counts in a field of 32 bits, but we are only concerned with a field of 24 bits, so we subtract 8.

```
    let shift = Math.clz32(last(divisor)) - 8;

    dividend = shift_up(dividend, shift);
    divisor = shift_up(divisor, shift);
    let place = dividend.length - divisor.length;
    let dividend_prefix = last(dividend);
    let divisor_prefix = last(divisor);
    if (dividend_prefix < divisor_prefix) {
        dividend_prefix = (dividend_prefix * radix) + next_to_last(dividend);
    } else {
        place += 1;
    }
    divisor = shift_up(divisor, (place - 1) * 24);
    let quotient = new Array(place + 1).fill(0);
    quotient[sign] = plus;
    while (true) {
```

The estimate will not be too small, but it might be too large. If it is too large then subtracting the product of the estimate and the divisor from the dividend produces a negative. When that happens, make the estimate smaller and try again.

```
let estimated = Math.floor(dividend_prefix / divisor_prefix);
if (estimated > 0) {
    while (true) {
        let trial = sub(dividend, mul(divisor, [plus, estimated]));
        if (!is_negative(trial)) {
            dividend = trial;
            break;
        }
        estimated -= 1;
    }
}
```

The corrected estimate is stored in the quotient. If that was the final place, then move on.

```
quotient[place] = estimated;
place -= 1;
if (place === 0) {
    break;
}
```

Prepare for the next place. Update dividend_prefix with the first two words of the remaining dividend, and scale down the divisor.

```
    if (is_zero(dividend)) {
        break;
    }
    dividend_prefix = last(dividend) * radix + next_to_last(dividend);
    divisor = shift_down(divisor, 24);
}
```

Fix the remainder.

```
quotient = mint(quotient);
remainder = shift_down(dividend, shift);
return [
    (
        quotient_is_negative
        ? neg(quotient)
        : quotient
    ),
    (
        remainder_is_negative
        ? neg(remainder)
        : remainder
    )
];
}

function div(dividend, divisor) {
    let temp = divrem(dividend, divisor);
    if (temp) {
        return temp[0];
    }
}
```

Raising an integer to an integer power is easy using the square and multiply method.

```
function power(big, exponent) {
    let exp = int(exponent);
    if (exp === 0) {
        return wun;
    }
    if (is_zero(big)) {
        return zero;
    }
    if (exp === undefined || exp < 0) {
        return undefined;
    }
    let result = wun;
    while (true) {
        if ((exp & 1) !== 0) {
            result = mul(result, big);
        }
        exp = Math.floor(exp / 2);
        if (exp < 1) {
            break;
        }
        big = mul(big, big);
    }
    return mint(result);
}
```

We will use the gcd function to reduce fractions.

```
function gcd(a, b) {
    a = abs(a);
    b = abs(b);
    while (!is_zero(b)) {
        let [ignore, remainder] = divrem(a, b);
        a = b;
        b = remainder;
    }
    return a;
}
```

We need functions for converting numbers and strings into big integers and back again. When converting to and from strings, we want to support decimal notation obviously, but we also want to support binary, octal, hexadecimal, Base32, and Base32 checksums. You can find more information about Base32 at crockford.com/wrmg /base32.html.

The digitset string allows us to map numbers to characters. The charset object maps characters to numbers. Hexadecimal, decimal, octal, and binary can use a subset of the same character mapping.

```
const digitset = "0123456789ABCDEFGHJKMNPQRSTVWXYZ*~$=U";
const charset = (function (object) {
    digitset.split("").forEach(function (element, element_nr) {
        object[element] = element_nr;
    });
    return Object.freeze(object);
}(Object.create(null)));
```

The make function takes a number or a string and an optional radix, and returns a big integer. These conversions are exact for all integer values.

```
function make(value, radix_2_37) {
```

The make function returns a big integer. The value parameter is a string and an optional radix, or an integer, or a big_integer.

```
let result;
if (typeof value === "string") {
    let radish;
    if (radix_2_37 === undefined) {
        radix_2_37 = 10;
        radish = ten;
    } else {
        if (
            !Number.isInteger(radix_2_37)
            || radix_2_37 < 2
            || radix_2_37 > 37
        ) {
            return undefined;
        }
        radish = make(radix_2_37);
    }
    result = zero;
    let good = false;
    let negative = false;
    if (value.toUpperCase().split("").every(
        function (element, element_nr) {
            let digit = charset[element];
            if (digit !== undefined && digit < radix_2_37) {
                result = add(mul(result, radish), [plus, digit]);
                good = true;
                return true;
            }
            if (element_nr === sign) {
                if (element === plus) {
                    return true;
                }
                if (element === minus) {
                    negative = true;
                    return true;
                }
            }
            return digit === "_";
        }
    ) && good) {
        if (negative) {
            result = neg(result);
        }
        return mint(result);
    }
    return undefined;
}
if (Number.isInteger(value)) {
    let whole = Math.abs(value);
    result = [(
        value < 0
```

```
                    ? minus
                    : plus
            )];
            while (whole >= radix) {
                let quotient = Math.floor(whole / radix);
                result.push(whole - (quotient * radix));
                whole = quotient;
            }
            if (whole > 0) {
                result.push(whole);
            }
            return mint(result);
        }
        if (Array.isArray(value)) {
            return mint(value);
        }
    }
```

The number function converts a big integer to a JavaScript number. The conversion is exact if the value is in the safe integer range.

```
    function number(big) {
        let value = 0;
        let the_sign = 1;
        let factor = 1;
        big.forEach(function (element, element_nr) {
            if (element_nr === 0) {
                if (element === minus) {
                    the_sign = -1;
                }
            } else {
                value += element * factor;
                factor *= radix;
            }
        });
        return the_sign * value;
    }
```

The string function converts a big integer into a string. The conversion is exact.

```
    function string(a, radix_2_thru_37 = 10) {
        if (is_zero(a)) {
            return "0";
        }
        radix_2_thru_37 = int(radix_2_thru_37);
        if (
            !Number.isSafeInteger(radix_2_thru_37)
            || radix_2_thru_37 < 2
            || radix_2_thru_37 > 37
        ) {
            return undefined;
        }
        const radish = make(radix_2_thru_37);
        const the_sign = (
            a[sign] === minus
            ? "-"
            : ""
        );
```

```
    a = abs(a);
    let digits = [];
    while (!is_zero(a)) {
        let [quotient, remainder] = divrem(a, radish);
        digits.push(digitset[number(remainder)]);
        a = quotient;
    }
    digits.push(the_sign);
    return digits.reverse().join("");
}
```

The population count function counts the number of '1' bits in a big integer. This can be used to compute the Hamming distance.

```
function population_32(int32) {
```

Produce the total count of 1 bits in a 32 bit integer.

Count 16 pairs of bits, producing 16 two bit counts (0, 1, or 2). For each pair, we subtract the higher bit from the pair, which converts the two bits into a count.

```
//                      HL - H = count
//                      00 - 0 = 00
//                      01 - 0 = 01
//                      10 - 1 = 01
//                      11 - 1 = 10

    int32 -= (int32 >>> 1) & 0x55555555;
```

Combine 8 pairs of two bit counts, producing 8 four bit counts, ranging from 0 thru 4.

```
    int32 = (int32 & 0x33333333) + ((int32 >>> 2) & 0x33333333);
```

Combine 4 pairs of four bit counts, producing 4 eight bit counts, ranging from 0 thru 8. Overflow into neighbor counts is no longer possible, so we only need a single masking operation after the addition.

```
    int32 = (int32 + (int32 >>> 4)) & 0x0F0F0F0F;
```

Combine 2 pairs of eight bit counts, producing 2 sixteen bit counts, ranging from 0 thru 16.

```
    int32 = (int32 + (int32 >>> 8)) & 0x001F001F;
```

Finally, combine the 2 sixteen bit counts, producing a number ranging number from 0 thru 32.

```
    return (int32 + (int32 >>> 16)) & 0x0000003F;
}

function population(big) {
```

Count the total number of 1 bits.

```
    return big.reduce(
        function (reduction, element, element_nr) {
            return reduction + (
                element_nr === sign
                ? 0
                : population_32(element)
            );
        },
        0
```

```
        );
    }

    function significant_bits(big) {
```

Count the total number of bits excluding leading zeros.

```
        return (
            big.length > 1
            ? make((big.length - 2) * log2_radix + (32 - Math.clz32(last(big))))
            : zero
        );
    }
```

Finally, all of this goodness is exported as a module.

```
    export default Object.freeze({
        abs,
        abs_lt,
        add,
        and,
        div,
        divrem,
        eq,
        gcd,
        is_big_integer,
        is_negative,
        is_positive,
        is_zero,
        lt,
        make,
        mask,
        mul,
        neg,
        not,
        number,
        or,
        population,
        power,
        random,
        shift_down,
        shift_up,
        significant_bits,
        signum,
        string,
        sub,
        ten,
        two,
        wun,
        xor,
        zero
    });
```

You can access the big integer object in your module by importing it.

```
    import big_integer from "./big_integer.js";
```

Chapter 4

How Big Floating Point Works

○ ○ ● ○ ○

Don't be a hero, young man.
There's no percentage in it.
Harlan Potter

A big integer system can solve many problems, but it is obviously constrained to just integers, and there are some problems that integers can not solve. So let's build a big floating point system. A floating point system is concerned with three numbers, a *coefficient*, an *exponent*, and a *basis*. The three numbers determine a value.

value = coefficient * (basis ** exponent)

The IEEE 754 format that JavaScript uses for its numbers has a basis of 2. This provides the benefit that hardware implementations in the 1950s were feasible. Moore's Law has eliminated the constraints that made 2 the only reasonable basis, so let's consider other possibilities.

Our Big Integer package has an affinity for `2 ** 24`. If we made 16777216 our basis, then some alignment operations would simply insert or delete elements from the array. That could provide very good performance. And it is consistent with the very popular practice of trading away correctness for performance.

I think the basis should be 10. If the basis is 10, then all decimal fractions can be represented exactly. That is important because most humans use decimal fractions, so a floating point system with a basis of 10 would be good for humanity.

Big integers are an ideal representation of the coefficient. Most of the weirdness of floating point systems is due to size constraints. If size is unbounded, there is little weirdness. Since weirdness can cause bugs, it is good to get rid of it when we can.

We could also use big integers for the exponent, but that would be overkill. JavaScript's numbers will be just fine. We would exhaust our gigabytes of memory long before `Number.MAX_SAFE_INTEGER` becomes a constraint.

We represent big floating point numbers as objects with `coefficient` and `exponent` properties.

Armed with big integers, floating point really isn't very complicated.

```
import big_integer from "./big_integer.js";
```

The `is_big_float` function is used to identify a big float object.

```
function is_big_float(big) {
    return (
        typeof big === "object"
        && big_integer.is_big_integer(big.coefficient)
        && Number.isSafeInteger(big.exponent)
    );
}

function is_negative(big) {
    return big_integer.is_negative(big.coefficient);
}

function is_positive(big) {
    return big_integer.is_positive(big.coefficient);
}

function is_zero(big) {
    return big_integer.is_zero(big.coefficient);
}
```

A single zero value represents all zeros.

```
const zero = Object.create(null);
zero.coefficient = big_integer.zero;
zero.exponent = 0;
Object.freeze(zero);

function make_big_float(coefficient, exponent) {
    if (big_integer.is_zero(coefficient)) {
        return zero;
    }
    const new_big_float = Object.create(null);
    new_big_float.coefficient = coefficient;
    new_big_float.exponent = exponent;
    return Object.freeze(new_big_float);
}

const big_integer_ten_million = big_integer.make(10000000);
```

The number function converts a big floating point number into a JavaScript number.
The conversion is not guaranteed to be exact if the number is outside of the safe
integer zone. We also try to make sense out of other types.

```
function number(a) {
    return (
        is_big_float(a)
        ? (
            a.exponent === 0
            ? big_integer.number(a.coefficient)
            : big_integer.number(a.coefficient) * (10 ** a.exponent)
        )
        : (
            typeof a === "number"
            ? a
            : (
                big_integer.is_big_integer(a)
                ? big_integer.number(a)
                : Number(a)
```

```
                )
            )
        );
    }
```

We need an absolute value function and a negation function.

```
    function neg(a) {
        return make_big_float(big_integer.neg(a.coefficient), a.exponent);
    }

    function abs(a) {
        return (
            is_negative(a)
            ? neg(a)
            : a
        );
    }
```

Addition and subtraction are really easy: We just add the coefficients together, but only if the exponents are equal. If the exponents are not equal, we must make them conform. Because addition and subtraction are so similar, I made a function that makes the add and sub functions. If you pass big_integer.add into conform_op, you get the floating point add function. If you pass big_integer.sub into conform_op, you get the floating point sub function.

```
    function conform_op(op) {
        return function (a, b) {
            const differential = a.exponent - b.exponent;
            return (
                differential === 0
                ? make_big_float(op(a.coefficient, b.coefficient), a.exponent)
                : (
                    differential > 0
                    ? make_big_float(
                        op(
                            big_integer.mul(
                                a.coefficient,
                                big_integer.power(big_integer.ten, differential)
                            ),
                            b.coefficient
                        ),
                        b.exponent
                    )
                    : make_big_float(
                        op(
                            a.coefficient,
                            big_integer.mul(
                                b.coefficient,
                                big_integer.power(big_integer.ten, -differential)
                            )
                        ),
                        a.exponent
                    )
                )
            );
        };
    }
```

```
const add = conform_op(big_integer.add);
const sub = conform_op(big_integer.sub);
```

Multiplication is even easier. We just multiply the coefficients and add the exponents.

```
function mul(multiplicand, multiplier) {
    return make_big_float(
        big_integer.mul(multiplicand.coefficient, multiplier.coefficient),
        multiplicand.exponent + multiplier.exponent
    );
}
```

The difficulty with division is knowing when to stop. Stopping is easy with integer division. You stop when you run out of digits. It is also easy with fixed size floating point. You stop when you run out of bits, but using big integers, there is no limit. We could continue to divide until we get an exact result, but there is no guarantee that such a result is ever attainable. So we will leave it up to the programmer. The div function takes an optional third argument which is the precision of the result. You indicate a decimal place. The units position is zero. Fractional positions are negative. The division returns at least as many decimal places as you specify. The default is -4, which is four digits after the decimal point.

```
function div(dividend, divisor, precision = -4) {
    if (is_zero(dividend)) {
        return zero;
    }
    if (is_zero(divisor)) {
        return undefined;
    }
    let {coefficient, exponent} = dividend;
    exponent -= divisor.exponent;
```

Scale the coefficient to the desired precision.

```
    if (typeof precision !== "number") {
        precision = number(precision);
    }
    if (exponent > precision) {
        coefficient = big_integer.mul(
            coefficient,
            big_integer.power(big_integer.ten, exponent - precision)
        );
        exponent = precision;
    }
    let remainder;
    [coefficient, remainder] = big_integer.divrem(
        coefficient,
        divisor.coefficient
    );
```

Round the result if necessary.

```
    if (!big_integer.abs_lt(
        big_integer.add(remainder, remainder),
        divisor.coefficient
    )) {
        coefficient = big_integer.add(
            coefficient,
```

```
            big_integer.signum(dividend.coefficient)
        );
    }
    return make_big_float(coefficient, exponent);
}
```

A big floating point number is normalized if the exponent is as close to zero as possible without losing significance.

```
function normalize(a) {
    let {coefficient, exponent} = a;
    if (coefficient.length < 2) {
        return zero;
    }
```

If the exponent is zero, it is already normal.

```
    if (exponent !== 0) {
```

If the exponent is positive, multiply the coefficient by 10 ** exponent.

```
        if (exponent > 0) {
            coefficient = big_integer.mul(
                coefficient,
                big_integer.power(big_integer.ten, exponent)
            );
            exponent = 0;
        } else {
            let quotient;
            let remainder;
```

While the exponent is negative, if the coefficient is divisible by ten, then we do the division and add 1 to the exponent.

To help this go a little faster, we first try units of ten million, reducing 7 zeros at a time.

```
            while (exponent <= -7 && (coefficient[1] & 127) === 0) {
                [quotient, remainder] = big_integer.divrem(
                    coefficient,
                    big_integer_ten_million
                );
                if (remainder !== big_integer.zero) {
                    break;
                }
                coefficient = quotient;
                exponent += 7;
            }
            while (exponent < 0 && (coefficient[1] & 1) === 0) {
                [quotient, remainder] = big_integer.divrem(
                    coefficient,
                    big_integer.ten
                );
                if (remainder !== big_integer.zero) {
                    break;
                }
                coefficient = quotient;
                exponent += 1;
            }
        }
```

```
        }
        return make_big_float(coefficient, exponent);
    }
```

The `make` function takes a big integer, or a string, or a JavaScript number, and convert it into big floating point. The conversion is exact.

```
    const number_pattern = /
        ^
        ( -? \d+ )
        (?: \. ( \d* ) )?
        (?: e ( -? \d+ ) )?
        $
    /;

    //  Capturing groups
    //       [1] int
    //       [2] frac
    //       [3] exp

    function make(a, b) {

    //       (big_integer)
    //       (big_integer, exponent)
    //       (string)
    //       (string, radix)
    //       (number)

        if (big_integer.is_big_integer(a)) {
            return make_big_float(a, b || 0);
        }
        if (typeof a === "string") {
            if (Number.isSafeInteger(b)) {
                return make(big_integer.make(a, b), 0);
            }
            let parts = a.match(number_pattern);
            if (parts) {
                let frac = parts[2] || "";
                return make(
                    big_integer.make(parts[1] + frac),
                    (Number(parts[3]) || 0) - frac.length
                );
            }
        }
    }
```

If `a` is a number, then we deconstruct it into its basis 2 exponent and coefficient, and then reconstruct as a precise big float.

```
        if (typeof a === "number" && Number.isFinite(a)) {
            if (a === 0) {
                return zero;
            }
            let {sign, coefficient, exponent} = deconstruct(a);
            if (sign < 0) {
                coefficient = -coefficient;
            }
            coefficient = big_integer.make(coefficient);
```

If the exponent is negative, then we can divide by 2 ** abs(exponent).

```
            if (exponent < 0) {
                return normalize(div(
                    make(coefficient, 0),
                    make(big_integer.power(big_integer.two, -exponent), 0),
                    b
                ));
            }
```

If the exponent is greater than zero, then we can multiply the coefficient by `2 **` exponent.

```
            if (exponent > 0) {
                coefficient = big_integer.mul(
                    coefficient,
                    big_integer.power(big_integer.two, exponent)
                );
                exponent = 0;
            }
            return make(coefficient, exponent);
        }
        if (is_big_float(a)) {
            return a;
        }
    }
```

The `string` function converts a big floating point number into a string. The conversion is exact. Most of the work involves inserting the decimal point and zero filling. A similar function for binary floating point would be vastly more complicated.

```
    function string(a, radix) {
        if (is_zero(a)) {
            return "0";
        }
        if (is_big_float(radix)) {
            radix = normalize(radix);
            return (
                (radix && radix.exponent === 0)
                ? big_integer.string(integer(a).coefficient, radix.coefficient)
                : undefined
            );
        }
        a = normalize(a);
        let s = big_integer.string(big_integer.abs(a.coefficient));
        if (a.exponent < 0) {
            let point = s.length + a.exponent;
            if (point <= 0) {
                s = "0".repeat(1 - point) + s;
                point = 1;
            }
            s = s.slice(0, point) + "." + s.slice(point);
        } else if (a.exponent > 0) {
            s += "0".repeat(a.exponent);
        }
        if (big_integer.is_negative(a.coefficient)) {
            s = "-" + s;
        }
        return s;
    }
```

There are two popular conventions for representing the decimal point: . *period* and , *comma*. Most countries use wun or the other. Within the borders of a country, it does not matter which. Both work well. But it is a hazard to international communication because 1,024 can have two very different interpretations. I predict that we will ultimately settle on . *period* as the international standard because programming languages use . *period* and ultimitely most information flows thru our programs written in those languages.

The `scientific` function converts a big floating point number into a string with the e notation.

```
function scientific(a) {
    if (is_zero(a)) {
        return "0";
    }
    a = normalize(a);
    let s = big_integer.string(big_integer.abs(a.coefficient));
    let e = a.exponent + s.length - 1;
    if (s.length > 1) {
        s = s.slice(0, 1) + "." + s.slice(1);
    }
    if (e !== 0) {
        s += "e" + e;
    }
    if (big_integer.is_negative(a.coefficient)) {
        s = "-" + s;
    }
    return s;
}
```

Finally, all of this goodness is exported as a module.

```
export default Object.freeze({
    abs,
    add,
    div,
    eq,
    fraction,
    integer,
    is_big_float,
    is_negative,
    is_positive,
    is_zero,
    lt,
    make,
    mul,
    neg,
    normalize,
    number,
    scientific,
    string,
    sub,
    zero
});
```

This is a library that is suitable for calculators, financial processing, or any other activity that requires correctness with decimal fractions. At this stage it is pretty minimal, but it could be enhanced with all of the functions and operators you could ever need.

I used this library to expose the truth in Chapter 2. Whilst it is very powerful, I think a more conventional fixed size decimal floating point type would be better suited to most applications. The problem with JavaScript's number type isn't its limited range or precision. The problem is that it can not accurately represent the numbers that are most interesting to humanity: the numbers made of decimal digits. So something like DEC64 would be a better choice for the next language. `www.DEC64.com`

Neither binary floating point nor decimal floating point can exactly represent things like `100/3`. We will consider that problem next.

## Chapter 5

How Big Rationals Work

○ ○ ● ○ ●

> I only took the regular course. Reeling and
> Writhing, of course, to begin with, and then
> the different branches of Arithmetic—
> Ambition, Distraction, Uglification, and
> Derision.
>
> *The Mock Turtle*

A rational number is a number that can be expressed as the ratio of two integers. If the two integers are big integers, this can be a very nice representation of numbers. It can exactly express everything that binary floating point can. It can exactly express everything that decimal floating point can. And it can exactly express all of the rational numbers that the other representations can not.

A rational system is concerned with two numbers, a numerator, and a denominator. The two numbers determine a value.

value = numerator / denominator

Our rational values are objects with `numerator` and `denominator` properties that are both big integers. The sign of the value is determined by the sign of the numerator. The denominator may not be negative.

This is a very nice way to do arithmetic. We can build an implementation on top of big integers.

```
import big_integer from "./big_integer.js";
```

We start with some predicate functions.

```
function is_big_rational(a) {
    return (
        typeof a === "object"
        && big_integer.is_big_integer(a.numerator)
        && big_integer.is_big_integer(a.denominator)
    );
}

function is_integer(a) {
    return (
        big_integer.eq(big_integer.wun, a.denominator)
        || big_integer.is_zero(
            big_integer.divrem(a.numerator, a.denominator)[1]
```

```
        )
    );
}

function is_negative(a) {
    return big_integer.is_negative(a.numerator);
}
```

These are constants that I found useful. We could easily make more.

```
function make_big_rational(numerator, denominator) {
    const new_big_rational = Object.create(null);
    new_big_rational.numerator = numerator;
    new_big_rational.denominator = denominator;
    return Object.freeze(new_big_rational);
}
const zero = make_big_rational(big_integer.zero, big_integer.wun);
const wun = make_big_rational(big_integer.wun, big_integer.wun);
const two = make_big_rational(big_integer.two, big_integer.wun);
```

We need an absolute value function and negation function. By convention, the sign is in the numerator. The denominator is always positive.

```
function neg(a) {
    return make(big_integer.neg(a.numerator), a.denominator);
}

function abs(a) {
    return (
        is_negative(a)
        ? neg(a)
        : a
    );
}
```

Addition and subtraction are really easy. If the denominators are equal, we can add or subtract the numerators. Otherwise, we do two multiplies, an addition, and another multiplication because

$$(a\ /\ b) + (c\ /\ d) = ((a * d) + (b * c))\ /\ (b * d)$$

Since addition and subtraction are so similar, I made a function that makes the **add** and **sub** functions.

```
function conform_op(op) {
    return function (a, b) {
        try {
            if (big_integer.eq(a.denominator, b.denominator)) {
                return make(
                    op(a.numerator, b.numerator),
                    a.denominator
                );
            }
            return normalize(make(
                op(
                    big_integer.mul(a.numerator, b.denominator),
                    big_integer.mul(b.numerator, a.denominator)
                ),
                big_integer.mul(a.denominator, b.denominator)
            ));
```

```
            } catch (ignore) {
            }
        };
    }

    const add = conform_op(big_integer.add);
    const sub = conform_op(big_integer.sub);
```

We can increment a rational number by adding the denominator to the numerator.

```
    function inc(a) {
        return make(
            big_integer.add(a.numerator, a.denominator),
            a.denominator
        );
    }

    function dec(a) {
        return make(
            big_integer.sub(a.numerator, a.denominator),
            a.denominator
        );
    }
```

Multiplication is easy. We just multiply the numerators and the denominators. Division is just multiplication with the second argument inverted. In a rational system, we rarely have to do long division. We just make the denominator bigger.

```
    function mul(multiplicand, multiplier) {
        return make(
            big_integer.mul(multiplicand.numerator, multiplier.numerator),
            big_integer.mul(multiplicand.denominator, multiplier.denominator)
        );
    }

    function div(a, b) {
        return make(
            big_integer.mul(a.numerator, b.denominator),
            big_integer.mul(a.denominator, b.numerator)
        );
    }

    function remainder(a, b) {
        const quotient = div(normalize(a), normalize(b));
        return make(
            big_integer.divrem(quotient.numerator, quotient.denominator)[1]
        );
    }

    function reciprocal(a) {
        return make(a.denominator, a.numerator);
    }

    function integer(a) {
        return (
            a.denominator === wun
            ? a
            : make(big_integer.div(a.numerator, a.denominator), big_integer.wun)
```

```
        );
    }

    function fraction(a) {
        return sub(a, integer(a));
    }
```

Our `normalize` function reduces the fraction so that there are no common factors. Factoring of large numbers is a hard problem. Fortunately, we do not need to factor in order to reduce. We just need to find the greatest common divisor, which then is divided out.

It is never necessary to normalize. The value is not changed by normalizing. The big integers inside the rational object might be made smaller, which might reduce memory consumption (which is rarely important) and might speed up subsequent arithmetic operations.

```
    function normalize(a) {
```

Normalize a big rational by dividing the two components by their greatest common divisor. If their gcd is 1, then the number was already normalized.

```
        let {numerator, denominator} = a;
        if (big_integer.eq(big_integer.wun, denominator)) {
            return a;
        }
        let g_c_d = big_integer.gcd(numerator, denominator);
        return (
            big_integer.eq(big_integer.wun, g_c_d)
            ? a
            : make(
                big_integer.div(numerator, g_c_d),
                big_integer.div(denominator, g_c_d)
            )
        );
    }
```

We do not need to normalize in order to determine if two values are equal. If

$$a \ / \ b = c \ / \ d$$

then

$$a * d = b * c$$

even if they are not normalized.

```
    function eq(comparahend, comparator) {
        return (
            comparahend === comparator
            ? true
            : (
                big_integer.eq(comparahend.denominator, comparator.denominator)
                ? big_integer.eq(comparahend.numerator, comparator.numerator)
                : big_integer.eq(
                    big_integer.mul(comparahend.numerator, comparator.denominator),
                    big_integer.mul(comparator.numerator, comparahend.denominator)
                )
            )
        );
    }
```

```
function lt(comparahend, comparator) {
    return (
        is_negative(comparahend) !== is_negative(comparator)
        ? is_negative(comparator)
        : is_negative(sub(comparahend, comparator))
    );
}
```

The make function takes a pair of things and makes an object containing a numerator and a denominator. The conversion is exact.

It takes wun or two big integers. It also takes strings like "33 1/3" and "98.6" and properly converts them. It also takes any finite JavaScript number and makes it rational with no additional loss.

```
const number_pattern = /
    ^
    ( -? )
    (?:
        ( \d+ )
        (?:
            (?:
                \u0020 ( \d+ )
            )?
            \/
            ( \d+ )
        |
            (?:
                \. ( \d* )
            )?
            (?:
                e ( -? \d+ )
            )?
        )
    |
        \. (\d+)
    )
    $
/;
```

```
function make(numerator, denominator) {
```

If there are two arguments, both will be converted to big integers. The return value is an object containing the numerator and the denominator.

If called with 1 argument, we will try to make sense of that argument. If the argument is a string, we will try to parse it as a mixed fraction or as a decimal literal. If the argument is a number, we will deconstruct it. Otherwise, we will assume that the missing argument was a 1.

```
        if (denominator !== undefined) {
```

Make a rational number from a numerator and a denominator. You may pass in big integers, integers, or strings.

```
            numerator = big_integer.make(numerator);
```

If the numerator is zero, we do not care about the denominator.

```
        if (big_integer.zero === numerator) {
            return zero;
        }
        denominator = big_integer.make(denominator);
        if (
            !big_integer.is_big_integer(numerator)
            || !big_integer.is_big_integer(denominator)
            || big_integer.zero === denominator
        ) {
            return undefined;
        }
```

If the denominator is negative, move the sign to the numerator.

```
        if (big_integer.is_negative(denominator)) {
            numerator = big_integer.neg(numerator);
            denominator = big_integer.abs(denominator);
        }
        return make_big_rational(numerator, denominator);
    }
```

Is the argument a string? If so, try to parse it.

```
    if (typeof numerator === "string") {
        let parts = numerator.match(number_pattern);
        if (!parts) {
            return undefined;
        }

// Capturing groups:
//      [1] sign
//      [2] integer
//      [3] top
//      [4] bottom
//      [5] frac
//      [6] exp
//      [7] naked frac

        if (parts[7]) {
            return make(
                big_integer.make(parts[1] + parts[7]),
                big_integer.power(big_integer.ten, parts[7].length)
            );
        }
        if (parts[4]) {
            let bottom = big_integer.make(parts[4]);
            if (parts[3]) {
                return make(
                    big_integer.add(
                        big_integer.mul(
                            big_integer.make(parts[1] + parts[2]),
                            bottom
                        ),
                        big_integer.make(parts[3])
                    ),
                    bottom
                );
            }
            return make(parts[1] + parts[2], bottom);
```

```
        }
        let frac = parts[5] || "";
        let exp = (Number(parts[6]) || 0) - frac.length;
        if (exp < 0) {
            return make(
                parts[1] + parts[2] + frac,
                big_integer.power(big_integer.ten, -exp)
            );
        }
        return make(
            big_integer.mul(
                big_integer.make(parts[1] + parts[2] + parts[5]),
                big_integer.power(big_integer.ten, exp)
            ),
            big_integer.wun
        );
    }
```

Is the argument a number? If so, deconstruct it and reconstruct it.

```
    if (typeof numerator === "number" && !Number.isSafeInteger(numerator)) {
        let {sign, coefficient, exponent} = deconstruct(numerator);
        if (sign < 0) {
            coefficient = -coefficient;
        }
        coefficient = big_integer.make(coefficient);
        if (exponent >= 0) {
            return make(
                big_integer.mul(
                    coefficient,
                    big_integer.power(big_integer.two, exponent)
                ),
                big_integer.wun
            );
        }
        return normalize(make(
            coefficient,
            big_integer.power(big_integer.two, -exponent)
        ));
    }
    return make(numerator, big_integer.wun);
}
```

The number function converts a big rational into a JavaScript number. The conversion is not guaranteed to be exact if the value is outside of the safe integer zone.

```
function number(a) {
    return big_integer.number(a.numerator) / big_integer.number(a.demoninator);
}
```

The string function converts a big rational into a string. The conversion is exact.

```
function string(a, nr_places) {
    if (a === zero) {
        return "0";
    }
    let {numerator, denominator} = normalize(a);
```

Divide the numerator by the demominator. If there was no remainder, then we have our result.

```
let [quotient, remains] = big_integer.divrem(numerator, denominator);
let result = big_integer.string(quotient);
if (remains !== big_integer.zero) {
```

If `nr_places` was provided, then the result will be in the decimal format. We scale the remains by a power of ten and do an integer division. If the residue is not less than half the denominator, then round up.

```
remains = big_integer.abs(remains);
if (nr_places !== undefined) {
    let [fractus, residue] = big_integer.divrem(
        big_integer.mul(
            remains,
            big_integer.power(big_integer.ten, nr_places)
        ),
        denominator
    );
    if (!big_integer.abs_lt(
        big_integer.mul(residue, big_integer.two),
        denominator
    )) {
        fractus = big_integer.add(fractus, big_integer.wun);
    }
    result += "." + big_integer.string(fractus).padStart(
        big_integer.number(nr_places),
        "0"
    );
} else {
```

The result will be in mixed fraction form.

```
    result = (
        (
            result === "0"
            ? ""
            : result + " "
        )
        + big_integer.string(remains)
        + "/"
        + big_integer.string(denominator)
    );
}
}
return result;
}
```

All of this goodness is exported as a module.

```
export default Object.freeze({
    abs,
    add,
    dec,
    div,
    eq,
    fraction,
    inc,
    integer,
    is_big_rational,
    is_integer,
```

```
        is_negative,
        lt,
        make,
        mul,
        neg,
        normalize,
        number,
        wun,
        reciprocal,
        remainder,
        string,
        sub,
        two,
        zero
});
```

You can access the big rational object in your module by importing it.

```
import big_rational from "./big_rational.js";
```

This rational library is small, simple, slow, and surprisingly powerful. It still can not exactly represent *pi* or the square root of two, but it can come as close as you desire. For example,

```
const pi = big_rational.make(
    "31415926535897932384626433832795028841971693993751058209749445923078164 06",
    "10000000000000000000000000000000000000000000000000000000000000000000000000"
);
const sqrt_two = big_rational.make(
    "14142135623730950488016887242096980785696718753769480731766797373990732478",
    "10000000000000000000000000000000000000000000000000000000000000000000000000"
);
```

That is good to 72 decimal places. If you need more, you can have more. As precision goes up, performance goes down. We are often too quick to trade away correctness for performance.

With this library you can perform computations in JavaScript that it has been said can not be done in JavaScript. So there is no real need to add new number types to JavaScript. Anything we need to do we can do with the language as it is.

It comes with some inconvenience. You must write `big_rational.add(a, b)` instead of `a + b`. I don't think that is a big deal, particularly if you are more concerned with good results than with typing time. Syntax is way overrated. But if you really need syntactic support, a transpiler could easily rewrite a pretty language into `big_rational` calls.

Chapter 6

How Booleans Work

○ ○ ● ● ○

> Truth is truth. You can't have opinions
> about truth.
>
> *Peter Schickele*

The boolean type was named after George Boole, an English mathematician who developed a system of algebraic logic. Claude Shannon adapted Boole's system for the design of digital circuits. That is why we call computer circuits *logic*.

The boolean type contains only two values, `true` and `false`. Boolean values are usually generated by the comparison operators; manipulated by the logical operators; and consumed by the ternary operator and the condition part of the `if`, `do`, `for`, and `while` statements.

The `typeof` operator returns `"boolean"` when its operand is `true` or `false`.

Relational Operators

`===` *equal sign equal sign equal sign*	equal
`!==` *exclamation point equal sign equal sign*	not equal
`<` *less than*	less than
`<=` *less than equal sign*	less than or equal
`>` *greater than*	greater than
`>=` *greater than equal sign*	greater than or equal

It is deeply unfortunate that the equality operator is `===` *equal sign equal sign equal sign* and not `=` *equal sign*. It is even more unfortunate that the not equal operator is `!==` *exclamation point equal sign equal sign* and not ≠ *not equal sign*. All of these operators do pretty much what you would expect, except there is also plenty of nonsense. Here are some examples of nonsense:

```
undefined < null                              // false
undefined > null                              // false
undefined === null                            // false

NaN === NaN                                   // false
NaN !== NaN                                   // true
```

```
"11" < "2"                                      // true
"2" < 5                                         // true
5 < "11"                                        // true
```

=== *equal sign equal sign equal sign* and !== *exclamation point equal sign equal sign* generally do the right thing except when both operands are NaN. === *equal sign equal sign equal sign* and !== *exclamation point equal sign equal sign* can be used to determine if a value is null or undefined or any value other than NaN. To test if x is NaN, always use Number.isNaN(x).

=== *equal sign equal sign equal sign* should not be used to test for the completion of a loop unless the induction variable is in the safe integer range. Even then, it is safer to use >= *greater than equal sign*.

< *less than* and <= *less than equal sign* and > *greater than* and >= *greater than equal sign* generally do the right thing when both operands are strings or when both operands are numbers. In most other cases, the result is nonsense. Avoid mixing types when doing comparisons. JavaScript does not prohibit mixing types in that way, so you need to bring your own discipline.

JavaScript also has some comparison operators that are even less reliable. I recommend never using == *equal sign equal sign* (and != *exclamation point equal sign*). They do type coercion before doing the comparison, and so are likely to produce false positives (and false negatives). Always use === *equal sign equal sign equal sign* (and !== *exclamation point equal sign equal sign*) instead. Always.

Boolish

JavaScript has a lovely boolean type but does not make good use of it. These are the positions in a program where the booleans do the most good:

- the condition position of an if statement
- the condition position of a while statement
- the condition position of a for statement
- the condition position of a do statement
- the operand of the ! *exclamation point* operator
- both operands of the && *ampersand ampersand* operator
- both operands of the || *vertical bar vertical bar* operator
- the first operand of the ? *question mark* : *colon* ternary operator
- the return value of the function argument to the Array methods filter, find, findIndex, indexOf

In a well designed language, only boolean values would be allowed in those positions. JavaScript instead allows any type in all of those positions. All values in the language are members of the boolish type. All values in the boolish type are either truthy or falsy.

The falsy values are

- `false`
- `null`
- `undefined`
- `""` (the empty string)
- `0`
- `NaN`

All other values are truthy, including empty objects, empty arrays, and strings that might look falsy, like `"false"` and `"0"`.

The falsy values often act like `false`, but most of them are not, strictly speaking, `false`. The truthy values often act like `true`, but most of them are not `true`. This boolishness was a mistake, but it was not an accident. It was done intentionally in order to permit idioms of the C language in JavaScript.

C is an inadequately typed language. It uses a single value to represent `0`, `FALSE`, `NULL`, end of string, and other things. They are all the same to C. So in the condition position of an `if` statement, C is looking to see if the expression is `0` or not. There is a style of C programming that exploits that by making the conditions terse.

JavaScript has a sound boolean type, but boolishness tosses much of the value away. A condition should be either `true` or `false`. Any other value should be an error, ideally a compile time error. That is not the case in JavaScript. Conditional expressions can be as terse and cryptic as in C. Values that accidentally fall into condition position are not flagged as errors. Instead, they can send the program off in unexpected directions. The Java language requires that conditions be booleans, and so eliminates a class of errors. I wish that JavaScript had done that too.

I recommend that you write programs as though JavaScript had been designed correctly. Use booleans in all conditions. If you write in the style of a better language, you will write better programs.

Logical Operators

The logical operators are also subject to boolishness.

`!` *exclamation point*	logical not	If the operand is truthy then the result is `false`. If the operand is falsy then the result is `true`.
`&&` *ampersand ampersand*	logical and	If the first operand is falsy, then the result is the first operand and the second operand is not evaluated. If the first operand is truthy, then the result is the second operand.
`||` *vertical bar vertical bar*	logical or	If the first operand is truthy, then the result is the first operand and the second operand is not evaluated. If the first operand is falsy, then the result is the second operand.

Not!

Logical expressions can get complicated. There are formal transformations that can simplify them. Unfortunately, boolishness and NaN can cause formal transformations to produce errors.

It is usually wise to simplify double negatives. In a logical system,

```
!!p === p
```

That is only true in JavaScript when p is a boolean. If p is of any other type, then !!p is equal to Boolean(p), not necessarily p.

Some of the comparison operators have opposites, so < is the opposite of >=, and > is the opposite of <=. So it should be possible to simplify !(a < b) as a >= b because

```
!(a === b) === (a !== b)
!(a <=  b) === (a >   b)
!(a >   b) === (a <=  b)
!(a >=  b) === (a <   b)
```

If either a or b is NaN, then the code transformation fails. This is because comparing any number to NaN produces a result of false, regardless of the comparison operator. So,

```
7 < NaN                          // false
NaN < 7                          // false
!(7 < NaN) === 7 >= NaN          // false
```

It might make sense if NaN were smaller than all other numbers or if comparing a number to NaN would raise an exception. JavaScript instead implements nonsense. The only meaningful operation on NaN is Number.isNaN(NaN). Avoid NaN in all other contexts.

The De Morgan Laws can be helpful in simplfying logical expressions. I use them frequently:

```
!(p && q) === !p || !q
!(p || q) === !p && !q
```

The laws are sound in JavaScript as long as p and q were not corrupted with nonsense. Boolish values should be avoided. Use booleans instead.

## Chapter 7

How Arrays Work

○ ○ ● ● ●

> Everything is numbered here.
> The monster is Zero.
> *The Controller of Planet X*

The array is the most venerable data structure. An array is a contiguous section of memory, divided into equal size chunks, each associated with and quickly accessed with an integer. JavaScript failed to include arrays in its first release. That omission was barely noticed because JavaScript's objects are so powerful. Ignoring performance issues, objects can do everything that arrays can do.

That is still the case. Any string can be used to index into an array. JavaScript's arrays are really objects. In today's JavaScript, arrays slightly differ from objects in four ways:

- Arrays have a magical `length` property. An array's `length` is not necessarily the number of elements in the array. It is instead the highest integer ordinal plus 1. This supports the pretense that JavaScript's arrays are truly arrays, allowing a JavaScript array to be processed using the same archaic `for` statement that you might find in a half century old C program.

- Arrays inherit from `Array.prototype` which contains a much better collection of methods than `Object.prototype`.

- Arrays are produced using array literals, not object literals. Array literals are syntactically much simpler: [*left bracket* and] *right bracket* surrounding zero or more expressions separated with , *comma*.

- `JSON` treats arrays and objects very differently even though JavaScript mostly treats them as the same.

JavaScript is itself confused about arrays. When given an array, the `typeof` operator returns the string `"object"`, which is obviously wrong. You should instead use the `Array.isArray(`*value*`)` function to determine if a *value* is an array.

```
const what_is_it = new Array(1000);
typeof what_is_it                              // "object"
Array.isArray(what_is_it)                      // true
```

Origin

Since the invention of counting, people have started numbering with whatever word they used to indicate 1. In the mid 1960s, a small but influential group of programmers determined that we should instead be starting with 0. Today virtually all programmers begin numbering with 0. The rest of humanity, including most of the mathematicians, still start with 1. Mathematicians usually label the origin as 0, but most label the first member of an ordered set as 1. How they do this is still a mystery.

There is an efficiency argument for starting at 0, but it is so weak as to be worthless. Similarly, there is a correctness argument that says that starting at 0 causes fewer off-by-wun errors, but that is also suspect. It seems that there should be a good reason for why programmers count differently than everywun else. Perhaps wun day we will discover why.

The place where this affects JavaScript is in the numbering of the elements of arrays, and to a lesser extent, in the numbering of the characters in a string. The idea that arrays should be processed wun element at a time goes back at least as far as FORTRAN. A more modern idea is to process arrays functionally. This simplifies code by eliminating explicit loop management and it creates the potential for distributing the work over multiple processors.

A well written program in a well designed language should not care if arrays start at 0 or 1. I would not accuse JavaScript of being a well designed language, but it is a significant improvement over FORTRAN, and in fact, by stepping away from the FORTRAN model, we do not usually need to care about how the elements are numbered.

Sometimes we do need to care. The word *first* becomes problematic because of its association with *wun* so instead I use *zeroth*. It makes my origin clear.

[0]	*zeroth*	*0th*
[1]	*wunth*	*1th*
[2]	*twoth*	*2th*
[3]	*threeth*	*3th*

Moving on from those, *fourth*, *fifth*, and *sixth* seem ambiguous, but by the time we have counted past the smallest integers, it should be clear what the origin was.

Initialization

There are two ways to make a new array.

- array literal
- new Array(*integer*)

```
let my_little_array = new Array(10).fill(0);
                // my_little_array is [0, 0, 0, 0, 0, 0, 0, 0, 0, 0]
let same_thing = [0, 0, 0, 0, 0, 0, 0, 0, 0, 0];

my_little_array === same_thing                           // false
```

Note that `my_little_array` and `same_thing` are exactly the same. They are also two separate, unique values. Unlike strings, but like objects, identical arrays are only equal if they are actually the same array.

Stacks and Queues

Arrays have methods that act on an array as a stack. The `pop` method removes and returns the last element of the array. The `push` method appends a new element to the array.

Stacks are often used in interpreters and calculators.

```
function make_binary_op(func) {
    return function (my_little_array) {
        let wunth = my_little_array.pop();
        let zeroth = my_little_array.pop();
        my_little_array.push(func(zeroth, wunth));
        return my_little_array;
    };
}

let addop = make_binary_op(function (zeroth, wunth) {
    return zeroth + wunth;
});

let mulop = make_binary_op(function (zeroth, wunth) {
    return zeroth * wunth;
});

let my_little_stack = [];            // my_little_stack is []
my_little_stack.push(3);             // my_little_stack is [3]
my_little_stack.push(5);             // my_little_stack is [3, 5]
my_little_stack.push(7);             // my_little_stack is [3, 5, 7]
mulop(my_little_stack);              // my_little_stack is [3, 35]
addop(my_little_stack);              // my_little_stack is [38]
let answer = my_little_stack.pop();  // my_little_stack is [], answer is 38
```

The `shift` method is similar to the `pop` method, except that it removes and returns the zeroth element instead of the last. The weirdly named `unshift` method is like `push` except that it prepends the new element at the front of the array, not at the end. The `shift` and `unshift` methods can be much slower than `pop` and `push`, especially if the array is large. Using `shift` and `push` together makes a queue, where you append new items to the back and ultimately harvest them from the front.

Searching

JavaScript provides methods for searching thru an array. The `indexOf` method takes a value that it compares to each of the elements of the array starting at the beginning. If your value matches an element, it stops its search and returns the ordinal of the element.

If it fails to find a match, it returns -1. Note that this is a type error that is waiting to happen because -1 is a number, much like every other number. If you use the return value of `indexOf` without first explicitly checking for -1, then the computation it contributes to could go wrong without warning. JavaScript has many bottom values. Wun of those should have been used instead.

The `lastIndexOf` function is similar to `indexOf` except that it starts at the end of the array and searches backward. It also uses -1 as the failure code.

The `includes` function is similar to `indexOf` except that it returns `true` if the value is found, and `false` if it is not found.

Reducing

The `reduce` method reduces an array to a single value. It takes a function that takes two arguments. The `reduce` method calls that function with pairs of values, over and over again, until there is just a single value that is the result.

There are two ways to design a `reduce` method. Wun way is to have it call the function for every element of the array. An initial value must be provided to get things started.

```
function add(reduction, element) {
    return reduction + element;
}

let my_little_array = [3, 5, 7, 11];

let total = my_little_array.reduce(add, 0);        // total is 26
```

For each element, the reduction value is passed to `add`, along with the current array element. We explicitly pass in the 0 which is the initial reduction value. The `add` function sees

```
(0, 3)                                        // 3
(3, 5)                                        // 8
(8, 7)                                        // 15
(15, 11)                                      // 26
```

Each value that `add` returns becomes the reduction on the next call to `add`.

The initial reduction will not always be 0. If we pass a multiply function to `reduce`, then the initial reduction should be 1. If we pass `Math.max` to `reduce`, the initial reduction should be -Infinity. This creates a hazard: You need to be careful in selecting the initial reduction value.

The other way to design `reduce` is to not require an initial reduction value. Instead, the function is called wun less time. The first time it is called, it receives the zeroth and wunth elements. The zeroth element becomes the initial reduction value.

```
total = my_little_array.reduce(add);          // 26
```

Now the `add` function sees

```
(3, 5)                                        // 8
(8, 7)                                        // 15
(15, 11)                                      // 26
```

The function is called wun fewer time, and there is no error possible in selecting the wrong initial reduction value.

The thing that JavaScript did that is kind of brilliant is that its `reduce` method works either way. If you pass in the initial reduction value, then the function is called for every element. If you do not pass in an initial reduction value, then your function is not called for the zeroth element. Instead, the first element is used as the initial reduction value. So both of the examples above of `reduce add` work.

The `reduceRight` function works the same way, except that it begins at the end of the array. I wish it had been named `reduce_reverse`.

I used `reduce` to compute the check digit of the ISBN number of this book.

```
function isbn_13_check_digit(isbn_12) {
    const string_of_digits = isbn_12.replace(/-/g, "");
    if (string_of_digits.length === 12) {
        const check = string_of_digits.split("").reduce(
            function (reduction, digit, digit_nr) {
                return reduction + (
                    digit_nr % 2 === 0
                    ? Number(digit)
                    : Number(digit) * 3
                );
            },
            0
        ) % 10;
        return (
            check > 0
            ? 10 - check
            : check
        );
    }
}
isbn_13_check_digit("978-1-94-981500")                        // 9
```

Iterating

Wun of the most common operations on arrays is to do something to each element. Historically this was done with the `for` statement. JavaScript offers a more modern approach.

The `forEach` method takes an array and a function. It calls that function for each element of the array. The function can have three parameters: `element`, `element_nr`, and `array`. The `element` parameter is an element of the array. The `element_nr` parameter is the ordinal of the element, which can be handy if there is another array in the computation and you need to coordinate. The `array` parameter was a mistake and should not be there. It is an invitation to modify the array that is being processed, which is usually a bad thing.

Unfortunately, there is not a method that can process the array in the reverse order (like `reduceRight` can). There is a `reverse` method that could be called first, but `reverse` is a destructive method that can not be used on frozen arrays.

The `forEach` method ignores the return value of the function it calls. Interesting methods can be made by paying attention to the return value.

> The `every` method looks at the return value. If it is falsy, the `every` method stops processing and returns `false`. If it is truthy, the `every` method continues processing. If the `every` method reaches the end of the array, it returns `true`.

> The `some` method is so similar to the `every` method that it isn't clear why it should even be in the language. If the function's return value is truthy, the `some` method stops processing and returns `true`. If it is falsy, the `some`

method continues processing. If the `some` method reaches the end of the array, it returns `false`.

The `find` method is like the `some` method, except that instead of returning `true` or `false`, it returns the element that was being processed when the function returned something truthy.

The `findIndex` method is like the `find` method, except that instead of returning the element, it returns the ordinal of the element that was being processed when the function returned something truthy.

The `filter` method is also like the `find` method, except it always processes to the end, and it returns an array collecting all of the elements for which the function returned a truthy value. So `find` returns the first match. The `filter` method returns all of the matches.

The `map` method is like the `forEach` method, except that it collects all of the return values and returns them in a new array. The `map` method is an ideal way of doing transformations by creating a new array that is a refinement or amplification of the original.

These methods are a better way of processing arrays without resorting to `for` loops. But the set of methods is incomplete.

`forEach` and `find` are able to exit early. (The exiting forms of `forEach` are `every` and `some`.) `map`, `reduce`, and `filter` do not have the option of exiting early.

The `reduce` method has the option of working backwards with `reduceRight`, but `forEach`, `map`, `filter`, and `find` do not have the option of working backwards.

These omissions are used as justification for not abolishing the `for` statement.

Sorting

JavaScript has a `sort` method. Unfortunately, it has some problems.

It sorts in place, modifying the array it sorts. That means it is not possible to sort a frozen array, and it is not safe to sort a shared array.

```
let my_little_array = ["unicorns", "rainbows", "butterflies", "monsters"];
my_little_array.sort()
        // my_little_array is ["butterflies", "monsters", "rainbows", "unicorns"]
```

Its default comparison function wants to arrange values as strings, even if they are numbers. For example,

```
let my_little_array = [11, 2, 23, 13, 3, 5, 17, 7, 29, 19];
my_little_array.sort();
        // my_little_array is [11, 13, 17, 19, 2, 23, 29, 3, 5, 7]
```

That isn't just terribly inefficient, it is also terribly wrong. Fortunately, we can mitigate this by passing a comparison function to `sort`. The function is given two elements. It is expected to return a negative number if the first element should come first, a positive number if the second element should come first, or a zero if the comparison function can not tell.

This comparison function could sort an array of numbers correctly (as long as all of the elements are finite numbers):

```
function compare(first, second) {
    return first - second;
}
```

If you want to compare numbers that are not finite (like NaN and Infinity) then your compare function will have to work harder.

Next on the list of problems with the sort function is the lack of stability. A sort is stable if elements that are equalish (your compare function returns zero) retain their original relative order. JavaScript does not guarantee stability. This is not a concern when sorting an array of strings or an array of numbers. It can be a concern when sorting an array of objects or an array of arrays. A complex sort might want to sort by last name, and when last names are the same, sort by first name. Wun way to do that would be to first sort by first name, and then sort again by last name. But that does not work because the sort is not stable, and the information added by the first name sort may be lost.

We can mitigate that by using a more complex comparison function. To make that easier, we make a factory that makes comparison functions.

```
function refine(collection, path) {
```

Take an array or object and a path in the form of an array of strings, and return the value at the end of the path. If there is no value, return undefined.

```
    return path.reduce(
        function (refinement, element) {
            try {
                return refinement[element];
            } catch (ignore) {}
        },
        collection
    );
}
```

```
function by(...keys) {
```

This factory creates a comparison function to help in sorting an array of objects or an array of arrays. The arguments are wun or more strings or integers that will identify the properties or elements to compare. If the first argument sees a tie, then try the second, and then the third...

Convert each key into an array of strings.

```
const paths = keys.map(function (element) {
    return element.toString().split(".");
});
```

Compare each pair of values until finding a mismatch. If there is no mismatch then the two values are equal.

```
    return function compare(first, second) {
        let first_value;
        let second_value;
        if (paths.every(function (path) {
            first_value = refine(first, path);
            second_value = refine(second, path);
            return first_value === second_value;
```

```
    })) {
        return 0;
    }
```

If the two values are of the same type, then we can compare the two values. If the
types are not the same, then we need some policy to cope with the weirdness. Our
simple policy here is to compare the names of the types, so boolean < number < string
< undefined. (It might be better to fail instead of sorting disagreeable types.)

```
        return (
            (
                typeof first_value === typeof second_value
                ? first_value < second_value
                : typeof first_value < typeof second_value
            )
            ? -1
            : 1
        );
    };
}
```

Example:

```
let people = [
    {first: "Frank", last: "Farkel"},
    {first: "Fanny", last: "Farkel"},
    {first: "Sparkle", last: "Farkel"},
    {first: "Charcoal", last: "Farkel"},
    {first: "Mark", last: "Farkel"},
    {first: "Simon", last: "Farkel"},
    {first: "Gar", last: "Farkel"},
    {first: "Ferd", last: "Berfel"}
];

people.sort(by("last", "first"));

// [
//     {"first": "Ferd", "last": "Berfel"},
//     {"first": "Charcoal", "last": "Farkel"},
//     {"first": "Fanny", "last": "Farkel"},
//     {"first": "Frank", "last": "Farkel"},
//     {"first": "Gar", "last": "Farkel"},
//     {"first": "Mark", "last": "Farkel"},
//     {"first": "Simon", "last": "Farkel"},
//     {"first": "Sparkle", "last": "Farkel"}
// ]
```

Potpourri

The `concat` method takes two or more arrays and concatenates them together to make a new array.

```
let part_zero = ["unicorns", "rainbows"];
let part_wun = ["butterflies", "monsters"];
let whole = part_zero.concat(part_wun);
            // whole is ["unicorns", "rainbows", "butterflies", "monsters"]
```

The `join` method takes an array of strings and a separator string. It makes a big string that combines everything. Use an empty string as the separator if you don't want separation. This is the inverse of the string `split` method.

```
let string = whole.join(" & ");
            // string is "unicorns & rainbows & butterflies & monsters"
```

The `reverse` method moves the elements around in an array so that they are in the opposite order. This is destructive, like the `sort` function.

```
whole.reverse();
            // whole is ["monsters", "butterflies", "rainbows", "unicorns"]
```

The `slice` method can make a copy of an array, or a copy of a part of an array. The zeroth parameter determines at what ordinal to start. The wunth parameter is the zeroth parameter plus the number of elements to copy. If the wunth parameter is omitted, all of the remaining elements are copied.

```
let element_nr = whole.indexOf("butterflies");
let good_parts;
if (element_nr !== -1) {
    good_parts = whole.slice(element_nr);
}
            // good_parts is ["butterflies", "rainbows", "unicorns"]
```

Pure and Impure

Some of the array methods are pure, not changing their inputs. Some of them are not. Some of them should have been pure, but are not. Some by their nature can not be pure, but are still valuable.

When coping with the pure/impure duality, it is important to know what is pure and what is not.

Pure methods:

```
concat
every
filter
find
findIndex
forEach
indexOf
join
lastIndexOf
map
reduce
reduceRight
slice
some
```

Impure methods:

```
fill
pop
push
shift
splice
unshift
```

Impure methods that should have been pure:

```
reverse
sort
```

Chapter 8

How Objects Work

○ ● ○ ○ ○

> Have gratitude for the things you're
> discarding. By giving gratitude, you're
> giving closure to the relationship with that
> object, and by doing so, it becomes a lot
> easier to let go.
> *Marie Kondo*

JavaScript overloads the word *object*. This is a language in which everything (except the two bottom values, `null` and `undefined`) is an object. But usually, especially in this chapter, *object* means something more specific.

JavaScript's primary data structure is called *object*. An object is a container of properties (or members). Each property has a name and a value. The name is a string. The value can be of any type. In other languages, this type of object might be called a hash table, map, record, struct, associative array, dictionary, or in some very rude languages, a dict.

A new object can be created with an object literal. An object literal creates a value that can be stored in a variable or object or array, or passed to a function, or returned from a function.

An object literal is delimited by { *left brace* and } *right brace*. Nestled inside can be zero or more properties, separated with , *comma*. A property can be:

- A string followed by : *colon* followed by an expression. The property's name is the string. The property's value is the value of the expression.

- A name followed by : *colon* followed by an expression. The property's name is the name converted into a string. The property's value is the value of the expression.

- A name. The property's name is the name converted into a string. The property's value is the value of the variable or parameter having the same name.

- A name followed by a parameter list wrapped in (*left paren* and) *right paren* followed by a function body wrapped in { *left brace* and } *right brace*. This is a contraction for a name followed by a colon followed by a function expression. This allows for omitting : `function` which, given the loss of clarity, hardly seems worth it.

So, for example,

```
let bar = "a long rod or rigid piece of wood or metal";
let my_little_object = {
    "0/0": 0,
    foo: bar,
    bar,
    my_little_method() {
        return "So small.";
    }
};
```

We can access a property of an object by using the dot notation with a name.

```
my_little_object.foo === my_little_object.bar              // true
```

We can also access a property of an object using the bracket notation. We can use the bracket notation to access a property whose name is not a valid identifier. We can also use the bracket notation to access computed property names. The expression in the brackets is evaluated and converted into a string if necessary.

```
my_little_object["0/0"] === 0                              // true
```

If we ask for a name with the dot or the bracket that can not be found in the object, then the bottom value undefined is provided instead. Asking for a non-existent or missing property is not considered an error. It is a normal operation that produces undefined.

```
my_little_object.rainbow                   // undefined
my_little_object[0]                        // undefined
```

New properties may be added to an object by assignment. The values of existing properties may also be replaced by assignment.

```
my_little_object.age = 39;
my_little_object.foo = "slightly frilly or fancy";
```

I recommend not storing undefined in objects. JavaScript allows it, and correctly gives back the undefined value, but it is the same undefined that means that the property is missing. This is a source of confusion that can easily be avoided. I wish that storing undefined would cause the property to be removed, but it does not. A property can be removed by the delete operator.

```
delete my_little_object["0/0"];
```

Sophisticated data structures can be built out of objects because references to objects can be stored in objects. All sorts of graphs and cyclic structures can be constructed. There is no limit on the depth of nesting, but don't go crazy.

When the typeof operator is given an object, it gives the string "object".

```
typeof my_little_object === "object"                       // true
```

Case

The matching of keys is case sensitive. So my_little_object.cat is not the same property as my_little_object.Cat or my_little_object.CAT. The === operator determines the string matching of property names.

Copy

The `Object.assign` function can copy the properties from an object to another. You can make a copy of an object by assigning to an empty object.

```
let my_copy = Object.assign({}, my_little_object);
my_copy.bar                // "a long rod or rigid piece of wood or metal"
my_copy.age                                                // 39
my_copy.age += 1;
my_copy.age                                                // 40
delete my_copy.age;
my_copy.age                                                // undefined
```

An object can be assigned material from many objects. In this way, a complex object can be constructed by the assembling of material from simpler objects.

Inheritance

In JavaScript, an object can be made that inherits from another object. This is a very different style of inheritance than is practiced in languages that have tightly coupled programmatic structures like classes. In JavaScript, it is the data that is coupled, which can significantly reduce the brittleness that can seize an application architecture.

`Object.create(`*prototype*`)` takes an existing object and returns a new object that inherits from the existing object. The existing object is the new object's *prototype*. Any object can be the prototype of a new object. An object that inherits from a prototype can also be the prototype of newer objects. There is no limit on the length of a prototype chain, but it is wise to keep them short.

If there is an attempt to access a missing property, before returning `undefined`, the system first goes to the prototype, and then its prototype, and so on. If a same named property is found in the prototype chain, then that is given as though it had been found in the object of interest.

When assigning to an object, only the top-most object is changed. No changes are made to objects on the prototype chain.

```
let my_clone = Object.create(my_little_object);
my_clone.bar               // "a long rod or rigid piece of wood or metal"
my_clone.age                                               // 39
my_clone.age += 1;
my_clone.age                                               // 40
delete my_clone.age;
my_clone.age                                               // 39
```

The most popular use of prototypes is as a place to store functions. JavaScript itself does this. When an object is made with an object literal, that object inherits from `Object.prototype`. Similarly, arrays inherit methods from `Array.prototype`. Numbers inherit methods from `Number.prototype`. Strings inherit methods from `String.prototype`. Even functions inherit methods from `Function.prototype`. The array and string methods are pretty useful, but the methods in `Object.prototype` are mostly useless.

Because we have inheritance, we now have two types of properties: *own* properties that live in the top-most object, and *inherited* properties that live in the prototype chain. Most of the time they work just the same. Sometimes you need to know if the property is truly the object's own. Most objects inherit a hasOwnProperty(*string*) function, but unfortunately, it has a reliability hazard. It takes a *string* and returns true if the object contains a property with that name *and* if the property is not inherited. Unfortunately, if the object has a property named hasOwnProperty, it will be called instead of the Object.prototype.hasOwnProperty method. That could cause a failure or other confusion. It would have been better had hasOwnProperty been an operator so that the state of an object could not cause the call to hasOwnProperty to fail. It would have been even better still if there were no inherited properties, which would make this troublesome method unnecessary.

```
my_little_object.hasOwnProperty("bar")                    // true
my_copy.hasOwnProperty("bar")                             // true
my_clone.hasOwnProperty("bar")                            // false
my_clone.hasOwnProperty = 7;
my_clone.hasOwnProperty("bar")                            // EXCEPTION!
```

If you have a property named hasOwnProperty, then you can not use the inherited hasOwnProperty method. You will be calling the own property instead.

Object.prototype.toString shares the same failure risk. But even when it works, it is a disappointment.

```
my_clone.toString                            // "[object Object]"
```

You don't need to be told that your object is an object. You probably already knew that. You want to be shown what it contains. If you want to convert an object into a string, JSON.stringify does a much better job.

The advantage of Object.create(*prototype*) over Object.assign(Object.create({}), *prototype*) is that less memory is used. In most cases, the savings are not significant. Prototypes can add weirdness without adding much benefit.

There is also a problem with unintended inheritance. You might want to use an object as you would use a hash table, but the object inherits names like "toString", "constructor", and other names that might be implementation dependent. These could potentially be confused with your properties.

Fortunately, Object.create(null) makes an object that inherits nothing. There is no confusion over inherited properties or unintended inheritance. There is nothing in the object except what you explicitly put into it. I am now making frequent use of Object.create(null).

Keys

The Object.keys(*object*) function can take all of the names of the own (but not inherited) properties in an *object* and return them as an array of strings. This allows you to use the array methods to process the properties of an object.

The strings in the array will be in the order in which they were inserted. If you need them in a different order, you can use the Array sort method.

Freeze

Object.freeze(*object*) can take an *object* and freeze it, making it immutable. Immutability can lead to more reliable systems. Wunce an object is constructed to your liking, it can be frozen, which guarantees that it can not be damaged or tampered with. This is not a deep freeze. Only the top level object is frozen.

Immutable objects might someday have valuable performance characteristics. If it is known that an object can never change, then a powerful set of optimizations become available to the language implementation.

Immutable objects have excellent security properties. This is important because current industry practices encourage the installation of untrustworthy code into our systems. Immutability might someday help that to become a safe practice. With immutability, we can give objects good interfaces with which to defend themselves.

Object.freeze(*object*) and the const statement do two very different things. Object.freeze operates on values. const operates on variables. If you put a mutable object in a const variable, you can still mutate the object, but you can not replace the object with a different value. If you put an immutable object in an ordinary variable, you can not change the object, but you can assign a different value to the variable.

```
Object.freeze(my_copy);
const my_little_constant = my_little_object;

my_little_constant.foo = 7;                          // allowed
my_little_constant = 7;                              // SYNTAX ERROR!
my_copy.foo = 7;                                     // EXCEPTION!
my_copy = 7;                                         // allowed
```

Prototypes And Freezing Do Not Mix

Wun use of prototypes is the creation of light copies of objects. We might have an object full of data. We want another object that is the same but with wun of the properties changed. We can do that with Object.create, as we have seen. This will save some time on the creation of the new object, but the retrieval of the properties might cost a little more because of looking thru the prototype chain.

Unfortunately, this does not work if the prototype is frozen. If a property in a prototype is immutable, then the instances can not have their own versions of that property. In some functional programming styles we want all objects to be frozen for the reliability benefits that come from immutability. So instead of making a copy to realize a change, it would have been nice if we could make an instance that inherits from the frozen prototype, update the instance, and then freeze the instance. But that just does not work. Updating the instance raises an exception. It also slows down the insertion of new properties in general. Whenever a new property is inserted, the whole prototype chain must be searched for that key to determine that there is not an immutable property in an ancestor. This search can be avoided by using Object.create(null) to make your objects.

WeakMap

Wun of the design errors in JavaScript is that the names of properties in objects must be strings. There are situations when you want to use an object or an array as a key. Unfortunately, JavaScript objects do the wrong thing in that case, converting the key object into a key string using the `toString` method, which we already saw is a disappointment.

Instead of giving us an object that works correctly for all keys, JavaScript gives us a second type of object called a WeakMap that allows objects as keys, but not strings, and with a completely different interface.

Object	WeakMap
`object = Object.create(null);`	`weakmap = new WeakMap();`
`object[key]`	`weakmap.get(key)`
`object[key] = value;`	`weakmap.set(key, value);`
`delete object[key];`	`weakmap.delete(key);`

It does not make sense that these two things which do the same thing are so syntactically different. It also does not make sense that these two things are not wun thing. Instead of a thing that allows only strings as keys and another thing that allows only objects as keys, there should have been a single thing that allows strings and objects as keys.

In spite of that, `WeakMap` is brilliant. Here are two examples of its use.

We want to put a secret property on an object. In order to access the secret property, you need access to the object and to the secret key. You can not access the property unless you have both. We can do this with a `WeakMap`. We treat the `WeakMap` as the secret key.

```
const secret_key = new WeakMap();
secret_key.set(object, secret);

secret = secret_key.get(object);
```

You must have access to both the object and the secret key in order to recover the secret. A nice thing about this technique is that we can effectively add secret properties to frozen objects.

We want to be able to give an object to some code that might do something useful for us, like catalog it or store it for later retrieval, but we do not want to also give that code the capability to alter the object or call any of its methods. In the real world, we want to allow a valet to park the car, but not empty the glove box and trunk or sell the car. The honor system can work for people in the real world, but not for code in a computer network.

So we make a device called a *sealer*. We give an object to a sealer and it returns a box that can not be opened. That box can be given to a valet. To recover the original object, give the box to the matching *unsealer*. We can easily make these functions using `WeakMap`.

```
function sealer_factory() {
    const weakmap = new WeakMap();
    return {
        sealer(object) {
            const box = Object.freeze(Object.create(null));
            weakmap.set(box, object);
            return box;
        },
        unsealer(box) {
            return weakmap.get(box);
        }
    };
}
```

The weakMap does not allow inspection of its contents. You can not get a value from it unless you also hold the key. WeakMap interacts well with JavaScript's garbage collector. If there are no copies of a key still in existence, then that key's property in the weakmap is automatically deleted. This can help avoid memory leaks.

JavaScript also has a similar thing called Map, but Map does not have the security and memory leak protection that WeakMap has. And whilst WeakMap is a terrible name, Map is even more confusing. It has no connection to the Array map method, and it could be confused with a cartography function. That is why I do not recommend Map. But I like WeakMap and the Array map function.

JavaScript has a thing called Symbol that can do wun of the things that WeakMap can do. I do not recommend Symbol because it is unnecessary. I am looking to simplify by eliminating the excessive features that I don't need.

## Chapter 9

How Strings Work

○ ● ○ ○ ●

> Not fair! Not fair! It isn't fair, my precious,
> is it, to ask us what it's got in its nassty
> little pocketses?
>
> *Gollum*

Computers are good at manipulating bit patterns. Humans are not. Strings bridge the gap between computers and humans. The mapping of characters onto integers was wun of the important advances in the development of digital computers. It was the first important step forward in the development of user interfaces.

We do not know why we call this type *string*. Why do we not call it *text* instead? No wun knows. A JavaScript string does not resemble a piece of string. We can talk about a *string of characters*, but we can as easily talk about a *string of statements*, or a *string of bits*, or even a *string of failures*. In the real world, we do not concatenate strings. We tie strings.

Foundation

A string is an immutable array of 16 bit unsigned integers ranging from 0 thru 65535. A string may be made with the `String.fromCharCode` function, which takes any number of numbers. The elements of a string can be accessed with `charCodeAt`. Elements may not be changed because strings are always frozen. Strings, like arrays, have a `length` property.

```
const my_little_array = [99, 111, 114, 110];
const my_little_string = String.fromCharCode(...my_little_array);
my_little_string.charCodeAt(0) === 99                           // true
my_little_string.length                                        // 4
typeof my_little_string                                        // "string"
```

The bracket notation can be used to obtain individual values from a string, but it does not deliver a number as an array would. Instead it returns a new string with a `length` of 1 whose content is the number.

```
my_little_string[0] === my_little_array[0]                     // false
my_little_string[0] === String.fromCharCode(99)               // true
```

`String.prototype` contains methods that act on strings. The `concat` and `slice` methods work very much like the array methods. But the `indexOf` method works very differently. The argument to `indexOf` is a string, not a number. It attempts to match all of the elements in the argument in sequence with elements in the first string.

```
my_little_string.indexOf(String.fromCharCode(111, 114))        // 1
my_little_string.indexOf(String.fromCharCode(111, 110))        // -1
```

The methods `startsWith`, `endsWith`, and `includes` are just wrappers around `indexOf` and `lastIndexOf`.

Strings containing similar contents are considered to be equal by the `===` operator. Similar arrays are only equal when they are the same array.

```
my_little_array === my_little_array                        // true
my_little_array === [99, 111, 114, 110]                    // false
my_little_string === String.fromCharCode(99, 111, 114, 110)   // true
```

The equality of strings is a very powerful feature. It eliminates the need for a symbol type because similar strings are considered to be the same object. This is not true in lesser languages like Java.

Unicode

JavaScript allows all 65536 of the 16 bit patterns as elements of strings. However, the usual practice is to consider each element to be a character, and the Unicode standard determines the encoding of characters. JavaScript has a lot of syntactic and methodic support for Unicode. The Unicode standard declares that some codes are not characters and should not be used. JavaScript does not care. It allows all 16 bit codes. If you intended to have your systems interact with systems that are written in lesser languages, then you should not abuse Unicode.

String literals are written by surrounding zero or more Unicode characters with `"` *double quote*. (`'` *single quote* can also be used, but is not recommended because it is unnecessary.) Each character is represented as a 16 bit element.

The `+` *plus sign* operator is used to do concatenation. We have already seen that `+` is also used to do addition. If you intend to do concatenation, then you need to assure that at least wun of the operands is a string. Wun way to do that is to make wun of the operands a string literal. Another way is to pass a value to the `String` function.

```
my_little_string === "corn"            // true
"uni" + my_little_string               // "unicorn"
3 + 4                                  // 7
String(3) + 4                          // 34
3 + String(4)                          // 34
```

A string literal must fit entirely on wun line. The `\` *backslash* is used as an escapement character that allows for including `"` *double quote*, `\` *backslash*, and line break in string literals.

Brackets can be used to retrieve characters from a string. The representation of a character is a string with a `length` of 1. There is no character type. A character can be represented as a number or a string.

Many languages do have a character type, and it is usually abbreviated as `char`, but there does not seem to be a standard pronounciation. I have heard it spoken as *car*, *care*, *chair*, *char*, and *share*.

All strings are frozen when they are created. Wunce made, a string can not be changed. Smaller pieces can be copied from strings. Each piece is a new string. New strings can be made by concatenating strings together.

```
const mess = "monster";
const the_four = "uni" + my_little_string + " rainbow butterfly " + mess;
                       // the_four is "unicorn rainbow butterfly monster"

const first = the_four.slice(0, 7);              // first is "unicorn"
const last = the_four.slice(-7);                 // last is "monster"
const parts = the_four.split(" ");               // parts is [
                                                 //     "unicorn"
                                                 //     "rainbow"
                                                 //     "butterfly"
                                                 //     "monster"
                                                 // ]
parts[2][0] === "b"                              // true
"*".repeat(5)                                    // "*****"
parts[1].padStart(10, "/")                       // "///rainbow"
```

More Unicode

Unicode's original goal was to represent all of the world's living languages in 16 bits. Its charter later changed to represent all of the world's languages in 21 bits. Unfortunately, JavaScript was designed during Unicode's 16 bit phase.

Unicode takes JavaScript's *character* and breaks it into two new terms: *code unit* and *code point*. A code unit is wun of those 16 bit characters. A code point is the number that corresponds to a character. A code point is formed from 1 or more code units.

Unicode defines 1,114,112 code points, divided into 17 planes of 65,536 code points. The original plane is now called the Basic Multilingual Plane (BMP). The remaining 16 planes are the supplementary planes. JavaScript can easily use the characters in the BMP because that is where a code point can be identified with a single code unit. The supplemental characters are more difficult.

JavaScript accesses the supplemental characters by use of surrogate pairs. A surrogate pair is formed by two special code units. There are 1024 high surrogate code units, and 1024 low surrogate code units. The high surrogate code units have lower codes than the low surrogate code units.

0xD800 thru 0xDBFF	high surrogate code units
0xDC00 thru 0xDFFF	low surrogate code units

When properly paired, each surrogate code unit contributes 10 bits to form a 20 bit offset, to which 65,536 is added to form the code point. (The addition was to eliminate confusion caused by having two different sequences of code units that could produce the same code point. I think this solution caused more confusion than it avoided. A simpler solution would have been to make it illegal to use a surrogate pair to represent a code point in the BMP. This would have yielded a 20 bit character set instead of a 21 bit character set.)

Consider the code point U+1F4A9 (or 128169 in decimal). We subtract 65,536 which yields 62,633 or 0xF4A9. The high 10 bits are 0x03D. The low 10 bits are 0x0A9. We add 0xD800 to the high bits, and 0xDC00 to the low bits, and we get a surrogate pair. So

JavaScript stores U+1F4A9 as U+D83D U+DCA9. From JavaScript's point of view, U+1F4A9 is two 16 bit characters. It will display as a single character if the operating system is competent. JavaScript is mostly unaware of the supplemental planes, but it is not overtly hostile to them.

There are two ways to write the code point U+1F4A9 with escapement in a string literal.

```
"\uD83D\uDCA9" === "\u{1F4A9}"                                    // true
```

They both produce the same string having a `length` of 2.

There is a `String.fromCodePoint` function that can make surrogate pairs.

```
String.fromCharCode(55357, 56489) === String.fromCodePoint(128169)  // true
```

The `codePointAt` method is similar to `charCodeAt` except that it may also look at the next character, and if they form a surrogate pair, it returns a supplemental code point.

```
"\uD83D\uDCA9".codePointAt(0)                                     // 128169
```

Most of the characters that people need for global communication can be found in the BMP, so the surrogate stuff is not usually needed. Even so, the supplemental characters can appear at any time, so your program should be expecting them.

Unicode contains combining and modifying characters that add accents and other modifications to letters. It also contains characters that control the writing direction and other services. Sometimes these can get complicated, so that two strings that appear to contain the same characters might not be equal. Unicode has normalization rules that specify the order in which things must appear, and when base characters with modifiers should be replaced with composite characters. Humans are not bound by those rules, so you might have to deal with denormal material. JavaScript wraps the normalization rules in a `normalize` method.

```
const combining_diaeresis = "\u0308";
const u_diaeresis = "u" + combining_diaeresis;
const umlaut_u = "\u00FC";

u_diaeresis === umlaut_u                                          // false
u_diaeresis.normalize() === umlaut_u.normalize()                  // true
```

Unicode contains many duplicates and lookalikes, so it is still possible to have strings that look the same but are not equal, even after normalization. This is a source of confusion and it is a security hazard.

Template String Literals

Templating is a very popular practice in the development of web applications. Since the web browser's DOM API is so misfeatured and error prone, the prevailing practice is to instead build HTML views using templating. Whilst this can be much easier than rassling the DOM, it is also the cause of XSS and other web security failures. JavaScript's template string literals were intended to provide support for templating whilst mitigating the security problems, and sometimes partly succeed.

Template string literals are string literals that can span multiple lines. The ` *grave accent* (also known as backtick) is used as the delimiter.

```
const old_form = (
    "Can you"
    + "\nbelieve how"
    + "\nincredibly"
    + "\nlong this"
    + "\nstring literal"
    + "\nis?"
);

const new_form = `Can you
believe how
incredibly
long this
string literal
is?`;

old_form === new_form                                      // true
```

Does the new form offer a significant advantage over the old form? There is a small notational advantage, but it comes at a cost: The largest syntactic structures in the language are delimited by the lightest optical character on the keyboard. The potential for errors is large. Also, a visual ambiguity is added. Is there a space after `incredibly`? With the old form, the answer is clearly no.

In most cases, long form textual material should not be stored in programs. It should instead be maintained with an appropriate tool, like a text editor or a JSON editor or a database tool, and then accessed by the program as a resource bundle. The new syntax is encouraging a bad practice.

It is very common to use strings to record human language. Such texts usually need to be translated to serve the global audience. We do not want to maintain a separate version of each program file in every language. We want to have a single version of each program file that can receive localized text. The new form makes this more difficult because it restricts the ways that template strings can be provided to programs.

The benefit of the new syntax is that it provides interpolation. Valid expressions can be placed inside of ${ *dollar sign left brace* } *right brace* inside a template string literal. The expressions are evaluated, converted into a strings, and inserted.

```
let fear = "monsters";

const old_way = "The only thing we have to fear is " + fear + ".";

const new_way = `The only thing we have to fear is ${fear}.`;

old_way === new_way                                        // true
```

The danger with both ways is that the content could be something nasty, like

```
fear = "<script src=https://themostevilserverintheworld.com/malware.js>";
```

The web provides lots of opportunities for enabling malicious material. Templating seems to increase vulnerability. Most templating tools provide mechanisms for mitigating the dangers, but still allow exploits to occur. And the worst, like template string literals with interpolation, are unsafe by default.

The mitigation affordance in this case is a special kind of function, called a *tag* function. Preceding a template string literal with a function expression causes the function to be called with the template string and the values of the expressions as its arguments. The idea is that the tag function is given all of the pieces which it then properly filters, encodes, assembles, and returns.

The `dump` function is a tag function that just returns all of the input material in a human readable form.

```
function dump(strings, ...values) {
    return JSON.stringify({
        strings,
        values
    }, undefined, 4);
}

const what = "ram";
const where = "rama lama ding dong";

`Who put the ${what} in the ${where}?`
                    // "Who put the ram in the rama lama ding dong?"

const result = dump`Who put the ${what} in the ${where}?`;
                    // The result is `{
                    //      "strings": [
                    //          "Who put the ",
                    //          " in the ",
                    //          "?"
                    //      ],
                    //      "values": [
                    //          "ram",
                    //          "rama lama ding dong"
                    //      ]
                    // }`
```

It is odd that the strings are passed together as an array, but the values are passed as individual arguments. Tag functions can mitigate XSS and other security hazards if they are constructed properly, and if the tag functions are actually used. But again, it is unsafe by default.

Template string literals added a lot of new syntax, mechanism, and complexity to the language. They encourage bad practices, but they do provide some benefit in providing large string literals.

Regular Expressions

These string methods can take regular expression objects as arguments: `match`, `replace`, `search`, `split`. The regular expression objects can also contain their own methods: `exec`, `test`.

Regular expression objects perform pattern matching on strings. Regular expressions are bafflingly terse, but powerfully expressive. As powerful as they are, there are many things that they can not do. Regular expression objects are not powerful enough to parse JSON text, for example. This is because JSON parsing requires some sort of a pushdown store to deal with the nested structures. Regular expression objects do not have pushdown stores. Regular expression objects are capable of breaking JSON text into tokens, which could significantly simplify the task of making a JSON parser.

Tokenization

Compilers tokenize source programs as a part of the compilation. There are other programs that also rely on tokenization, including editors, code decorators, static analyzers, macro processors, and minifiers. Highly interactive programs, like editors, need to tokenize quickly. Unfortunately, JavaScript is a very difficult language to tokenize.

This is due to the interaction between regular expression literals and automatic semicolon insertion. This causes ambiguities that make programs difficult to interpret. For example,

```
    return /a/i;                     // return a regular expression object

    return b.return /a/i;            // return ((b.return) / a) / i
```

This shows that it is not possible in general to correctly tokenize JavaScript programs without simultaneously doing a full parse.

This gets much worse with the template string literals. An expression can be embedded inside of a literal. Another template string literal can be nested inside of that expression. This can go to any depth. The expressions can also contain regular expression literals and strings that contain backticks. It can be very difficult to determine if a backtick is closing the current literal or opening a nested literal. It can be very difficult to determine what the structure of a thing is.

```
    `${`${"\"}`"}`}`
```

It gets even worse. Those expressions can also contain functions that can contain regular expression literals and missing semicolons and more template string literals.

Tools like editors will assume that programs are well behaved. There is a subset of JavaScript that can be tokenized without also doing a full parse. If you go crazy with this stuff, you should expect to see your tools fail.

I hope that the next language will be trivial to tokenize. In the meantime, I recommend not using interpolation with template string literals.

Fulfill

Let's consider an alternative to template string interpolation: a function called `fulfill`. It takes a string that may contain symbolic variables, and an object or an array containing values that should replace the symbolic variables. It can also take either a function or an object of functions that can encode the replacements.

A potential problem with template strings is that everything that is in scope is available for inclusion. That is very convenient but it is also a security hazard. The `fulfill` function only has access to the container of values that you explicitly pass to it, so it is safer. The default encoder removes characters that are known to be hazardous in some contexts, so in an HTML context, it is safe by default, unlike template strings which are unsafe by default. But like template string interpolation, it may be unsafe if you misuse the encoders.

The string can come from any source, such as a JSON payload or a string literal. It does not need to be colocated in the JavaScript file. This better suits the needs of localized applications.

A symbolic variable is wrapped in { *left brace* }*right brace*. It can not contain any spaces or braces. It can contain a path, and optionally a colon followed by the name of an encoding. A path is wun or more names or numbers, separated by . *period*.

```
{a.very.long.path:hexify}
```

The container is an object or array that holds the values that will replace the symbolic variables. It can contain nested objects and arrays. The values will be found with the path. If the replacement value is a function, it is called and its return value is the replacement value. The container itself can be a function. It is called, passing the path and encoding to get the replacement value.

The replacement value can then be transformed by an encoder. This is primarily to mitigate the security problems that come with templating, but it can have other uses.

The optional encoder argument can be an object containing encoder functions. The encoding part of a symbolic variable chooses wun of the encoders. If the encoder object does not have a matching function, then the original symbolic variable is not replaced. The encoder argument can also be an encoder function that is called with all of the symbolic variables. An encoder function is passed the replacement candidate, the path, and the encoding. If it does not return a string or a number, then the original symbolic variable is not replaced.

If a symbolic variable does not specify an encoding, then the "" encoding is assumed.

A path contains a number that corresponds to an element in the values array, or the name of a property in the values object. The path can contain dots so that properties from nested objects and arrays can be found.

Symbolic variables are only replaced if they are well formed, and if there is a replacement value, and if the encoding is specified and implemented correctly. If anything is not right, then the symbolic variable is left in place. Literal braces can be placed in the string without need for escapement. If they are not part of a symbolic variable, they are left alone.

```
const example = fulfill(
    "{greeting}, {my.place:upper}!  :{",
    {
        greeting: "Hello",
        my: {
            fabulous: "Unicorn",
            insect: "Butterfly",
            place: "World"
        },
        phenomenon : "Rainbow"
    },
    {
        upper: function upper(string) {
            return string.toUpperCase();
        },
        "": function identity(string) {
            return string;
```

```
        }
    }
);      // example is "Hello, WORLD!   :{"
```

The `entityify` function makes text safe for insertion into HTML.

```
function entityify(text) {
    return text.replace(
        /&/g,
        "&amp;"
    ).replace(
        /</g,
        "&lt;"
    ).replace(
        />/g,
        "&gt;"
    ).replace(
        /\\/g,
        "&bsol;"
    ).replace(
        /"/g,
        "&quot;"
    );
}
```

We now fill a template with dangerous data.

```
const template = "<p>Lucky {name.first} {name.last} won ${amount}.</p>";

const person = {
    first: "Da5id",
    last: "<script src=https://enemy.evil/pwn.js/>"
};

// Now we call the fulfill function.

fulfill(
    template,
    {
        name: person,
        amount: 10
    },
    entityify
)
// "<p>Lucky Da5id &lt;script src=enemy.evil/pwn.js/&gt; won $10.</p>"
```

The `entityify` encoder rendered the evil script tag harmless to HTML.

And now I will show you the code I used to prepare the chapter list of the book you are reading right now!

The chapter list is in the form of a JSON text. There are literal braces in the templates but that presents no problem. It shows nested calls to `fulfill` that avoid the lexical complexity of nested template strings.

```
const chapter_names = [
    "Read Me First!",
    "How Names Work",
    "How Numbers Work",
    "How Big Integers Work",
```

```
        "How Big Floating Point Works",
        "How Big Rationals Work",
        "How Booleans Work",
        "How Arrays Works",
        "How Objects Work",
        "How Strings Work",
        "How Bottom Values Work",
        "How Statements Work",
        "How Functions Work",
        "How Generators Work",
        "How Exceptions Work",
        "How Programs Work",
        "How this Works",
        "How Class Free Works"
        "How Tail Calls Work",
        "How Purity Works",
        "How Eventual Programming Works",
        "How Date Works",
        "How JSON Works",
        "How Testing Works",
        "How Optimizing Works",
        "How Transpiling Works",
        "How Tokenizing Works",
        "How Parsing Works",
        "How Code Generation Works",
        "How Runtimes Work",
        "How Wat! Works",
        "How This Book Works"
    ];
    const chapter_list = "<div>[</div>{chapters}<div>]</div>";
    const chapter_list_item = `{comma}
<a href="#{index}">{"number": {index}, "chapter": "{chapter}"}</a>`;

    fulfill(
        chapter_list,
        {
            chapters: chapter_names.map(function (chapter, chapter_nr) {
                return fulfill(
                    chapter_list_item,
                    {
                        chapter,
                        index: chapter_nr,
                        comma: (chapter_nr > 0)
                            ? ","
                            : ""
                    }
                ).join("");
            })
        },
        entityify
    )                          // See the Chapter List at the front of this book
```

The fulfill function is not very big.

```
    const rx_delete_default = /[ < > & % " \\ ]/g;
    const rx_syntactic_variable = /
        \{
        (
```

```
            [^ { } : \s ]+
        )
        (?:
            :
            (
                [^ { } : \s ]+
            )
        )?
        \}
    /g;

    //  Capturing groups:
    //      [0] original (symbolic variable wrapped in braces)
    //      [1] path
    //      [2] encoding

    function default_encoder(replacement) {
        return String(replacement).replace(rx_delete_default, "");
    }

    export default Object.freeze(function fulfill(
        string,
        container,
        encoder = default_encoder
    ) {
```

The `fulfill` function takes a string containing symbolic variables, a generator function or an object or array containing values to replace the symbolic variables, and an optional encoder function or object of encoder functions. The default encoder removes all angle brackets.

Most of the work is done by the string `replace` method that finds the symbolic variables, presenting them as the original substring, a path string, and an optional encoding string.

```
        return string.replace(
            rx_syntactic_variable,
            function (original, path, encoding = "") {
                try {
```

Use the path to obtain a single replacement from the container of values. The path contains wun or more names (or numbers) separated by periods.

```
                    let replacement = (
                        typeof container === "function"
                        ? container
                        : path.split(".").reduce(
                            function (refinement, element) {
                                return refinement[element];
                            },
                            container
                        )
                    );
```

If the replacement value is a function, call it to obtain a replacement value.

```
                    if (typeof replacement === "function") {
                        replacement = replacement(path, encoding);
                    }
```

If an encoder object was provided, call wun of its functions. If the encoder is a function, call it.

```
replacement = (
    typeof encoder === "object"
    ? encoder[encoding]
    : encoder
)(replacement, path, encoding);
```

If the replacement is a number or boolean, convert it to a string.

```
if (
    typeof replacement === "number"
    || typeof replacement === "boolean"
) {
    replacement = String(replacement);
}
```

If the replacement is a string, then do the substitution. Otherwise, leave the symbolic variable in its original state.

```
return (
    typeof replacement === "string"
    ? replacement
    : original
);
```

If anything goes wrong, then leave the symbolic variable in its original state.

```
            } catch (ignore) {
                return original;
            }
        }
    );
});
```

## Chapter 10

How Bottom Values Work

○ ● ○ ● ○

> You're romance,
> you're the steppes of Russia
> You're the pants,
> on a Roxy usher
> I'm a broken doll, a fol-de-rol, a blop
> But if, baby, I'm the bottom
> you're the top!
> *Cole Porter*

Bottom values are special values that indicate the end of a recursive data structure or the absence of a value. In programming languages, bottom values can have names like `nil`, `none`, `nothing`, and `null`.

JavaScript has two bottom values: `null` and `undefined`. The `NaN` value could also be considered to be a bottom value, indicating the absence of a number. The abundance of bottom values should be regarded as a design error.

`null` and `undefined` are the only values in JavaScript that are not objects in the vague sense. Attempting to get a property value from them raises an exception.

In some ways `null` and `undefined` are very similar to each other, but in some ways they behave differently. They are partially, but not completely interchangable. Having two things that can be seen as the same thing but that sometimes act differently is a source of confusion. Time is wasted in trying to decide which to use when, and those groundless theories lead to even more confusion, and confusion leads to bugs.

We can make better programs if we eliminate wun of them. We can not eliminate wun from the language, but we can profitably eliminate wun from our own programs. We should eliminate `null` and use `undefined` exclusively.

Ordinarily, when forced to choose between two words, I tend to prefer the shorter wun. `null` has a known meaning in the context of programming and data structures, and `undefined` has not. Furthermore, `undefined` is a confusing name. It does not mean what mathematicians mean by *undefined*. It does not even mean what programmers mean by *undefined*.

So given that `null` seems to be a more suitable name, why do I prefer `undefined`? I prefer `undefined` because `undefined` is the value that JavaScript itself uses. If you define a variable using `let` or `var` and do not explicitly initialize it, JavaScript implicitly initializes it with `undefined`, which is confusing because the newly defined variable has `undefined` as its value. If you do not pass enough arguments into a function, the extra parameters are set to `undefined`. If you get the value of a property of an object and the object lacks that property, it gives `undefined`. If you get an element of an array that the array lacks, it gives `undefined`.

The only place I use `null` is in using `Object.create(null)` to create a new empty object. A specification error forbids the use of `Object.create()` and `Object.create( undefined)`.

`null` and `undefined` can be tested for with the equality operator.

```
function stringify_bottom(my_little_bottom) {
    if (my_little_bottom === undefined) {
        return "undefined";
    }
    if (my_little_bottom === null) {
        return "null";
    }
    if (Number.isNaN(my_little_bottom)) {
        return "NaN";
    }
}
```

You may sometimes see old-timers writing (`typeof my_little_bottom === "undefined"`), which also works. But (`typeof my_little_bottom === "null"`) fails because `typeof null` returns `"object"`, not `"null"`. This is bad because (`typeof my_little_object === "object"`) gives a false positive when `my_little_object` is `null`, leading to the error that the test was intended to prevent. This is another reason to avoid using `null`.

`undefined` is strictly better to use than `null`, but it also suffers from the path problem. You recall that the value of missing properties is `undefined`, which would be a good thing if `undefined` were a frozen empty object, but it is not. `undefined` is not an object, so attempting to get a property from it raises an exception. This makes it tricky to write path expressions. For example,

```
my_little_first_name = my_little_person.name.first;
```

throws an exception if `my_little_person` does not have a `name` property or if `my_little_person` is `undefined`. So you can not think of a chain of `.` *dot* and `[ ]` *subscript* as a path. You must think of it as a sequence of individual operations, any wun of which might fail. This has led to code like:

```
my_little_first_name = (
    my_little_person
    && my_little_person.name
    && my_little_person.name.first
);
```

The `&&` *logical and* operator is used to avoid evaluating the stuff to the right if the stuff to the left is falsy. That is big and ugly and slow, but it avoids the exceptions, and usually does what

```
my_little_first_name = my_little_person.name.first;
```

would do if `undefined` worked like an object and not like an anti-object.

## Chapter 11

How Statements Work

○ ● ○ ● ●

> When I nod my head, you hit it with a
> hammer.
>
> *Bullwinkle J. Moose*

We can sort most programming languages into two classes: expression languages and statement languages. A statement language has statements and expressions. An expression language has only expressions. The proponents of expression languages have a body of theory that argues that expression languages are vastly superior. There does not appear to be much theory to justify statement languages. Even so, all of the popular languages, including JavaScript, are statement languages.

Early programs were simply lists of instructions, sometimes resembling sentences, even ending with a period in some languages. Unfortunately, periods were confused with decimal points, so in later languages the statement ending characters became semicolons.

Structured programming destroyed the idea of simple lists of statements, allowing lists of statements to be nested in other statements. ALGOL 60 was wun of the first languages of the structured generation, having `BEGIN` and `END` to delimit blocks of statements. BCPL introduced `{` *left brace* and `}` *right brace* to replace `BEGIN` and `END`. This bit of sixties fashion has remained in vogue for many decades.

Declaration

JavaScript has three statements that are used to declare variables in a function or a module: `let`, `function`, and `const`. There is also an obsolete statement, `var`, that is used with Internet Explorer, an unloved web browser.

Let's talk about `let`. The `let` statement declares a new variable in the current scope. Every block (a string of statements wrapped in `{` *left brace* and `}` *right brace*) creates a scope. Variables declared in a scope are not visible outside of the scope. The `let` statement also allows, but does not require, initialization. If a variable is not initialized, it is given the default value `undefined`. A `let` statement is allowed to declare several variables at wunce, but I recommend declaring each variable in its own `let` statement. This improves readability and ease of maintenance.

The `let` statement also allows destructuring. This is a tricky bit of syntax that defines and initializes multiple variables with the contents of an object or array. So

```
let {huey, dewey, louie} = my_little_object;
```

is a shorthand for

```
let huey = my_little_object.huey;
let dewey = my_little_object.dewey;
let louie = my_little_object.louie;
```

Similarly,

```
let [zeroth, wunth, twoth] = my_little_array;
```

is a shorthand for

```
let zeroth = my_little_array[0];
let wunth = my_little_array[1];
let twoth = my_little_array[2];
```

Destructuring is not an important feature but it can improve some patterns. It is also easily misused. There are syntactic affordances for renaming and default values but they introduce too much visual complexity.

The `function` declaration creates a function object and a variable to contain it. Unfortunately, it has the same syntax as function expressions which is a source of confusion.

```
function my_little_function() {
    return "So small.";
}
```

is a shorthand for

```
let my_little_function = undefined;

my_little_function = function my_little_function() {
    return "So small.";
};
```

Notice that the `function` declaration does not end in a semicolon, but the `let` and assignment statements do.

The `function` declaration gets hoisted. The pieces are removed from where you placed the declaration and moved to the top of the function body or module. All of the `let` statements created by `function` declarations get hoisted to the top, followed by all of the assignments of function objects to those variables.

That is why a `function` declaration should not be placed in a block. It is good to put a `function` declaration in a function body or a module, but it is bad to put a `function` declaration in an `if` statement, `switch` statement, `while` statement, `do` statement, or `for` statement. Functions will be discussed in Chapter 12.

The `const` statement is like the `let` statement but with two important differences: the initialization is required, not optional, and the variable may not be assigned to later. When I have a choice, I prefer to use `const` because it encourages greater purity (Chapter 19).

The word `const` is obviously short for *constant*. That word is troublesome because it implies permanence or timelessness. A `const` is an ephemeral thing that may disappear when the function returns. It may have a different value each time the program is run or the function is called. Also be aware that if the value of a `const` is a mutable value like an unfrozen object or unfrozen array, then the value can be assigned to whilst the variable can not be assigned to. `Object.freeze` works on values, not on variables, and `const` works on variables, not on values. It is important to understand the difference between variables and values: variables contain references to values. Values never contain variables.

```
let my_littlewhitespace_variable = {};
const my_little_constant = my_littlewhitespace_variable;
my_little_constant.butterfly = "free";              // {butterfly: "free"}
Object.freeze(my_littlewhitespace_variable);
my_little_constant.monster = "free";                         // FAIL!
my_little_constant.monster                                   // undefined
my_little_constant.butterfly                                 // "free"
my_littlewhitespace_variable = Math.PI;    // my_littlewhitespace_variable is
approximately π
my_little_constant = Math.PI;                                // FAIL!
```

Expression

JavaScript allows any expression to appear in statement position. This is a sloppy-but-popular practice in language design. JavaScript has three expression types that make sense in statement position: assignments, invocations, and `delete`. Unfortunately, all other expression types are also allowed in statement position which degrades a compiler's ability to identify errors.

An assignment statement replaces the reference in a variable, or modifies a mutable object or array. An assignment statement contains four parts.

0. An *lvalue*, an expression that receives the value. It can be a variable or an expression that produces an object or array value and a refinement: a . *period* followed by a property name, or a [*left bracket* followed by an expression that produces a property name or an element number followed by a] *right bracket*.

1. An assignment operator:

   = *assignment*

   += *add assignment*

   -= *subtract assignment*

   *= *multiply assignment*

   /= *divide assignment*

   %= *remainder assignment*

   **= *exponentiation assignment*

   >>>= *shift right assignment*

   >>= *shift right sign extended assignment*

   <<= *shift left assignment*

   &= *bitwise and assignment*

   |= *bitwise or assignment*

   ^= *bitwise xor assignment*

2. An expression, whose value will be stored.

3. A ; *semicolon*.

I do not recommend use of the increment operators ++ *plus plus* or -- *minus minus*. They were created in antiquity for doing pointer arithmetic. We have since discovered that pointer arithmetic is harmful, so modern languages no longer allow it. The last popular language to boast of having pointer arithmetic was C++, a language so bad that it was named after ++ *plus plus*.

We got rid of pointer arithmetic, but we are still stuck with ++. Now it adds 1 to something. Why do we think we need a different syntactic form to add 1 than to add every other value? How does that make any sense?

The answer is: **It does not make any sense**.

Making matters worse, ++ has a pre-increment form and a post-increment form. It is very easy to get them reversed, and that can be very difficult to debug. And ++ has been implicated in buffer overrun errors and other security failures. We should discard features that are unnecessary and hazardous.

Expression statements are impure. Assignment statements and `delete` are obviously causing mutation. An invocation that discards the return value relies on side-effects. The expression statement is the only statement that does not start with an identifying keyword. This syntactic optimization encourages impurity.

Branching

JavaScript has two branching statements, `if` and `switch`, which is either wun too many or two too many.

I do not recommend use of `switch`, an unholy hybrid of C. A. R. Hoare's `case` statement and FORTRAN's computed `goto` statement. There is nothing that can be written with the `switch` statement that can not be written (usually more compactly) with the `if` statement. The `switch` statement offers an implicit switch variable, but suffers from a fallthru hazard that can lead to errors and bad practices. And there is the stylistic problem: Should a `case` be aligned with the `switch` or should it be indented? There does not seem to be a correct answer.

An object can be used as an alternative to the `switch` statement. Fill an object with functions that implement the behavior for each case. The value matching the `case` variable is the key.

```
const my_little_result = my_little_object[case_expression]();
```

Your *case_expression* selects wun of the functions from your object, which can then be called. If the *case_expression* does not match wun of your functions, an exception is raised for you.

Unfortunately, this form also comes with a potential security hazard because of the binding of `this`. There will be more of `this` in Chapter 16.

The `if` statement is strictly better than the `switch` statement. Its `else` is not a statement, it is a clause, so it should not be indented like a statement. The `else` should be placed on the same line as the } *right brace* that closed the previous block.

JavaScript expects the condition part to be a boolish value. I think that was a mistake. JavaScript should have insisted on a boolean. I recommend that you provide booleans even though the language invites you to be sloppier.

The `else if` form allows the `if` statement to replace the `switch` statement without wildly indenting across the screen. It can be misused which can lead to confusing control flows. The `else if` form should only be used in case-like constructions. If an `else` clause starts with an `if`, it might be better to not use `else if` and instead put the if in the else block. The else if form should not be used if the previous block ended in a disruption.

When writing in a pure functional style, it can be better to use the ternary operator. The ternary operator is often misused, which has given it a bad reputation. Wrap the entire ternary expression in parens. Put a line break after the open paren and align the condition and the two consequences.

```
let my_little_value = (
    is_mythical
    ? (
        is_scary
        ? "monster"
        : "unicorn"
    )
    : (
        is_insect
        ? "butterfly"
        : "rainbow"
    )
);
```

Looping

JavaScript has three looping statements, for, while, and do, which is either two too many or three too many.

The for statement is a descendant of FORTRAN's DO statement. Both were used to process arrays wun element at a time, pushing most of the work of managing the induction variable onto the programmer. We should instead be using array methods like forEach that manage the induction variable automatically. I expect that in future versions of the language, the array methods, when given pure functions to apply to the elements, will be able to do most of the work in parallel. Incompetent programs using the for statement will still be processing the elements wun at a time.

I found when teaching programming to beginners that the three-part control (*initialization*; *condition*; *increment*) was baffling. It is not obvious what the clauses are or why they are in that particular order, and there are no syntactic affordances to make it easy to discover or remember.

I do not recommend using the for statement.

The while statement and the do statement are both used for general looping. They are very different syntactically, but operationally the only difference is that the while statement checks its condition at the top of the loop and the do statement checks its condition at the bottom. It is weird that a large visual difference has such a small operational difference.

I find that many of my loops do not want to break exclusively at the top or bottom. They usually want to break in the middle. So many of my loops have this shape:

```
while (true) {
    // do some work
    if (are_we_done) {
        break;
    }
    // do some more work
}
```

The best way to write loops is to use tail recursion (Chapter 18).

Disruption

JavaScript has four disruptive statements that alter the control flow, and none of them are goto! They are break, continue, throw, and return.

The break statement is used to leave a loop. It could also be used to leave a switch statement if we used a switch statement, but that gets complicated if a switch statement is in a loop.

The continue statement is a goto statement that jumps to the top of a loop. I have never seen a program that contained continue that was not improved by its removal.

The throw statement raises an exception (Chapter 14).

My favorite of the disruptive statements is return. It ends the execution of a function and designates the return value. There is a school that teaches that a function should have only wun return statement. I have never seen any evidence that shows that that teaching is beneficial. I think it makes more sense to have a function return when it knows it needs to, and not have to first funnel down to a unique exit point.

JavaScript does not have a goto statement, but it does allow all statements to have labels. I think that was a mistake. Statements should not need labels.

Potpourri

The throw statement, the try statement, and the catch clause will be discussed in Chapter 14.

The import and export statements will be discussed in Chapter 15.

The debugger statement may cause a suspension of execution, similar to reaching a breakpoint. The debugger statement should only be used during development. It should be removed before moving a program into production.

Punctuation

JavaScript allows `if` and `else` and the looping statements to take either a single statement or a block. Always use a block, even if the block contains a single statement. This makes the code more resilient. It will be easier to improve the code without introducing errors into it. Do not be setting syntactic traps in your code that might trip up your teammates. Code as if it is important that the code always works well.

The expression statements, the `do` statement, the disruptive statements, and the `debugger` statement are all concluded with a ; *semicolon*. JavaScript has a misfeature called Automatic Semicolon Insertion that was intended to make coding easier for beginners by allowing them to leave the ; *semicolon* out. Unfortunately, it can fail in bad ways, so write like a professional. It would have been better if JavaScript had been designed with a semicolon-free grammar, but it wasn't, so do not pretend that it was. That confusion can cause errors.

If a statement is too long to fit on a line, then it needs to be broken. I break after a (*left parenthesis*, [*left bracket*, or { *left brace*. The matching) *right parenthesis*,] *right bracket*, or } *right brace* starts a new line at the same indentation as the line that began the break. The material in between will be indented four spaces.

## Chapter 12

How Functions Work

○ ● ○ ○

> The fact is that, if proper procedures were
> available, everybody would use them; the
> advantages in their use in program
> construction are, in practice, overwhelming.
>
> *Ian F. Currie*

The first programs were called *routines*. A routine was a list of orders (or instructions). A routine was loaded into a machine along with some data, and in time, with some luck, an answer was output.

It was observed that it was difficult to manage a routine as a single list. Some sequences of orders might appear in multiple routines, or might appear multiple times in the same routine. So subroutinues were invented. A set of useful subroutines could be collected into a library. Each subroutine would be given a call number, similar to the call number on a library book. (Names were an extravagance.)

Grace Murray Hopper developed a routine called A-0. It was the first compiler. It would take a list of orders and call numbers and a tape containing a library of subroutines. It would find the subroutines that corresponded to the call numbers, and compile them into a new program. The sense of *compile* was the literary sense: producing a work by assembling information from other sources. This gave us many terms of art that are still used today: assembler, compiler, library, source, and most importantly, call. We call for a subroutine as we might call for a book in a library. We do not commence or activate a subroutine. We call for it. Grace Murray Hopper helped establish much of the jargon in our profession. It is because of Grace Murray Hopper that we call these machines *computers* and not *electronic brains*. It is because of Grace Murray Hopper that I am proud to call myself a *programmer*.

It was observed that subroutines were related to mathematical functions. FORTRAN II had a `SUBROUTINE` declaration and a `CALL` statement for activating them, and it also had a `FUNCTION` declaration that could return a result that could contribute a value to an expression.

The C language unified the subroutine and the function, all informally called functions. C did not use a descriptive keyword. JavaScript does: `function`.

The `function` operator makes function objects. The `function` operator takes a parameter list and a body, which is block of statements.

Each name in the parameter list is a variable that is initialized by an expression from the argument list. Each name can optionally be followed by = *equal sign* and an expression. If the value of the argument is undefined, then the value of the expression is used instead.

```
function make_set(array, value = true) {

// Make an object by taking property names from an array of strings.

    const object = Object.create(null);
    array.forEach(function (name) {
        object[name] = value;
    });
    return object;
}
```

A function object is called with an argument list containing zero or more expressions, separated by commas. Each of those expressions is evaluated and bound to a parameter of the function.

The argument list and parameter list do not have to have the same length. Excess arguments are ignored. Missing arguments give the undefined value.

The ... *ellipsis* operator is allowed in argument lists and parameter lists. In argument lists it is called *spread*. It takes an array and spreads it out so that each element of the array is treated as a separate argument. In parameter lists it is called *rest*. All of the rest of the arguments are packed into an array that is bound to that parameter name. The rest parameter must be the last parameter in the parameter list. This allows a function to handle a variable number of arguments.

```
function curry(func, ...zeroth) {
    return function (...wunth) {
        return func(...zeroth, ...wunth);
    };
}
```

When a function is called, an activation object is created. The activation object is not visible to you. It is a hidden data structure that holds the information and bindings that the function needs to execute, and the return address of the activation of the calling function.

In languages like C, activation objects are allocated on a stack. They are deallocated (or popped off) when the function returns. JavaScript does this differently. JavaScript allocates activation objects on a heap, like ordinary objects. Activation objects are not automatically deactivated when functions return. Instead, the activation object can survive as long as there is a reference to it. Activation objects are garbage collected like ordinary objects.

The activation object contains:

- A reference to the function object.
- A reference to the activation object of the caller. This is used by return to give control back.
- Resumption information that is used to continue execution after a call. This is usually the address of an instruction that is immediately after a function call.

- The parameters of the function, initialized with the arguments.
- The variables of the function, initialized with `undefined`.
- Temporary variables that the function uses to evaluate complex expressions.
- `this`, which might be a reference to the object of interest if the function object was called as a method.

A function object is like ordinary mutable objects in that it can be a container of properties. This is not a good thing. Ideally, function objects should be immutable objects. In some security scenarios, shared mutable function objects can be used to facilitate collusion.

A function object has a `prototype` property. This is used in the (not recommended) pseudoclassical model. The `prototype` property contains a reference to an object that contains a `constructor` property that contains a reference back to the function object, and a delegation link to `Object.prototype`. There will be more about this in Chapter 16.

A function object has a delegation link to `Function.prototype`. By this link, a function object inherits the unnecessary methods `apply` and `call`.

A function object also contains two hidden properties.

- A reference to the function's executable code.
- A reference to the activation object that was active at the time the function object was created. This is what makes closure possible. A function can use that hidden property to access the variables of the function that created it.

The term *free variable* is sometimes used to describe the variables that a function uses that were declared outside of the function. The term *bound variable* is sometimes used to describe the variables that were declared inside of the function including the parameters.

Functions can be nested. When an inner function object is created it contains a reference to the activation object of the outer function that created it.

This mechanism, a function object holding a reference to the activation object of the outer function, is called *closure*. It is the most important discovery so far in the history of programming languages. It was discovered in the Scheme language. It reached the mainstream with JavaScript. It is what makes JavaScript an interesting language. Without it, JavaScript would just be a steaming pile of good intentions, blunders, and classes.

## Chapter 13

How Generators Work

○ ● ● ○ ●

> The present day composers refuse to die.
> *Edgard Varèse*

JavaScript introduced a feature in ES6 called *generators*. They were added during a time when the standards process suffered from serious Python envy. I can not recommend using ES6 generators for several reasons.

What the code does is very different from how the code looks. They look like ordinary functions, but they work very differently. They produce a function object that produces an object that contains a `next` method that is made of the `function*` body. It has a `yield` operator that resembles a `return` statement, but it doesn't produce the expected value. Instead it produces an object that contains a `value` property that contains the expected value. A tiny `*` asterisk can cause huge changes in behavior.

They can have very complex control flow. We learned in the Structured Revolution that control flows should be straight forward and predictable. Generators can have complicated control flows because generators can be suspended and resumed. They can also have confusing interactions with `finally` and `return`.

They encourage use of loops. As we move away from objects and toward functions, we should be moving away from loops. These generators instead require *more* loops. Most generators contain a loop with a `yield` in the middle of it to produce the values. Most users of that generator use a `for` loop to consume them. That is two loops where none are needed.

Generators use a clumsy OOP interface. The factory produces an object, and the generator produces an object. (In a functional design, the factory produces a generator function, and the generator function produces a value. The functional design is simpler, cleaner, and easier to use.)

And finally, worst of all, ES6 generators are unnecessary. I do not recommend using features when there are better options available.

This is an example of ES6 generators:

```
function* counter() {
    let count = 0;
    while (true) {
        count += 1;
        yield count;
    }
}

const gen = counter();

gen.next().value                                    // 1
gen.next().value                                    // 2
gen.next().value                                    // 3
```

This is what I recommend you do instead:

```
function counter() {
    let count = 0;
    return function counter_generator() {
        count += 1;
        return count;
    };
}

const gen = counter();

gen()                                               // 1
gen()                                               // 2
gen()                                               // 3
```

So instead of writing something that looks like a function that yields a value but is actually a function that returns an object that contains a `next` method that yields an object that contains a `value` property that contains a value, simply write a function that returns a function that returns a value.

A Better Way

Generators are a really good thing to have. So let's do it right. We start with a function that returns a function. The outer function is a *factory*. The inner function is a *generator*. This is the general pattern:

```
function factory(factory's parameters) {

    Initialization of the generator's state

    return function generator(generator's parameters) {

        update the state

        return value;
    };
}
```

Of course, there can be many variations. The state of the generator is held securely in the factory's variables.

The simplest useful instance of this pattern is the `constant` factory. It takes a value, and returns a generator that always returns that value.

```
function constant(value) {
    return function constant_generator() {
        return value;
    };
}
```

A more useful example is the `integer` factory. It returns a generator that returns the next integer in a sequence each time it is called. At the end of the sequence it returns `undefined`. We use `undefined` as the sentinel that communicates the end of a sequence.

```
function integer(from = 0, to = Number.MAX_SAFE_INTEGER, step = 1) {
    return function () {
        if (from < to) {
            const result = from;
            from += step;
            return result;
        }
    };
}
```

The `element` factory takes an array and returns a generator that returns an element of that array each time it is called. It returns `undefined` when there are no more elements. The factory can take an optional second argument: a generator that produces the element numbers that are used to retrieve the elements. By default, it retrieves all of the elements in order.

```
function element(array, gen = integer(0, array.length)) {
    return function element_generator(...args) {
        const element_nr = gen(...args);
        if (element_nr !== undefined) {
            return array[element_nr];
        }
    };
}
```

The `property` factory does the same thing for objects. It returns each property of the object in the form of an array containing the key and the value. It returns `undefined` when there are no more properties. The factory can take an optional second argument: a generator that produces the keys that are used to retrieve the properties. By default, it retrieves all of the own properties in insertion order.

```
function property(object, gen = element(Object.keys(object))) {
    return function property_generator(...args) {
        const key = gen(...args);
        if (key !== undefined) {
            return [key, object[key]];
        }
    };
}
```

The `collect` factory takes a generator and an array. It returns a generator that works exactly like the generator it receives except that it also appends the interesting return values to the array. All of the arguments that are passed to the new function are passed to the old wun.

```
function collect(generator, array) {
    return function collect_generator(...args) {
        const value = generator(...args);
        if (value !== undefined) {
            array.push(value);
        }
        return value;
    };
}
```

We can use the `repeat` function as a driver. It receives a function and calls it until it returns `undefined`. This is the only loop we need. We could write it with a `do` statement, but I prefer to write it with tail recursion (Chapter 18).

```
function repeat(generator) {
    if (generator() !== undefined) {
        return repeat(generator);
    }
}
```

We can use `collect` to capture data.

```
const my_array = [];
repeat(collect(integer(0, 7), my_array)); // my_array is [0, 1, 2, 3, 4, 5, 6]
```

We could join `repeat` and `collect` together to make `harvest`. The `harvest` function is not a factory or a generator, but it takes a generator as its argument.

```
function harvest(generator) {
    const array = [];
    repeat(collect(generator, array));
    return array;
}
```

```
const result = harvest(integer(0, 7));  // result is [0, 1, 2, 3, 4, 5, 6]
```

The `limit` factory takes a function and returns a function that can be used only a limited number of times. When the count is exhausted, the new function does nothing but return `undefined`. The second argument to the factory is the number of times the new function may be called.

```
function limit(generator, count = 1) {
    return function (...args) {
        if (count >= 1) {
            count -= 1;
            return generator(...args);
        }
    };
}
```

The `limit` factory can be used with any function. For example, if you pass a function that grants wishes and 3 to `limit`, you get a function that grants 3 wishes.

The `filter` function takes a generator and a predicate function. A predicate function is a function that returns `true` or `false`. It returns a new generator that works like the old wun except that it only delivers the values for which the predicate returns `true`.

```
function filter(generator, predicate) {
    return function filter_generator(...args) {
        const value = generator(...args);
```

```
            if (value !== undefined && !predicate(value)) {
                return filter_generator(...args);
            }
            return value;
        };
    }

    const my_third_array = harvest(filter(
        integer(0, 42),
        function divisible_by_three(value) {
            return (value % 3) === 0;
        }
    ));
    // my_third_array is [0, 3, 6, 9, 12, 15, 18, 21, 24, 27, 30, 33, 36, 39]
```

The concat factory can take two or more generators and concatenate them together to
make a generator that combines their sequences. It takes values from the first generator until it produces undefined. It then switches to the next generator. The concat
factory uses the element factory that we saw earlier to smartly work thru the generators.

```
function concat(...generators) {
    const next = element(generators);
    let generator = next();
    return function concat_generator(...args) {
        if (generator !== undefined) {
            const value = generator(...args);
            if (value === undefined) {
                generator = next();
                return concat_generator(...args);
            }
            return value;
        }
    };
}
```

The join factory takes a function and wun or more generators and returns a new
generator. Each time the new generator is called, it calls all of the old generators and
pass their results to the function. You can use join with repeat to do all of the things
you used to do with for of. The function argument to join does the work of the block.
The join factory can work with multiple generator streams at wunce.

```
function join(func, ...gens) {
    return function join_generator() {
        return func(...gens.map(function (gen) {
            return gen();
        }));
    };
}
```

We can use all of this to make a map function that works like the array map method. It
takes a function and an array, and returns a new array where each element contains
the result of calling the function with each element of the array.

```
function map(array, func) {
    return harvest(join(func, element(array)));
}
```

The `objectify` factory gives us another way to construct data objects.

```
function objectify(...names) {
    return function objectify_constructor(...values) {
        const object = Object.create(null);
        names.forEach(function (name, name_nr) {
            object[name] = values[name_nr];
        });
        return object;
    };
}

let date_marry_kill = objectify("date", "marry", "kill");
let my_little_object = date_marry_kill("butterfly", "unicorn", "monster");
            // {date: "butterfly", marry: "unicorn", kill: "monster"}
```

Generators live at the frontier between pure and impure functions. The generators made by the `constant` factory are pure, but most generators are impeccably impure. Generators can be stateful, but they keep their state hidden in the closure of the factory. The state can only be updated by calling the generator. They are free of the side effects that plague most impure functions. This allows generators to compose really well.

It is good to make as much of our programs as pure as possible. Programs that interact with the universe can not be completely pure because the universe is not pure. How do we know what can be pure and what must be impure? Generators can show us a way.

## Chapter 14

How Exceptions Work

○ ● ● ● ○

No! Try not. Do, or do not.
There is no try.

Yoda

Programmers are optimists. There is often an implicit assumption in our programs that everything will always go right, but even an optimist knows that sometimes things can go wrong.

There is a possibility that the function we call might fail in an unexpected way. This is especially a concern when using code from third parties. Wun of the dimensions of coupling is failure modes. So what should happen when it fails? Should the whole program fail? Should we try calling the function again and hope for a better outcome? And how should the failure be communicated?

The most popular approach to this problem is exception handling which attempts to free us to program optimistically. We do not have to check for obscure error codes in every return value. We do not have to poll a global *defcon* register to find out if the program has become unstable. Instead we assume that everything works correctly. If something unexpected happens, the current activity will stop and our exception handler will determine what the program will do next.

JavaScript's exception management was inspired by Java. Java's exception management was inspired by C++. C++ is a language without adequate memory management, so when something goes wrong, every function in the call chain needs to explicitly release any memory that it had allocated. JavaScript has very good memory management, but it assumes the implications of C++'s faulty memory model.

A failure is signalled with the `throw` statement. C++ would have had a `raise` statement like the Ada language, but the word **raise** had already been used in C libraries, so C++ instead reserved a word that no wun had ever wanted to use.

JavaScript allows you to `throw` any value. It is common to `throw` something made by the `Error` constructor, but that is not required. You can throw literally anything. In C++ and Java, the exception object is the macguffin. In well written JavaScript, the exception object is superfluous.

```
throw "That does not compute.";
```

The `try` statement attaches an exception handler to a block. The exception handler is packaged as a `catch` clause. It is allowed wun parameter, which is how it receives whatever it was that `throw` threw.

```
try {
    here_goes_nothing();
} catch {
    console.log("fail: here_goes_nothing");
}
```

If anything raises an exception in the `try`, then the `catch` clause runs.

The design of `try` allows very fine-grained exception management. Every statement in a function could have its own `try` and its own `catch`. It even allows `try` statements to contain `try` statements. And even worse, it allows `catch` clauses to contain `try` statements, and `try` statements and `catch` clauses can contain `throw` statements. A function should not contain more than wun `try`.

Unwinding

An important goal that exception management managed to keep is that it does not impose a performance penalty on correctly running programs. A performance hit might occur when an exception is raised, but that should happen rarely, and even then it is not significantly expensive.

The JavaScript compiler produces a catchmap for every function that it compiles. The catchmap maps instruction locations in the function body to the `catch` that handles those locations. The catchmap is not used during normal program execution.

When a `throw` statement is executed, raising an exception, the catchmap for the current function is consulted. If there is a designated `catch` clause, then it gets control and execution resumes from there.

If there is not a designated `catch` clause, then we look at the caller. The caller is now the current function, and the statement that invoked the previous function is now the location of the failure. The catchmap is again consulted. If there is a designated `catch` clause, then it gets control and execution resumes from there.

And so it goes, down the virtual call stack, until a `catch` clause is found. When the call stack is empty, we have an uncaught exception.

It is a simple and elegant mechanism. It allows a style of programming that puts most focus on success without totally ignoring failure. But it is easily misused.

Ordinary Exceptions

The most popular misuse of exceptions is to use them to communicate normal results. For example, given a function that reads a file, a *file not found* error should not be an exception. It is a normal occurence. Exceptions should only be used for problems that should not be anticipated.

The Java language encourages misuse of exceptions as a way to get around problems in its type system. A Java method can only return a single type of result, so exceptions are used as an alternate channel to return the ordinary results that the type system does not allow. This can lead to several `catch` clauses attached to a single `try` block. It can be confusing because the ordinary results get jumbled up with the real exceptions.

It resembles a FORTRAN assigned GOTO statement, in which a variable contains the address of the destination of the jump. The catch clauses must be properly ordered to make sure the right clause is selected. Selection is not based on any type of equality, as with the switch statement, but is instead based on the typecasting rules, which are themselves an abomination. Any type system that requires explicit casting is broken.

The control paths are dictated by the method that created the exception object. That creates a tight coupling between the thrower and the catcher that works against clean modular design.

There can be a great many paths thru this tangle, which can make the job of releasing allocated resources quite challenging. So the finally clause was added to help mitigate this. The finally clause is a parameterless function that is called implicitly from every exit point of the try and each of the catch clauses.

JavaScript, on the other hand, provides a much cleaner approach. If the try was successful, then we obtained either a good result or a good explanation. JavaScript's type system is flexible enough to handle all expected cases.

If something truly unexpected happens, then the catch clause starts and an alternate story begins, either shutting things down or starting things over. We go with Plan A. If that succeeds, we are good. If it fails, we go straight to Plan B.

```
try {
    plan_a();
} catch {
    plan_b();
}
```

Reasoning about error recovery is difficult, and testing it is even more difficult. So we should go with the pattern that is simple and reliable. Make all of the expected outcomes into return values. Save the exceptions for the exceptions.

The problem is that there are a lot of programs that were developed by people who were damaged by their experience with those other languages. They use throw when they should return. They make complex catch clauses that attempt to solve insolvable problems and maintain unmaintainable invariants. And they use finally, which JavaScript has but does not need, to try to clean up their mess.

Eventuality

Exceptions work by unwinding the stack. Thrown values are communicated to function invocations that are lower on the stack. In eventual programming, the stack is emptied after each turn. Time travel is not available for transmitting a thrown value to an activation that no longer exists. Exceptions have limited usefulness. They can only report local problems in the current time frame. We will explore this in Chapter 20.

Security

There is an important model of security that limits the destructive power of functions by giving them only the references they need to do their work and nothing more. Exceptions, as currently practiced, provide a channel thru which two untrusted functions can collude.

It goes like this: Thing 1 and Thing 2 are two packages that we carelessly installed on our server. By doing so we are taking a terrible risk, but we consider it to be an acceptable risk because Thing 1 and Thing 2 are sometimes useful. We give Thing 1 access to a network socket. We give Thing 2 access to our private key. If they are unable to communicate with each other, we are fine.

Thing 1 needs to have something decrypted as part of its usefulness, but we do not want it to communicate directly with Thing 2. So we create a trusted intermediary function. We allow Thing 1 to call the intermediary. The intermediary calls Thing 2. Thing 2 returns a value to the intermediary. The intermediary inspects the return value, verifies that it is the expected plaintext, and returns it to Thing 1.

If Thing 2 instead does this:

```
throw top_secret.private_key;
```

and if the intermediary does not catch it, or catches and throws it again (a terrible practice that C++ made popular), then Thing 1 can catch the private key and can transmit it to the bad guys. There was collusion.

Reliability

When something goes seriously wrong, what can a program be expected to do about it? A function calls another with an expectation that it is going to work. But suppose it does not work. The exception object tells the function that an argument was out of range, or that an object was immutable, or some other mistake was made. It is not reasonable to expect, at our current level of technology, that the function can take corrective action.

The details in the exception object might be important and useful for the programmer to know. That information is instead delivered to a function that can make no good use of it. We have corrupted the information flow. That information should be sent to the programmer, perhaps in the form of a journal entry. Instead it is sent down the call stack, where it can be misunderstood and forgotten. Exceptions have caused us to misdesign our systems. The exception mechanism itself is causing unreliability.

Chapter 15

How Programs Work

○ ● ● ● ●

> Greetings, programs!
>
> *Kevin Flynn*

JavaScript is delivered to the execution site in source form. JavaScript's first job was to add some interactivity to web pages. Since HTML is a text format, it was decided to embed JavaScript in web pages as source text. This is fairly unusual. Programs in most other languages are delivered to the execution site in each particular machine's instruction code, or in a more portable format such as a byte-coded instruction stream that will be fed to an interpreter or code generator.

A JavaScript engine at the execution site compiles the JavaScript source code, producing machine code or interpreted code or both. This makes JavaScript a very portable language. Programs have no dependence on the architecture of the underlying machine. A single version of a JavaScript program can run on any JavaScript engine, regardless of what lies beneath.

The JavaScript compiler can quickly and easily verify some important security properties of a program: it can assure that the program can not compute memory addresses or jump to restricted locations or violate type restrictions. Java attempts to do something similar with its bytecode verifier, but it is not as fast or as easy or as certain.

Some of the syntactic features of JavaScript make parsing unnecessarily difficult. Even so, JavaScript engines are able to compile, load, and launch much faster than Java can load and launch from `.jar` files.

JavaScript is distributed in source units. A source unit is usually a `.js` file, but it could also be a source string from a JSON object, or a source text from a database or source management system.

In web browsers in olden times, source units were parts of a page, like the contents of a `<script>` tag or an inline event handler. In the following example, `alert("Hi");` is a source unit.

```
<img src=hello.png onclick=alert("Hi");>
```

It is now accepted that embedding JavaScript source units into an HTML page is a bad practice. It is bad for design because there is no separation between presentation and behavior. It is bad for performance because code in a page can not be gzipped or cached. It is very bad for security because it enables the poorly named Cross

Site Scripting (XSS) attacks. W3C's Content Security Policy (CSP) should be used consistently to prevent all use of inline source.

A source unit is treated like the body of a function with no parameters. It is compiled as a function and then invoked. It may cause function objects to be created, and possibly executed.

That could be the end of the program. But in JavaScript it is typical for a source unit to register to receive events or messages, or to export a function that another source unit might use. JavaScript does not demand that programs be written this way, but this is a great way to write programs and JavaScript supports this style better than most languages.

(Historical note: Inline event handlers worked a little differently. The source unit was still treated as a function body, but the event handler function this created was not invoked immediately. Instead it was bound to a DOM node, and it was invoked as events were fired.)

Primordials

There are objects and functions that are made available automatically to every source unit. We have already seen some of these, such as `Number`, `Math`, `Array`, `Object`, and `String`. There are many more, all provided by the ECMAScript Standard. In addition, the host environment (for example, the browser or Node.js) may add many more. All of this stuff can be used by all of the functions in your source unit.

Global

In the ancient browser programming model, all variable declarations outside of a function were added to the *page* scope, also known as the *global* scope (was that grandiose or what?). That scope also contained the variables `window` and `self` that contained references to the page scope. All of the variables in the page scope were visible to all of the source units on that page.

This was a bad thing. It encouraged a style of programming that exploited shared global variables. This resulted in programs that were brittle and buggy. It caused unexpected errors when two independent source units accidentally used the same variable name. And it caused terrible security problems. It is what fuels the XSS exploits.

Global variables are evil.

Fortunately, things are much better now.

Module

It is better to have all variable declarations outside of a function be added to the *module* scope, which is only visible to all of the functions in the source unit. This is a good thing because it leads to stronger designs, greater safety, and better security.

Cooperation with other source units is now explicit, using the `import` and `export` statements. These statements can be used to make good programs. They can also be used to make bad programs. I focus on the good.

By exporting, a module is making an exportation available to other modules. A module should export wun thing, typically a function or an object full of functions. The exportation may be consumed by several other modules, so it is a good idea to freeze the exportation to prevent accidents or cross contamination. An exportation is an interface. Interfaces should be simple and clean.

The source unit's code body is only executed wunce, which means that all of the importers share the same exportation. This can be a problem if the exportation is stateful and each importer is expecting something pristine and unshared. In that case, export a factory function that can make the pristine and unshared instances. The `export` statement does not make the instances.

The `export` statement looks like this:

```
export default exportation;
```

It is really unfortunate that that `default` word is there stinking things up. The *exportation* expression is the frozen object or function that you are exporting.

Importing allows your source unit to receive a function or an object from another source unit. You choose the name of the new variable that you want to receive the import. You also specify the supplier with a " *double quote* string literal containing some sort of name or address that your system can use to locate the source unit, and if necessary, read it, compile it, load it, invoke it, and deliver its exportation.

You can think of the `import` statement as a special `const` statement that gets its initialization value from some other place. It looks like this:

```
import name from string literal;
```

I recommend having a single `export`, but you can use as many `import` statements as you need. Put your imports at the top of the file and your export at the bottom.

Cohesion and Coupling

Good programming at the micro level depends on good coding conventions that help increase the visual distance between good code and bad so that the errors are easier to spot.

Good programming at the macro level depends on good module design.

Good modules have strong cohesion. That means that all of the elements are related and working together to accomplish a specific thing. Bad modules have weak cohesion, often from poor organization and trying to do too much. JavaScript's functions can be powerful here because we can pass in a function to take care of specific details that the module should not be concerned with.

Good modules are loosely coupled. You should only need limited knowledge of a module's interface in order to make good use of it. You should not need details of its implementation. A good module hides its implementation. A leaky module invites tight coupling. JavaScript offers many invitations for tight coupling. Mutually dependent modules are very tightly coupled indeed. That is nearly as bad and as grandiose as global variables.

Make your module interfaces simple and clean. Minimize dependencies. Good architecture is necessary to give programs enough structure to be able to grow large without collapsing into a puddle of confusion.

The concepts of cohesion and coupling were introduced in two excellent books:

- *Reliable Software Through Composite Design*. Glenford Myers. John Wiley & Sons, 1975.
- *Structured Design*. Edward Yourdon and Larry L. Constantine. Yourdon Press, 1979.

Both books came out before Object Oriented Programming became a thing so they went out of fashion and have been largely forgotten. But their teachings about strong cohension and loose coupling are still true and important.

## Chapter 16

How this Works

● ○ ○ ○ ○

> I invented the term *Object-Oriented*, and I
> can tell you I did not have C++ in mind.
> *Alan Kay*

The Self language was a dialect of Smalltalk that replaced classes with prototypes. An object could inherit directly from another object. The classical model suffers from brittleness and bloat due to the tight coupling of classes via **extends**. Self's prototypes were a brilliant simplification. The prototypal model is lighter and more expressive.

JavaScript implements a weird variation of the prototypal model.

When an object is created, a prototype can be designated that holds some or all of the new object's contents.

```
const new_object = Object.create(old_object);
```

Objects are just containers of properties, and prototypes are just objects. Methods are just functions that are stored in objects.

If we try to retrieve the value of a property that an object does not have, the result is the **undefined** value. However, if the object has a prototype (as **new_object** has above) then the result is the value of the prototype's property. If that also fails, and if the prototype has a prototype, then the result is the value of the prototypes's prototype's property. And down and down it goes.

It is possible for many objects to share a prototype. Those objects could be viewed as instances of a class, but they are really just individual objects that happen to share a prototype.

The most common use of prototypes is as a place to store methods. Similar objects would likely all have similar methods, so there might be a memory savings if the methods are put in a single shared prototype and not in every object.

How does a function in a prototype know which object to work on? This is where **this** comes in.

Syntactically, a method call is a ternary operation using **.** *dot* and **( )** *invoke* or **[ ]** *subscript* and **( )** *invoke*. The three sub-expressions in the ternary expression are:

- The object of interest.
- The method name.
- The argument list.

The object and its prototype chain are searched for the named method. If a function is not found, an exception is raised. This is a very good thing. This encourages use of polymorphism. You shouldn't care about an object's heredity. You should only care about its abilities. If an object lacks the ability, then it raises an exception. If the object has the ability, we use it, not caring how it was acquired.

If a function is found, then it is called with the argument list. The function also receives this as an implied parameter bound to the object of interest.

If a method contains an inner function, the inner function does not get access to this because inner functions are called as functions, and only method calls get the this binding.

```
old_object.bud = function bud() {
    const that = this;

// lou can not see bud's this, but lou can see bud's that.

    function lou() {
        do_it_to(that);
    }
    lou();
};
```

this binding only works on method calls, so

```
new_object.bud();
```

succeeds, but

```
const funky = new_object.bud;
funky();
```

does not. Here funky contains a reference to the same function as new_object.bud, but funky is called as a function, so there is no this binding.

this is also peculiar in that it is bound dynamically. All other variables are bound statically. This is a source of confusion.

```
function pubsub() {

// The pubsub factory makes a publish/subscribe object. Code that gets
// access to the object can subscribe a function that receives
// publications, and can publish stuff that will be delivered to all of
// the subscribers.

// The subscribers array is used to hold the subscriber functions. It is
// hidden from the outside by the pubsub function's scope.

    const subscribers = [];
    return {
        subscribe: function (subscriber) {
            subscribers.push(subscriber);
        },
        publish: function (publication) {
```

```
            const length = subscribers.length;
            for (let i = 0; i < length; i += 1) {
                subscribers[i](publication);
            }
        }
    };
}
```

A subscriber function gets a `this` binding to the `subscribers` array because

```
            subscribers[i](publication);
```

is a method call. It might not look like a method call, but it is. It gives every subscriber function access to the `subscribers` array, which could allow a subscriber to do very bad things, like delete all of the other subscribers or intercept or alter their messages.

```
  my_pubsub.subscribe(function (publication) {
      this.length = 0;
  });
```

`this` can be a security and reliability hazard. When a function is stored into an array and later called, it is given `this` which is bound to the array. If we do not intend for functions to have access to the array, which we usually don't, then there is a new opportunity for things to go wrong.

The `publish` function can be repaired by replacing the `for` with `forEach`.

```
        publish: function (publication) {
            subscribers.forEach(function (subscriber) {
                subscriber(publication);
            }
        }
```

All variables are statically bound, which is good. Only `this` is dynamically bound, which means that the caller of the function, not the maker of the function, determines its binding. This deviation is a source of confusion.

A function object has two prototype properties. It has its delegation link to `Function.prototype`. And it also contains a `prototype` property that contains a reference to an object that is used as the prototype of objects constructed by the function when it is called with the `new` prefix.

A constructor call is written by placing the `new` prefix in front of a function call. This is what the `new` prefix does:

- Make a `this` value with `Object.create(`*function*`.prototype)`
- Call the *function* with `this` bound to the new object.
- If the *function* does not return an object, force it to return `this`.

A sort of inheritance is possible by using the `Object.assign` function to copy methods from wun prototype to another. A much more common practice is to replace a function object's `prototype` property with an object constructed by another constructor.

Since every function is a potential constructor, it is difficult to know at any instant if a call should use a `new` prefix. Even worse, there is no warning when it is required but forgotten.

This is why we have a convention: Functions that are intended to be called as constructors with the new prefix must be named with initial caps. Nothing else should be written with initial caps.

JavaScript also has more conventional looking `class` syntax that was designed specifically for developers who do not know nor ever will know how JavaScript works. It allows transfer of skills from lesser languages with no new learning.

The `class` syntax, despite its looks, does not implement classes. It is just syntactic sugar on top of the pseudoclassical constructor weirdness. It preserves the very worst aspect of the classical model, `extends`, which tightly couples classes together. That tight coupling causes brittleness and faulty designs.

This Free

In 2007, there were several research projects that were trying to develop a secure subset of JavaScript. Wun of the biggest problems was the managing of `this`. In a method call, `this` is bound to the object of interest, which is sometimes good thing. But if that same function object is called as a function, then `this` could be bound to the global object, which was a very bad thing.

My solution to this problem was to outlaw `this` entirely. My argument was that `this` is problematic and unnecessary. If we remove `this` from the language, the language is still Turing Complete. So I began programming in a `this`-free dialect to get a sense of how painful it would be to give `this` up.

I was very surprised to discover that it was easier, not harder, and my programs were smaller and better.

That is why I recommend the elimination of `this`. You will be a better, happier programmer if you can learn to do without `this`. I am not taking anything away from you. I am offering you a way to live better by writing better programs.

The coders using `class` will go to their graves never knowing how miserable they were.

`this` is not a good thing.

This is a demonstrative pronoun. Just having **this** in the language makes the language harder to talk about. It is like pair programming with Abbott and Costello.

## Chapter 17

How Class Free Works

●○○○●

> And you think you're so clever and classless
> and free
>
> *John Lennon*

Wun of the key insights in the development of Object Oriented Programming was the model of how the parts of a program communicate with each other. Think of a method name and its arguments as a message. Calling the method sends the message to the object. Each object has its own behavior that is triggered when it receives particular messages. The sender assumes that the receiver knows what to do with the message.

Wun of the things that falls out of this is polymorphism. Every object that recognizes a particular message is eligible to receive that message. What happens next depends on the specialization of the object. This is a really powerful idea.

Unfortunately, we have become distracted by inheritance. Inheritance is a powerful code reuse pattern. Code reuse is important because it allows us to reduce the amount of effort to develop a program. Inheritance builds on the idea of *same as except*. We can say that some object or class of objects is the same as some other object or class of objects except for some important differences. This works really well when things are simple. It should be remembered that modern OOP began with Smalltalk, a programming language for children. As things get complicated, inheritance becomes problematic. Inheritance causes the tight coupling of classes. A change in wun class can cause dependent classes to fail. Classes tend to be bad modules.

We also see too much attention placed on the properties and not on the objects. There is an over emphasis on getter and setter methods for each individual property, or in the worst designs, the properties are public and can be changed without the object's awareness. It is possible to practice good design, where the properties are hidden and the methods process transactions and not just property mutation, but it does not happen often enough.

There is also an overdependence on types. Types were a feature of FORTRAN and later languages where it was a convenience for the compiler writer. Since then, a mythology has grown up about types, with extravagant claims that types protect programs from errors. Despite devotion to types, errors still manage to happen every day.

Types get credit and deserve credit for the bugs that are found early by the compiler. The sooner a bug is found, the less it costs. But if the program is tested properly, all of those bugs are found very quickly. So the bugs that types identify are the low value bugs.

Types are not blamed for the bugs they fail to find, the expensive bugs. And types do not get blamed for the problems they cause by requiring circumvention. Types can induce us to embrace cryptic, intricate, and dubious coding practices.

Types are like weight loss diets. A diet gets credit for the weight that is lost. A diet is not blamed when the weight goes back on and increases. And a diet is not blamed for the misery or health problems it causes. Diets give us faith that we can attain a healthy weight and still eat unhealthy food.

Classical inheritance allows us to think that we are writing good programs whilst we continue to create more bugs and crufty legacies. If you ignore the negatives, types look like a big win. The benefits are real. But if you look at types systematically, the cost exceeds the benefit.

Constructor

In Chapter 13, we worked with factories (functions that return functions). We can now do something similar with constructors (functions that return objects containing functions).

We start by making a counter_constructor that is similar to the counter generator. It has two methods: up and down.

```
function counter_constructor() {
    let counter = 0;

    function up() {
        counter += 1;
        return counter;
    }

    function down() {
        counter -= 1;
        return counter;
    }

    return Object.freeze({
        up,
        down
    });
}
```

The object that is returned is frozen. The object can not be damaged or corrupted. The object has state. The counter variable is the object's private property. It can only be accessed thru the methods. And we do not have to use this.

This is important. The interface of the object is its methods and only its methods. The object has a very hard shell. This gives us the best kind of encapsulation. There is no direct access to the data. This is good modular design.

A constructor is a function that returns an object. The constructor's parameters and variables become the private properties of the object. There are no public data properties. The constructor's inner functions become the object's methods. They close over the private properties. The methods that go into the frozen object are the public methods.

The methods should implement transactions. For example, suppose we have a `person` object. We might want support for changing the person's address. We should not do this by having a separate set of functions for changing each individual item in the address. Instead we should have a single method that takes an object literal that can describe all of the parts of the address that need to change.

Wun of the brilliant ideas in JavaScript is the object literal. It is a pleasant and expressive syntax for clustering information. By making methods that consume and produce data objects, we can reduce the number of methods, increasing object integrity.

So we have two types of objects:

- Hard objects containing only methods. These objects defend the integrity of the data held in closure. They give us polymorphism and encapsulation.
- Soft data objects containing only data. These have no behavior. They are just convenient collections that can be manipulated by functions.

Wun view of OOP is that we started with the adding of procedures to COBOL records to provide behavior. I think the mingling of methods and data properties was an important step forward, but it should not have been the last step.

You should include a `toJSON` method if the hard object needs to be stringified. Otherwise, `JSON.stringify` sees it as an empty object, ignoring the methods and the hidden data (Chapter 22).

Constructor Parameters

I wunce wrote a constructor that took ten arguments. It was very difficult to use because no wun could remember the order. Later we noticed that no wun made good use of the twoth argument. I wanted to remove it from the parameter list but that would break all of the code that we had already developed.

Had I been smart, I would have had the constructor take a single object as its parameter. This would usually be from an object literal, but it could also come from other sources, such as a JSON payload.

This would have provided many benefits:

- The key strings makes the code self-documenting. It is easier to read the code because the code tells you what each argument at the call site is.
- The arguments can be in any order.
- New arguments can be added in the future without breaking existing code.
- Obsolete parameters can be ignored.

The most common use of a parameter is to initialize a private property. We can do it like this.

```
function my_little_constructor(spec) {
    let {
        name, mana_cost, colors, type, supertypes, types, subtypes, text,
        flavor, power, toughness, loyalty, timeshifted, hand, life
    } = spec;
```

This creates and initializes 15 private variables using same named properties from spec. If spec does not contain a matching property, then the new variable is initialized with undefined. That gives us the ability to fill in missing values with defaults.

Composition

JavaScript is so expressively powerful that you can write in the classical paradigm even though it is not a classical language. JavaScript also lets us do something better. We can work with functional composition. So instead of *same as except* we can get *a little bit of this and a little bit of that*. This is the general form of a constructor:

```
function my_little_constructor(spec) {
    let {member} = spec;
    const reuse = other_constructor(spec);
    const method = function () {
        // It can use spec, member, reuse, method
    };
    return Object.freeze({
        method,
        goodness: reuse.goodness
    });
}
```

Your constructor can call as many other constructors as you need to get access to the state management and behavior that they provide. We can even pass the same spec object to them. When we document our spec parameters, we list the properties that my_little_constructor needs, and the properties that the other constructors need.

In some cases we can simply add some of the methods we acquired to the frozen object. In other cases, we have our new methods call the acquired methods. This accomplishes code reuse similar to inheritance, but without the tight coupling. Calling a function is the original code reuse pattern, and it is still the best.

Size

This approach to object construction uses more memory than the prototypal approach because every hard object contains all of the object's methods, whilst a prototypal object contains a reference to a prototype containing the methods. Is the difference in memory consumption significant? No, not in proportion to recent improvements in memory capacity. We used to count memory in kilos. We now count memory in gigas. The difference is in the noise.

The differences may be mitigated by the improvements in modularity. Emphasis on transactions over properties tends to reduce the number of methods whilst improving cohesion.

The classical model is a wun size fits all model. Every object must be an instance of a class. JavaScript frees us from that restriction. Not all objects need hardness.

For example, I don't think it makes sense that points have to be hard objects with methods. A point can just be a simple container of two or three numbers. Points get passed to functions that can do the projection or interpolation or whatever it is we do with points. That can be much more productive than subclassing points to give them specific behaviors. Let the functions do the work.

## Chapter 18

How Tail Calls Work

● ○ ○ ● ○

> There comes a time in the affairs of man
> when he must take the bull by the tail and
> face the situation.
>
> *W. C. Fields*

We depend on optimizations in our systems to make our programs go faster. An optimization is a breaking of the rules, but breaking them in such a way that the breakage is not observable. An optimization is not allowed to change a good program into a bad wun. Optimizations are not allowed to inject bugs.

The most important of the optimizations not only does not inject new bugs, it eliminates a class of bugs from good programs, enabling new paradigms of programming. I am talking about *The Tail Call Optimization*. Some experts consider this optimization to be so important that we should not trivialize it by calling it an optimization. They call it *Proper Tail Calls*. Any other way of implementing tail calls is improper.

I prefer to call it an optimization because most coders put little importance on propriety but they love optimizations even when they have no substantive effect. I want them to want this feature.

A tail call happens when the last thing a function does is return the result of calling a function. In the following example, `continuize` is a factory that takes `any` type of function and returns a `hero` function. The `hero` calls `any`, and passes the return value to the `continuation` function.

```
function continuize(any) {
    return function hero(continuation, ...args) {
        return continuation(any(...args));     // <-- a tail call
    };
}
```

When a function returns the result of calling a function, we call that call a *tail call*. It is a shame that we call that call a *tail call* and not a *return call*.

The tail call optimization is a simple wun, but it has big implications. Using traditional instruction sets as a metaphor, the code generated for `continuize` might include these machine instructions:

```
call    continuation    # call the continuation function
return                   # return to the function that called hero
```

The `call` instruction pushes the address of the next instruction (which in this case happens to be the `return` instruction) onto the call stack. It then transfers control to the function whose address is in the register labelled as `continuation`. When the `continuation` function is done, it pops the address of the `return` from the stack and jumps to it. The `return` instruction will again pop the stack and jump to the instruction after the instruction that called `hero`.

The optimization replaces those two instructions with a single instruction:

```
jump     continuation     # go to the continuation function
```

Now we do not push the address of the `return` instruction onto the call stack. The `continuation` function returns to the function that called `hero`, not `hero` itself. A tail call is like a `goto` with arguments, but without any of the dangers of the `goto` that led to its elimination.

So it appears that the optimization saved wun instruction, a push, and a pop. That does not seem like a big deal. To better understand the benefit, let's look at how calls actually work in JavaScript. When you call a function, these things happen:

- Evaluate the argument expressions.
- Create an activation object of sufficient size to hold all of the function's parameters and variables.
- Store a reference to the function object that is being called in the new activation object.
- Store the values from the arguments into parameters in the new activation object. Missing arguments are treated as `undefined`. Excess arguments are ignored.
- Store `undefined` into all of the variables in the new activation object.
- Set the `next instruction field` in the activation to indicate the instruction immediately after the call.
- Set the `caller` field in the new activation to the current activation. There is not actually a call stack. Instead, there is a linked list of activations.
- Make the new activation the current activation.
- Begin execution of the called function.

The optimization acts a little differently.

- Evaluate the argument expressions.
- If the current activation is large enough,
    - Use the current activation object as the new activation object.
  Otherwise,
        - Create an activation object of sufficient size to hold all of the function's parameters and variables.
        - Copy the `caller` field from the current activation object to the new activation object.
        - Make the new activation object the current activation.
- Store a reference to the function object that is being called in the new activation object.

- Store the values from the arguments into parameters in the new activation object. Missing arguments are treated as `undefined`. Excess arguments are ignored.
- Store `undefined` into all of the variables in the new activation object.
- Begin execution of the called function.

The important difference is that if the activation object is big enough, and it usually is, then we do not need to allocate another. We can reuse the current activation object now. Call stack chains are not long, usually on the order of a few hundred, so it makes sense for implementations to always allocate activation objects in a single maxy size when tail calls are imminent. The reduction of time in memory allocation and garbage collection can be significant. But there is more.

With tail call optimization, recursive functions can become as fast as loops. This is important from a functional perspective because loops are inherently impure. Purity comes with recursion. With this optimization, the performance argument against recursion is defeated.

This is the general structure of a loop.

```
while (true) {
    do some stuff
    if (done) {
        break;
    }
    do more stuff
}
```

A tail recursive function might be like this

```
(function loop() {
    do some stuff
    if (done) {
        return;
    }
    do more stuff
    return loop();                                    // <-- tail call
}());
```

That demonstrates a correspondence between loops and recursive functions. Recursive functions will generally be more elegant, passing updated state in parameters and return values instead of using assignment.

We can now have recursion go to any depth without fear of memory exhaustion or synthetic stack overflow errors. So good recursive functions will now work correctly. *Proper Tail Calls* isn't a feature, it's a bug fix. The standard requires the implementation of this optimization because it is important to prevent the failure of good programs.

Tail Position

A call is a tail call if the value a function returns is returned. So

```
return (
    typeof any === "function"
    ? any()                                 // <-- tail call
    : undefined
);
```

is a tail call. Return expressions made of && *logical and* and || *logical or* can also be tail calls, but

```
return 1 + any();                           // <-- not a tail call
```

is not a tail call. The last thing the function did was return the result of an addition.

```
any();                                      // <-- not a tail call
return;
```

That was not a tail call because it is returning **undefined**, not the return value of a function.

```
const value = any();                        // <-- not a tail call
return value;
```

That was also not a tail call because it is returning the contents of **value**. We know that the value of **value** is the result of any(), but the call was not in tail position.

Recursion in general is not a tail call.

```
function factorial(n) {
    if (n < 2) {
        return 1;
    }
    return n * factorial(n - 1);            // <-- not a tail call
}
```

The recursive call to **factorial** is not in tail position so it generates an activation record on each iteration, but we can move the call to tail position:

```
function factorial(n, result = 1) {
    if (n < 2) {
        return result;
    }
    return factorial(n - 1, n * result);    // <-- tail call
}
```

This version will be optimized. The recursive calls will not generate activation objects. Instead they jump to the top of the function. It uses arguments instead of assignment to refresh the parameters.

Returning a new function object is not a tail call...

```
return function () {};                       // <-- not a tail call
```

unless you immediately invoke the new function object.

```
return (function () {}());                   // <-- tail call
```

Exclusions

There are situations where the optimization must be cancelled to protect good programs from going bad.

A tail call inside of a `try` block can not be optimized. The optimization would save time and memory by not linking the activation object for this invocation into the call stack. But `try` might send control back to this invocation's `catch`, and in order for that to happen, the activation object must not be optimized away. This is another good reason to avoid misuse of exceptions.

If this function creates a new function object that has any free variables, then the new function object must have access to the activation object of its creator, so the activation object must not be optimized away.

Continuation Passing Style

In Continuation Passing Style, functions take an additional `continuation` parameter, which is a function that receives the result. The `continuize` factory at the top of this chapter can turn any function into a function that also takes a `continuation`. In this style, a `continuation` is a function that represents the continuation of the program. The flow of the program is always going forward, rarely needing to revisit previous states. It is a very effective tool for managing eventuality. It has uses in transpiling and other applications. It is only possible with the tail call optimization.

Debugging

The elimination of activations in the call stack can make debugging more difficult because you can no longer see all of the steps that led to the current predicament, but a good debugger can mitigate that by offering a mode in which it copies the state of each activation object and always retains a small set of the most recent. This does not interfere with the benefits of the optimization, but still allows inspection of the traditional stack trace.

Chapter 19

How Purity Works

● ○ ○ ● ●

> The price of purity is purists.
> *Calvin Trillin*

Functional programming is defined sensibly as *programming with functions*. Unfortunately, it is an ambiguous definition. It could mean programming with mathematical functions, which map domains of values to ranges of values. Or it could mean programming with software functions, which in most programming languages means parameterized strings of statements.

The mathematical functions are considered to be more pure than the software kind. Purity is corrupted by mutation. A pure function does not cause mutation. A pure function is not influenced by mutation. A pure function's result is determined only by its inputs. It performs no action other than to provide an output. A given input always produces the same output.

JavaScript, on the other hand, seems like a celebration of mutation. Assignment operators are the principle mutation devices, and JavaScript has 15 of them, or 17 if you count the dreaded ++ and -- twice, which you should:

= *assignment*
+= *add assignment*
-= *subtract assignment*
*= *multiply assignment*
/= *divide assignment*
%= *remainder assignment*
**= *exponentiation assignment*
>>>= *shift right assignment*
>>= *shift right sign extended assignment*
<<= *shift left assignment*
&= *bitwise and assignment*
|= *bitwise or assignment*
^= *bitwise xor assignment*
++ *pre-increment*
++ *post-increment*
-- *pre-decrement*
-- *post-decrement*

Like most mainstream languages, JavaScript loves the slop, preferring mutation to clarity. JavaScript chose to give = *equal sign* to mutation (impurity), not to equality (purity).

The Blessings of Purity

Purity comes with some valuable benefits.

Purity usually implies excellent modularity. Pure functions have extremely strong cohesion. Everything in the function is there to help provide a single result. There is nothing else happening on the side that could weaken cohesion. Pure functions have extremely loose coupling. A pure function depends only on its inputs. The making of good modules can be very difficult, but with purity, good modularity comes for free.

Pure functions can be much easier to test. Since they depend only on their arguments, there is no need to mock, fake, or stub. Wunce we have seen a pure function return the correct output from an input, we know that no mutation in the environment can ever cause the pure function to return any other value. The bugs that seem to go away when you turn the power off and on are due to impurity.

Pure functions are very composable. Since they have no side effects and no external dependencies or influences, it is easy to assemble them into larger, more complex functions that can be pure and composable as well.

Someday purity will provide huge increases in performance. Purity provides an excellent solution to the reliability and performance problems that plague threads. In multi-threaded systems, if two threads attempt to access the same section of memory at the same time, then a race may occur that can result in data corruption or system failure. Such races can be very difficult to diagnose. Mutual exclusion can mitigate races, but it can also cause delays, deadlocks, and system failures.

Pure functions can make threads safe and efficient. Since pure functions cause no mutation, memory sharing creates no risk. An array `map` method, given a pure function, could distribute the array's elements over all of the available cores. The computation could proceed very quickly. Performance improvements could be linear. The more cores, the faster it goes. There is a large class of programs that could significantly benefit.

There are always lots of silly features that are being considered for inclusion into JavaScript. A lot of them get in. They are all distractions. The parallelization of pure functions is the wun we need.

Getting Pure

There are clearly enormous benefits that come with purity. So can we add purity to the language? No. Purity is not a feature that can be added. It is like reliability and security. We can not add reliability to a system. Instead we must remove unreliability. We can not add security. We must remove insecurity. And we can not add purity. We must remove the impurities. The impurities are the corruptions that deviate from the mathematical model of functions.

ECMA is powerless to remove the bad parts from JavaScript, which is why the number of bad parts keeps increasing, but *you* can simply stop using the badness. We can make the language pure for ourselves by bringing more discipline to the process. If we decide to never use an impure feature, then that feature can no longer sap and impurify the essence of our function bodies.

So let's do a quick survey of the impurities of the language.

Obviously, we must purge all of the assignment operators, as well as the `var` and `let` statements. We can keep the `const` statement. It creates and initializes a variable, but does not allow it to be mutated.

We must get rid of the operators and methods that modify objects, including the `delete` operator and methods like `Object.assign`. We must also get rid of the array mutating methods like `splice` and `sort`. The array `sort` method could have been a pure function, but its implementation modifies the original array, so out it goes.

We must get rid of getters and setters. The setters are obviously instruments of mutation, and both exist for creating side effects. All side effects are corruptions and must be eliminated.

The RegExp `exec` method mutates the `lastIndex` property, so it goes. It could have been designed better, but it wasn't.

The purpose of the `for` statement is to mutate the induction variable, so it has to go. We should get rid of `while` and `do` as well. Tail recursion is the purest form of iteration.

We must get rid of the `Date` constructor. Every time we call it, we get a different value. That is not pure. We should also get rid of `Math.random`. You never know what value it is going to give you.

We must get rid of the users. Every interaction with a human can return a different result. Humans are not pure.

And finally, we must get rid of the network. The Lambda Calculus has no way of expressing information that exists on wun machine and not on another. Similary, the Universal Turing Machine does not have WiFi connectivity.

The Problem With The Universe

The universe is not pure. The universe is eventual, fully distributed, and highly parallel. Our programming model should embrace this truth. If our programs are to interact with the universe, particularly with the universe's human agents, then some parts of our programs may have to be impure.

We should try to make our programs as pure as possible because the benefits of purity are real. Objects are still valuable even though they have state, and state is only interesting if it is changeable. We should design our objects so that the changing of their state is disciplined and tightly controlled.

Continuum

Purity would be easier to reason about if it were binary: A function is either pure or impure. Unfortunately, it is more complicated than that. There are a number of ways that we can think about purity.

Mutation is impure, but ultimately, even the purest systems have some impurity under the hood. A functional system is always creating new activation objects, and the business of moving objects from available memory to active memory and back again requires mutation. That is not a bad thing. Generally, we want as much stuff as possible to be pure, and the stuff that is not pure should be hidden.

The generators of Chapter 13 and the objects of Chapter 17 hide their state well. Code on the outside can only change the state thru the discipline imposed by the generator function and by the methods. The generators and objects can not be mutated by external assignment. They are not completely pure, but they are a significant improvement over the other patterns of OOP. They are examples of how we can manage the purity frontier.

Wun definition of purity is freedom from assignment and other mutators. So is this pure?

```
function repeat(generator) {
    if (generator() !== undefined) {
        return repeat(generator);
    }
}
```

The repeat function takes a generator function and calls it until it returns undefined. It is pure of body, but not of spirit. It commits no impure acts of its own, but it enables the impurity of the generator. Many higher order functions are in this middle ground.

It is possible for a function to do assignment and still be considered pure. If a function declares local variables, and uses loops and assignments to modify those variables, then it might look impure. But we could give such a function to the parallel map function and it will work just fine. It is pure of spirit but not of body. Viewed as a black box, it is pure. It is only impure if we look inside.

So there is a continuum of purity, with mathematical functions on top, and then functions that are pure enough for parallel application, then pure higher order functions, then stateful higher order functions, and then the miles of slop that pollute the web: the classical, the procedural, and at the very bottom, everything using global variables.

## Chapter 20

How Eventual Programming Works

● ○ ● ○ ○

> Moe! Larry! The cheese!
> *Jerome Lester Horwitz*

In the beginning there was *sequential* programming. The first computers were just automatic calculators. You would feed a computer some data and a routine, and it would execute the orders, wun at a time, until it produced a result and halted. This wun-at-a-time execution model worked well for calculation and bulk data processing.

The first programming languages were developed during the sequential era. Those languages were so influential that most modern languages are still firmly rooted in the sequential paradigm. The old paradigm did not anticipate what our programs do now, making programming of modern systems unnecessarily difficult, unreliable, and insecure.

A typical feature of sequential languages is blocking input and output. When a program attempts to read from a file or from the network, it is blocked until the input operation finishes. This made sense for FORTRAN. A program would block when it needed to read data from cards in the card reader. The program had nothing to do until the data was ready, so blocking was not a problem. Most modern languages still implement the FORTRAN I/O model. JavaScript does not. JavaScript's first job was to interact with humans, so it instead favors a better model. JavaScript is less stuck in the sequential model than most other languages.

Concurrency

The sequential model broke down when computers started interacting with people, and then with other computers. That required *concurrent* programming, the ability to do multiple things at wunce.

Homogeneous concurrency provides support for many similar operations happening at the same time. We saw an example of this with array methods that take pure functions, processing every element of the array at wunce.

Heterogeneous concurrency supports the cooperation of specialized processes that each has a different responsibility, but that all work together as a team. The difficulty is to make sure that the team members do not act like The Three Stooges. This is a real concern. Stooge behavior is an inevitable consequence of bad architecture. Nyuck nyuck.

Threads

Threads are wun of the oldest heterogeneous concurrency mechanisms, and are still widely used. Threads are (real or virtual) CPUs that all run at the same time whilst sharing the same memory. Threads work well when running pure functions. If the functions are not pure, then the stooges come out.

Here we see two threads, *Moe* and *Larry*, that share a `variable`. *Moe* adds 1 to the `variable` and *Larry* adds 2. As you would expect, the result is 3.

Moe	Larry	variable
		0
variable += 1		1
	variable += 2	3

In this trial, *Moe* mutated first. It could also happen that *Larry* is first to mutate. In this particular case, it does not matter who wins the race because the operations are commutative. If Larry used `*=` *asterisk equal sign* instead of `+=` *plus sign equal sign* then the result would depend on the race. There are other outcomes that are more problematic.

Looking at this code at a lower level, the `+=` *plus sign equal sign* assignment statement could be compiled into three simple machine instructions: `load`, `add`, and `store`.

Moe	Larry	variable
		0
load variable		0
add 1	load variable	0
store variable	add 2	1
	store variable	2

This demonstrates a read-modify-write race. *Moe* and *Larry* both fetch the `variable` whilst its state is 0. They both add to the value they fetched, and then they both store their sums. This time, *Moe*'s modification is overwritten. Another time, *Larry*'s modification is overwritten. Perhaps most of the time, *Moe* and *Larry* do not both fetch the same value, so the code usually works correctly.

It is possible for that code to run correctly, but it is also possible that it does not. It is difficult to see the potential error in these two extremely simple wun line programs. In complex programs, these errors can hide very well.

Computational load can change the interleaving of instructions. The code might work correctly during development and testing, but fail in production. Or it might run well all year and then fail in December. Temporal bugs in threads are the worst, most expensive of all bugs. When the behavior of a program can be influenced by cosmic randomness, reproduction of error conditions can be virtually impossible. Type checking does not find them. Tests do not find them. The errors might occur very infrequently, which makes them extremely difficult to debug, or to have confidence that the fix did not make things worse.

The dangers of thread races can be mitigated by means of mutual exclusion, which can lock critical sections of memory, blocking the threads, preventing them from executing when there is contention. The operation of the locks can be computationally expensive. There might be a blocked thread that is not able to release its locks. This is called *deadlock*, another failure mode that is difficult to prevent, replicate, or repair.

The biggest design error in Java (and many similar languages) was that it could not decide if it wanted to be a systems language or an application language. Because it tried to be both, it requires the use of threads in applications, which is inexcusable.

Threads in operating systems can be a necessary evil. Threads in applications are just evil. Fortunately, JavaScript does not use threads in this way. There is a better way to get concurrency.

Eventual Programming

An *eventual function* is a function that returns immediately, possibly before the work that is requested of it is finished. The result will be communicated eventually in the future thru a callback function or message send, but not as an immediate return value.

Eventuality provides a way of managing lots of activity without exposing applications to threads. In fact, there are systems that have application threads that depend on eventuality to manage their user interfaces just because it is an easier and more reliable way of dealing with events over time. Eventual programming is built on two ideas: callback functions and a processing loop.

A callback function is a function that will be called in the future when something interesting happens, such as:

- A message has arrived.
- Some work has finished.
- A human has communicated with the program.
- A sensor has observed something.
- Time has passed.
- Something has gone wrong.

A callback function is passed to a function that is starting or monitoring an activity. In more primitive systems, the callback function is attached to an object that represents an activity. In web browsers, a callback function can be attached to a DOM node by assigning the callback to a particular property of the DOM node...

```
my_little_dom_node.onclick = callback function;
```

or by calling an event registration method on the object.

```
my_little_dom_node.addEventListener("click", callback function, false);
```

Both forms work. When the user clicks on a particular DOM node, the *callback function* (aka *event handler*) is called, probably performing some useful action in response to the event.

The other idea in eventual programming is the processing loop, also known as the event loop or the message loop. The processing loop takes the highest priority event or message from a queue, and calls the callback function that is registered to receive the event or message. The callback function runs to completion. The callback does not need to bother with memory locks or mutual exclusion. The callback is not interrupted, so there is no chance of races. When the callback function returns, the processing loop takes the next thing from the queue, and on it goes. It is a very reliable programming model.

The processing loop maintains a queue, known as the event queue or message queue, that holds incoming events or messages. The events or messages can be originated by callback functions as part of their responses. More likely, the events or messages come from ancillary threads that are managing the user inputs, the network, the I/O system, and interprocess communication. The way to communicate with the main thread where your JavaScript program runs is with the queue. Mutual exclusion is limited to this wun point of contact, so eventual systems tend to be very efficient and reliable.

A surprising benefit of this model is that JavaScript programs in the web browser are remarkably resilient. When you open a debugger and then go surf the web, you see an almost constant stream of exceptions and failures. This might be because many web developers are not very good at what they do. And yet, most everything seems to work.

In systems with threads, if wun thread has an exception, its stack gets unwound. That thread might now be in an inconsistent state relative to the other threads, which could lead to cascading thread failure.

JavaScript uses a single thread. Most of its vital state is in the closure of its functions, not on the stack. So things tend to keep running. As long as there is a button that works, users can still make progress, unaware of the multitude of errors that are happening behind the scenes.

The Law of Turns

Each iteration of the processing loop is called a *turn*, which comes from games like Chess and Poker, where at any moment only wun player is allowed to play. The player makes a move, and having moved, the player's turn ends and, while the game is unfinished, another player's turn begins.

Games have rules, and the eventual model has rules: **The Law of Turns**.

Never wait. Never block. Finish fast.

The Law of Turns applies to callback functions that the processing loop calls, and to every function that they call, directly and indirectly. A function is not allowed to loop while waiting for something to happen. A function is not allowed to block the main thread. In the web browser, functions like `alert` are not allowed. In Node.js, functions whose names contain the malodorous `-Sync` suffix are not allowed. A function that takes a long time to do its work is not allowed.

Violations of the **The Law of Turns** turn a high performance eventual system into a very low performance system. Violations cause delays not just for the current callback, but for everything in the queue. These delays can accumulate, which can cause the queue to grow longer. The system is no longer fast and responsive.

So any violating function must either be corrected or isolated in a separate process. A process is like a thread that does not share its memory. So it is reasonable for a callback to send some work to a process, and for that process to send a message when it has completed. The message goes into the queue and is eventually delivered.

JavaScript does not know about processes. Processes are services that can be provided by systems in which JavaScript runs. Processes are an important part of the eventual model, so it is likely that processes will be a first-class feature of the next language.

Trouble In Serverland

JavaScript was created for event loops and it performs really well. Unfortunately, message loops have been more of a struggle. This is because the nature of the work that a server does is quite different. In the browser, most of a program's work is responding to UI events. An event handler is called, it does some work, updates the display, and is done.

The typical workflow for a server is much more complex. A message receiver or handler is called, which may need to communicate with other systems, possibly located on other machines, before it can transmit its response. Sometimes what it learns from wun system must be communicated to another. These operations can be in long chains. And the results of interacting with the other systems will be communicated with callbacks. There is an elegant programming solution to this, but first let's look at three popular mistakes.

The first mistake is called *Callback Hell*. This is a pattern in which each callback function contains the code to request the next unit of work. That request provides a callback that also requests another unit of work, and so on. Programs written this way are difficult to read, difficult to maintain, and brittle.

The second mistake is called *Promises*. In their original form, promises were brilliant. They were created to support the development of secure, distributed programs. Unfortunately, when promises migrated to JavaScript, they lost all of their new paradigm features. All that is left is an awkward control flow mechanism. Promises were not designed to manage local control flow, which is why they do not do it very well. They are definitely an improvement over callback hell, but they are not satisfactual.

The third mistake is called *Async Await*. It is a pair of keywords that are used to decorate ordinary sequential code and magically transform it into eventual code. It is similar to ES6 generators in that the code you write is quite different than the code you get. To its credit, it masks much of the disappointment of promises. The thing that is most liked about async await is that you can continue to write in the style of the old paradigm. That is also the biggest problem with it.

The new paradigm is important. Understanding the new paradigm can be difficult because it is new, but that is how we make progress. Async await gives us a way to be productive without actually making progress. Its users are writing code that they do not fully understand. That is never a good thing. A growing problem is coders who are putting the `async` and `await` decorators everywhere. Because they do not understand what they do, they do not understand how to use them well. We should not be trying to deny or hide the next paradigm. We should be embracing it.

Something that all three mistakes have in common is the tight coupling of logic and control flow. That yields poor cohesion because too many disparate activities are pasted together. It is better to separate them.

Requestors

We should design modularly. Each unit of work, which might be making a request of some server or database or launching a process, should be a separate function. A function that just performs a unit of work has strong cohesion. These functions also take a callback function as their first argument. When the unit of work is completed, the result is passed to the callback. This reduces dependence on other code, giving us loose coupling. This is a good modular design practice that helps us in the new paradigm.

We use the word *requestor* to describe a function that takes a callback and performs a unit of work that might not be completed until a future turn.

```
function my_little_requestor(callback, value)
```

A *callback* function takes two arguments: *value* and *reason*. *value* is the requestor's result, or **undefined** if the requestor failed. The optional *reason* can be used to document failures.

```
function my_little_callback(value, reason)
```

A requestor function may optionally return a cancel function. This function can be called to cancel the work for any reason. It is not an undo. It is only intended to stop unnecessary work. So if a requestor starts an expensive operation on another server, and if the operation is no longer required, then calling the requestor's cancel function might send a cease message to the server.

```
function my_little_cancel(reason)
```

Requestor Factories

Much of your work is making factories that take arguments and return requestors.

This factory is a simple wrapper that can take any wun argument function and return a requestor.

```
function requestorize(unary) {
    return function requestor(callback, value) {
        try {
            return callback(unary(value));
        } catch (exception) {
            return callback(undefined, exception);
        }
    };
}
```

This factory makes a requestor that can read a file on Node.js.

```
function read_file(directory, encoding = "utf-8") {
    return function read_file_requestor(callback, value) {
        return fs.readFile(
            directory + value,
```

```
        encoding,
        function (err, data) {
            return (
                err
                ? callback(undefined, err)
                : callback(data)
            );
        }
    );
};
}
```

The most interesting factories make requestors that communicate with other services in dialogs that may extend over many turns. They can take this form:

```
function factory(service_address, arguments) {

// The factory function returns a requestor function that can do a unit of work.

    return function requestor(callback, value) {

// It starts the work in a 'try' block just in case the function that sends the
// message to the worker service fails.

        try {

// When the requestor function is called, it sends a message to the service,
// telling it to start work. When a result is obtained, it will be delivered
// by the 'callback' function. In this example, we assume that the message
// system will send its result using the '(result, exception)' convention.

            send_message(
                callback,
                service_address,
                start,
                value,
                arguments
            );
        } catch (exception) {

// If an exception is caught, we signal failure.

            return callback(undefined, exception);
        }

// We are allowed to return a 'cancel' function that will attempt to cancel
// the request when the result is no longer needed.

        return function cancel(reason) {
            return send_message(
                undefined,
                service_address,
                stop,
                reason
            );
```

```
            };
        };
    }
```

Parseq

I developed the Parseq library to manage the flow between requestor functions. The Parseq factories package arrays of your requestor functions together with a control flow: parallel, sequence, fallback, or race. Each factory returns a new requestor. This makes requestors highly composable.

The Parseq library can deal with time limits. It might be that some work must be completed in 100 milliseconds. If it is late, then we should consider the work a failure and go on to an alternate response. This is something that is very difficult to do using any of the three mistakes. Using Parseq, all you have to do is specify a time limit in milliseconds.

```
parseq.sequence(
    requestor_array,
    milliseconds
)
```

The **sequence** factory takes an array of requestor functions and an optional time limit and returns a requestor that causes each of the requestors in the array to be called. The *value* passed to the new requestor is passed to the zeroth requestor in the array. The value it produces is passed to the wunth requestor. In this way, values flow from requestor to requestor. The result of the last requestor is the result of the sequence.

```
parseq.parallel(
    required_array,
    optional_array,
    milliseconds,
    time_option,
    throttle
)
```

The **parallel** factory starts all of its requestors at wunce. It does not add parallelism to JavaScript. Instead, it allows JavaScript to exploit the natural parallelism of the universe. This allows for spreading the computational load onto many servers. This can provide a huge performance advantage. If we process all of the requestors in parallel, the time taken is the time of the slowest requestor, not the total time of all of the requestors. This is an important optimization.

The **parallel** factory should only be used when the requestors have no interdependence. All of the requestors are given the same *value*. The result is an array containing the results of all of the requestors. In that way it resembles the array **map** method.

The **parallel** factory can take two arrays of requestors. The first array contains the required requestors. All of the required requestors must complete successfully for the parallel operation to succeed. The second array contains the optional requestors. They may fail without causing the parallel operation to fail.

A time limit in milliseconds can be provided. It determines how much time the required requestors have to complete their work. The time option parameter determines how the time limit affects the optional requestors.

time_option	Effect
undefined	The optional requestors must finish before the required requestors finish. The required requestors must finish before the time limit, if there is wun.
true	The required requestors and the optional requestors must all finish before the time limit.
false	The required requestors have no time limit. The optional requestors must finish before the required requestors finish and the time limit, whichever is later.

By default, all of the requestors are started at wunce. Unfortunately, this can overwhelm badly designed systems. So there is an optional throttle that limits the number of requestors that are active at wunce.

```
parseq.fallback(
    requestor_array,
    milliseconds
)
```

The fallback factory is like the sequence factory, but it is successful when any of the requestors has a successful result. If a requestor fails, it just tries the next wun. A fallback fails if every requestor fails.

```
parseq.race(
    requestor_array,
    milliseconds,
    throttle
)
```

The race factory is like the parallel factory, but it declares success on the first successful requestor result. If wun requestor succeeds, then the race succeeds.

Example:

```
let getWeather = parseq.fallback([
    fetch("weather", localCache),
    fetch("weather", localDB),
    fetch("weather", remoteDB)
]);

let getAds = parseq.race([
    getAd(adnet.klikHaus),
    getAd(adnet.inUFace),
    getAd(adnet.trackPipe)
```

```
    ]);

    let getNav = parseq.sequence([
        getUserRecord,
        getPreference,
        getCustomNav
    ]);

    let getStuff = parseq.parallel(
        [getNav, getAds, getMessageOfTheDay],
        [getWeather, getHoroscope, getGossip],
        500,
        true
    );
```

Exceptions

Exceptions are too weak to deal with failures happening over many turns. An exception can unwind a stack, but nothing in a stack survives from turn to turn. Exceptions do not have the power to communicate to a future turn that something failed in an earlier turn, nor can exceptions travel back in time to the origin of the failing request.

A factory is allowed to throw an exception because the caller of the factory is still on the stack. Requestors are never allowed to throw exceptions because there is nothing on the stack to catch them. Requestors must not allow stray exceptions to escape. All exceptions must be caught and passed to the *callback* function as a *reason*.

Parseq Implementation

Let's look at the implementation of Parseq. It is not very big. It contains four public functions and four private functions.

The first private function is make_reason. It makes an error object.

```
    function make_reason(factory_name, excuse, evidence) {
```

Make a reason object. These are used for exceptions and cancellations. They are made from Error objects.

```
        const reason = new Error("parseq." + factory_name + (
            excuse === undefined
            ? ""
            : ": " + excuse
        ));
        reason.evidence = evidence;
        return reason;
    }
```

A callback is a function with two parameters.

```
    function check_callback(callback, factory_name) {
        if (typeof callback !== "function" || callback.length !== 2) {
            throw make_reason(factory_name, "Not a callback.", callback);
        }
    }
```

Make sure that all of the elements in an array are requestor functions.

```
function check_requestor_array(requestor_array, factory_name) {
```

A requestor array contains only requestors. A requestor is a function that takes wun or two arguments: `callback` and optionally `initial_value`.

```
    if (
        !Array.isArray(requestor_array)
        || requestor_array.length < 1
        || requestor_array.some(function (requestor) {
            return (
                typeof requestor !== "function"
                || requestor.length < 1
                || requestor.length > 2
            );
        })
    ) {
        throw make_reason(
            factory_name,
            "Bad requestors array.",
            requestor_array
        );
    }
}
```

The `run` function is the heart of Parseq. It launches the requestors and manages timing, cancellation, and throttling.

```
function run(
    factory_name,
    requestor_array,
    initial_value,
    action,
    timeout,
    time_limit,
    throttle = 0
) {
```

The `run` function does the work that is common to all of the Parseq factories. It takes the name of the factory, an array of requestors, an initial value, an action callback, a timeout callback, a time limit in milliseconds, and a throttle.

If all goes well, we call all of the requestor functions in the array. Each of them might return a cancel function that is kept in the `cancel_array`.

```
    let cancel_array = new Array(requestor_array.length);
    let next_number = 0;
    let timer_id;
```

We need `cancel` and `start_requestor` functions.

```
    function cancel(reason = make_reason(factory_name, "Cancel.")) {
```

Stop all unfinished business. This can be called when a requestor fails. It can also be called when a requestor succeeds, such as `race` stopping its losers, or `parallel` stopping the unfinished optionals.

If a timer is running, stop it.

```
        if (timer_id !== undefined) {
            clearTimeout(timer_id);
            timer_id = undefined;
        }
```

If anything is still going, cancel it.

```
        if (cancel_array !== undefined) {
            cancel_array.forEach(function (cancel) {
                try {
                    if (typeof cancel === "function") {
                        return cancel(reason);
                    }
                } catch (ignore) {}
            });
            cancel_array = undefined;
        }
    }


    function start_requestor(value) {
```

The `start_requestor` function is not recursive, exactly. It does not directly call itself, but it does return a function that might call `start_requestor`.

Start the execution of a requestor, if there are any still waiting.

```
        if (
            cancel_array !== undefined
            && next_number < requestor_array.length
        ) {
```

Each requestor has a number.

```
            let number = next_number;
            next_number += 1;
```

Call the next requestor, passing in a callback function, saving the cancel function that the requestor might return.

```
            const requestor = requestor_array[number];
            try {
                cancel_array[number] = requestor(
                    function start_requestor_callback(value, reason) {
```

This callback function is called by the `requestor` when it is done. If we are no longer running, then this call is ignored. For example, it might be a result that is sent back after the time limit has expired. This callback function can only be called wunce.

```
                        if (
                            cancel_array !== undefined
                            && number !== undefined
                        ) {
```

We no longer need the cancel associated with this requestor.

```
                            cancel_array[number] = undefined;
```

Call the `action` function to let the requestor know what happened.

```
                            action(value, reason, number);
```

Clear `number` so this callback can not be used again.

```
                            number = undefined;
```

If there are any requestors that are still waiting to start, then start the next wun. If
the next requestor is in a sequence, then it gets the most recent `value`. The others get
the `initial_value`.

```
                    return start_requestor(
                        factory_name === "sequence"
                        ? value
                        : initial_value
                    );
                }
            },
            value
        );
```

Requestors are required to report their failure thru the callback. They are not allowed
to throw exceptions. If we happen to catch wun, it is treated as a failure.

```
        } catch (exception) {
            action(undefined, exception, number);
            number = undefined;
            start_requestor(value);
        }
    }
}
```

With the `cancel` and the `start_requestor` functions in hand, we can now get to work.

If a timeout was requested, start the timer.

```
    if (time_limit !== undefined) {
        if (typeof time_limit === "number" && time_limit >= 0) {
            if (time_limit > 0) {
                timer_id = setTimeout(timeout, time_limit);
            }
        } else {
            throw make_reason(factory_name, "Bad time limit.", time_limit);
        }
    }
```

If we are doing `race` or `parallel`, we want to start all of the requestors at wunce.
However, if there is a `throttle` in place then we start as many as the `throttle` allows,
and then as each requestor finishes, another is started.

The `sequence` and `fallback` factories set `throttle` to 1 because they process wun at a
time and always start another requestor when the previous requestor finishes.

```
    if (!Number.isSafeInteger(throttle) || throttle < 0) {
        throw make_reason(factory_name, "Bad throttle.", throttle);
    }
    let repeat = Math.min(throttle || Infinity, requestor_array.length);
    while (repeat > 0) {
        setTimeout(start_requestor, 0, initial_value);
        repeat -= 1;
    }
```

We return `cancel` which allows the requestor to cancel this work.

```
    return cancel;
}
```

And now, the four public functions:

The `parallel` function is the most complicated because of the array of optional requestors.

```
function parallel(
    required_array,
    optional_array,
    time_limit,
    time_option,
    throttle,
    factory_name = "parallel"
) {
```

The parallel factory is the most complex of these factories. It can take a second array of requestors that get a more forgiving failure policy. It returns a requestor that produces an array of values.

```
    let number_of_required;
    let requestor_array;
```

There are four cases because `required_array` and `optional_array` can both be empty.

```
    if (required_array === undefined || required_array.length === 0) {
        number_of_required = 0;
        if (optional_array === undefined || optional_array.length === 0) {
```

If both are empty, then there is probably a mistake.

```
            throw make_reason(
                factory_name,
                "Missing requestor array.",
                required_array
            );
        }
```

If there is only `optional_array`, then it is the `requestor_array`.

```
        requestor_array = optional_array;
        time_option = true;
    } else {
```

If there is only `required_array`, then it is the `requestor_array`.

```
        number_of_required = required_array.length;
        if (optional_array === undefined || optional_array.length === 0) {
            requestor_array = required_array;
            time_option = undefined;
```

If both arrays are provided, we concatenate them together.

```
        } else {
            requestor_array = required_array.concat(optional_array);
            if (time_option !== undefined && typeof time_option !== "boolean") {
                throw make_reason(
                    factory_name,
                    "Bad time_option.",
                    time_option
                );
            }
        }
    }
```

We check the array and return the requestor.

```
        check_requestor_array(requestor_array, factory_name);
        return function parallel_requestor(callback, initial_value) {
            check_callback(callback, factory_name);
            let number_of_pending = requestor_array.length;
            let number_of_pending_required = number_of_required;
            let results = [];
```

run gets it started.

```
            let cancel = run(
                factory_name,
                requestor_array,
                initial_value,
                function parallel_action(value, reason, number) {
```

The action function gets the result of each requestor in the array. `parallel` wants to return an array of all of the values it sees.

```
                    results[number] = value;
                    number_of_pending -= 1;
```

If the requestor was wun of the requireds, make sure it was successful. If it failed, then the parallel operation fails. If an optionals requestor fails, we can still continue.

```
                    if (number < number_of_required) {
                        number_of_pending_required -= 1;
                        if (value === undefined) {
                            cancel(reason);
                            callback(undefined, reason);
                            callback = undefined;
                            return;
                        }
                    }
```

If all have been processed, or if the requireds have all succeeded and we do not have a `time_option`, then we are done.

```
                    if (
                        number_of_pending < 1
                        || (
                            time_option === undefined
                            && number_of_pending_required < 1
                        )
                    ) {
                        cancel(make_reason(factory_name, "Optional."));
                        callback(
                            factory_name === "sequence"
                            ? results.pop()
                            : results
                        );
                        callback = undefined;
                    }
                },
                function parallel_timeout() {
```

When the timer fires, work stops unless we were under the **false** time option. The **false** time option puts no time limits on the requireds, allowing the optionals to run until the requireds finish or the time expires, whichever happens last.

```
                const reason = make_reason(
                    factory_name,
                    "Timeout.",
                    time_limit
                );
                if (time_option === false) {
                    time_option = undefined;
                    if (number_of_pending_required < 1) {
                        cancel(reason);
                        callback(results);
                    }
                } else {
```

Time has expired. If all of the requireds were successful, then the parallel operation is successful.

```
                    cancel(reason);
                    if (number_of_pending_required < 1) {
                        callback(results);
                    } else {
                        callback(undefined, reason);
                    }
                    callback = undefined;
                }
            },
            time_limit,
            throttle
        );
        return cancel;
    };
}
```

The `race` function is much simpler than `parallel` because it does not need to accumulate all of the results. It only needs a single result.

```
function race(requestor_array, time_limit, throttle) {
```

The `race` factory returns a requestor that starts all of the requestors in `requestor_array` at wunce. The first success wins.

```
    const factory_name = (
        throttle === 1
        ? "fallback"
        : "race"
    );

    check_requestor_array(requestor_array, factory_name);
    return function race_requestor(callback, initial_value) {
        check_callback(callback, factory_name);
        let number_of_pending = requestor_array.length;
        let cancel = run(
            factory_name,
            requestor_array,
            initial_value,
            function race_action(value, reason, number) {
                number_of_pending -= 1;
```

We have a winner. Cancel the losers and pass the value to the `callback`.

```
                if (value !== undefined) {
                    cancel(make_reason(factory_name, "Loser.", number));
                    callback(value);
                    callback = undefined;
                }
```

There was no winner. Signal a failure.

```
                if (number_of_pending < 1) {
                    cancel(reason);
                    callback(undefined, reason);
                    callback = undefined;
                }
            },
            function race_timeout() {
                let reason = make_reason(
                    factory_name,
                    "Timeout.",
                    time_limit
                );
                cancel(reason);
                callback(undefined, reason);
                callback = undefined;
            },
            time_limit,
            throttle
        );
        return cancel;
    };
}
```

A fallback is just a throttled race.

```
    function fallback(requestor_array, time_limit) {
```

The fallback factory returns a requestor that tries each requestor in requestor_array, wun at a time, until it finds a successful wun.

```
        return race(requestor_array, time_limit, 1);
    }
```

A sequence is just a throttled parallel with propagated values.

```
    function sequence(requestor_array, time_limit) {
```

A sequence runs each requestor in order, passing results to the next, as long as they are all successful. A sequence is a throttled parallel.

```
        return parallel(
            requestor_array,
            undefined,
            time_limit,
            undefined,
            1,
            "sequence"
        );

    }
```

You can access Parseq in your module by importing it.

```
    import parseq from "./parseq.js";
```

English

Edsger Dijkstra was wun of the first to recognize the problems with threads in 1962. He worked out the first mutual exclusion mechanism, *semaphores*. A semaphore was implemented as two functions, P and V. P would attempt to lock the critical section, blocking the caller if it is already locked. V would release the lock, allowing a waiting thread to lock the critical section and run.

Per Brinch Hansen and C. A. R. Hoare integrated semaphores into classes to make *monitors*, a syntactic form that was hoped to provide greater convenience and error resistance.

The Java language did a similar thing called *synchronized*. It used a `synchronized` keyword to decorate code that needed semaphores inserted. Unfortunately, the word they selected does not make sense.

Synchronous means to exist at the same time or to be using the same clock. Musicians in an orchestra are synchronized because they are all playing to the conductor's beat. When Java was created, the designers looked for a word that had something to do with time. Unfortunately, they did not look hard enough.

When Microsoft was looking to add deeply wrong-headed eventual support to C#, they looked to Java, taking a wrong word and making it wronger by giving it an **a-** prefix to create an opposite. `async` makes no sense.

Most programmers have little training or experience with concurrent programming. Simultaneous management of multiple streams of activity is unfamiliar and strange. Giving them jargon that is fundamentally wrong does not make this easier. It is the uninformed leading the even less informed.

Chapter 21

How Date Works

●○●○●

When you open the door, will your mystery
date be a dream, or a dud?
Milton Bradley

Our calendar maps the movement of the sun and the moon onto the steady passage of time, but it was designed long before we discovered how the Solar System works. It has been patched many times, but never completely repaired. Our misshapen calendar was imposed on larger and larger communities by means of conquest and commerce. Ultimately it was imposed on the global community without first correcting it or replacing it with a more suitable design. It works, and the whole world runs on it, but it could be better.

Our modern calendar is based on the Roman calendar which originally had ten months and a bonus winter season that held the year's leftover days. March (named for Mars, the god of war) was the first month. December (which means *the tenth month*) was the tenth month. The winter season was replaced by two new months, January and February. Days were sometimes stolen from February and used to extend other months for political purposes. The calendar drifted a day every four years or so because the number of the days in a year is not an integer. (It was not Rome's fault that the number of days in a tropical year is not an integer.) They attempted to expediently realign their calendar by declaring January the first month. December (which still means *the tenth month*) became the twelfth month.

Julius established the standard of adding a leap day to February every four years. This reduced the seasonal drift, but did not completely eliminate it. Gregory standardized a better leap year algorithm, but a simpler, more accurate algorithm was never adopted. The Gregorian algorithm:

> Add a leap day in years divisible by 4, unless they are also divisible by 100, but add the leap day anyway if the year is divisible by 400.

That yields an average year of 365.2425 days, which is fairly close to the tropical year, about 365.242188792 days.

There is a better algorithm:

> Add a leap day in years divisible by 4, unless they are also divisible by 128.

That yields a year of 365.2421875 which is much closer to the tropical year. The incorporation of two powers of 2 in the algorithm seems to me as a programmer to be miraculous, although I would be much more impressed if it exactly matched the real year. If the number of days in a year were an integer, I might think that there could possibly be some truth in the idea of Intelligent Design.

The next year in which the 4|100|400 and 4|128 algorithms disagree is 2048. We should standardize the 4|128 algorithm before then.

The leap day used to be added at the end of the year. Unfortunately, when January became the first month, they did not move the leap day from February to December (which still means *the tenth month*).

Minutes and seconds are zero origin values, which is great, and they are both modulo 60, which is not so great. Hours are zero origin, but the 12 hour clock replaces 0 with 12, which is bizarre.

(If I could, I would instead have a 10 hour day, where an hour is 100 minutes, and a minute is 100 seconds. My second would be slightly shorter, being 86.4% of the present second. The tempo of the seconds would be a nice adagio, a gentle improvement in the pace of life over the current largo.)

Months and days are wun origin values because they were standardized before zero was discovered. Months are modulo 12. The Romans attempted to make months modulo 10, but they could not make it work. Days per month are modulo 30 or 31 or 28 or 29, depending on the month and year. Years were wun origin, but the current numbering of years was adopted many centuries after the Common Era epoch, so we can safely ignore that inconvenience.

The Date Function

The weirdness in the standards for timekeeping are a hazard for programs that must process time. Java's `Date` class provided support for dates. It should have been a simple thing, but it was very complex, demonstrating wun of the worst design patterns of classical programming. JavaScript could have done something significantly better, but instead it just copied Java's very bad example.

Today's JavaScript `Date` objects come with an awful lot of methods. Most of them are just getters and setters.

getDate	setDate	toDateString
getDay	setFullYear	toISOString
getFullYear	setHours	toJSON
getHours	setMilliseconds	toLocaleDateString
getMilliseconds	setMinutes	toLocaleString
getMinutes	setMonth	toLocaleTimeString
getMonth	setSeconds	toString
getSeconds	setTime	toTimeString
getTime	setUTCDate	toUTCString
getTimezoneOffset	setUTCFullYear	
getUTCDate	setUTCHours	
getUTCDay	setUTCMilliseconds	
getUTCFullYear	setUTCMinutes	
getUTCHours	setUTCMonth	
getUTCMilliseconds	setUTCSeconds	
getUTCMinutes	setYear	
getUTCMonth		
getUTCSeconds		
getYear		

There is a getDate method that returns the day of the month from a date object. You can see immediately that the word Date has two very different meanings in the same method. Compounding the confounding, there is also a getDay method, which returns the day of the week.

The getMonth method corrects the month to be zero origin because programmers like to act on things that are zero origin. So getMonth returns a number between 0 and 11. The getDate method does not correct the day, so it returns a number between 1 and 31. This loose inconsistency is a source of errors.

The getYear and setYear methods do not work correctly after 1999 and should not be used. Java was released in 1995 and contained date methods that would fail in 2000. Had they not heard of the Y2K problem? Or did they doubt that Java would survive in the market long enough for that to matter? We may never know. What we do know is that Java inexplicably survived, and that JavaScript made exactly the same mistake. Always use getFullYear and setFullYear instead.

Date demonstrates a very bad practice in classical programming. An object should encapsulate something. Interactions with objects should be transactions and other high level activities. Date is exposing a very low level view with getters and setters for each individual component of time. This approach does not use the objects well.

ISO 8601

The new Date constructor can take a string that represents a date and produce an object for that date. Unfortunately, the ECMAScript standard does not specify what the parsing and recognition rules are, so according to the standard, it is not guaranteed to work.

Except for ISO dates.

ISO 8601 is an international standard for the representation of dates and times. JavaScript is required to correctly parse ISO dates like 2018-11-06. Putting the most significant stuff first and the least significant stuff last makes so much sense, certainly more sense than the US standard 11/06/2018. For example, we can sort ISO date strings.

A Different Approach

It is of course much too late to do the right thing. JavaScript should not have copied Java. That is always a mistake. Much of what is wrong in JavaScript came from Java. If doing the right thing were an option, this is what I would propose:

There should be three representations of a date:

- The number of milliseconds since the epoch.
- A data object that can contain these properties:

  ```
  year
  month
  day
  hour
  minute
  second
  zone
  week
  weekday
  ```

- A string in some standard format.

We do not need classical `Date` objects with methods. We just need simple functions to do conversion between the three representations.

`Date.now()` returns the current time as a number. This function already exists. JavaScript makes this function available to all code, but I think it should be a privilege that is only given to trusted code. A piece of impure malicious code could use `Date.now()` or `Math.random()` to alter its behavior, allowing it to avoid detection.

`Date.object()` would take either a number or a string and return an object containing the information that can be extracted. When the argument is a string, there could be additional optional arguments that determine the time zone and the formatting standard that drives the parse.

`Date.string()` would take a number or a data object and an optional formatting standard and time zone, and return a human readable string representation of the time.

`Date.number()` would take a data object or string and an optional formatting standard and time zone, and return the number representation of the time.

This approach would be much simpler, much easier to use, more error resistant, and (not that it matters any more) Y2K ready. It is just wun impure function and three pure functions instead of that big pile of low level impure methods. Java could not do this because it lacked JavaScript's lovely object literals. I don't know why JavaScript doesn't do this. I hope that the next language will.

The epoch used by JavaScript is the Unix epoch: 1970-01-01. There are 32 bit Unix systems that will fail in 2038 when the bits are all used up and the clock overflows. It turns out that 32 bits are not enough for running a system clock at seconds resolution.

I would prefer to use 0000-01-01 as the epoch. JavaScript numbers will not fail to accumulate milliseconds until the year 285426. We will either devise a better calendar by then, or we will be extinct. Have a nice day.

## Chapter 22

How JSON Works

● ○ ● ● ○

> For the payload format, XML has to be the
> mainstay, not because it's technically
> wonderful, but because of the extraordinary
> breadth of adoption that it has succeeded in
> achieving. This is where the JSON (or
> YAML) folks are really missing the point by
> proudly pointing to the technical
> advantages of their format: any damn fool
> could produce a better data format than
> XML.
>
> *James Clark*

Here, for the first time in print, I tell the true story of the origin of the world's best loved data interchange format.

Discovery

JSON was discovered in 2001 in a shed behind Chip Morningstar's house. Chip and I had started a company to develop a platform for single page web applications. Our pitch was that with a good JavaScript library (that I wrote) and an efficient and scalable session server (that Chip wrote) it was possible to produce web pages that worked as well as installable applications. Or better, because our platform also supported multiuser collaboration, which is something the web hasn't caught up to yet.

I am still really impressed with Chip's session server. He has reimplemented it many times over the years. The most recent iteration is called Elko. `elkoserver.org`

The only thing wrong with Elko is that it is written in Java. My dream is that someday soon somewun will pay Chip to do it wunce again, but this time in JavaScript. That would put us way ahead of where we are right now with Node.js. We would get better security, better scalability, and support for a broader range of applications.

Back to the shed. We needed a way of sending information between the browser and the server. At that time, the software industry had completely committed to XML. Giants like Microsoft, IBM, Oracle, Sun, HP, and others had decided that the next generation of software was going to be built on XML, and their satellites and customers were falling in line.

We wanted to exchange data between programs written in two different languages. We looked at XML and decided it was a poor fit for our problem. The usage pattern with XML was that you first send a query to the server, which responded with an XML document. Then to get the data, you make further queries of the XML document. Why can't the server just send the data in a form that our programs could immediately use? Our data simply did not look like documents.

There were a lot of improved XML variants and replacements available at the time, but none of them were getting any traction. We thought about rolling our own. And then I had an epiphany. We could use JavaScript object literals. They were built into JavaScript, so it was really convenient on the JavaScript side. And the subset we needed was not difficult to parse on the Java side. It was certainly less effort than XML.

We wanted our platform to work with both Microsoft's Internet Explorer and Netscape Navigator. That was really difficult because both companies were inventing their own features. There was little commonality. Microsoft added an `XMLHttpRequest` function that could be used for communication with the server. Unfortunately, Netscape had nothing like it, so we could not use it.

Both browsers had JavaScript (ES3) and both had framesets. So we used those together to forge a communication channel. This was the first JSON message sent to a browser:

```
<html><head><script>
document.domain = "fudco.com";
parent.session.receive({to: "session", do: "test", text: "Hello world"});
</script></head></html>
```

A web page contained an invisible frame that could be navigated. Doing a `POST` on the hidden frame sent a message to the server. The server responded by transmitting a document that contained a script that called the `receive` method of the `session` object in the main frame. We had to alter `document.domain` to enable inter-frame communication. The JavaScript compiler parsed the message.

I wish I could tell you that the first message was delivered successfully, but it failed. It failed because of ES3's terrible reserved word policy. These were the reserved words at that time:

```
abstract boolean break byte case catch char class const continue debugger
default delete do double else enum export extends false final finally float for
function goto if implements import in instanceof int interface long native new
null package private protected public return short static super switch
synchronized this throw throws transient true try typeof var void volatile
while with
```

The ES3 reserved word policy said that none of those words could be used as variable names, or as parameter names, or as property names in dot position, or as *property names in object literals*. The message contained a `do` property, so the script had a syntax error and did not run.

I am happy to report that this was corrected in ES5. The reserved word list was shortened, and the restrictions on property names were eliminated, but in 2001 we had to put quotes around "do" to make it work. Chip put the reserved word list into his encoder, and we had no more problems with that.

We discovered that a string containing the character sequence </ *less than slash* could cause failure. That was because the browser assumed that it was the closing of the script tag, so JavaScript would not receive the entire payload, resulting in a syntax error. Our workaround was to escape the slash. The browser was happy with <\/ *less than backslash slash*.

We called it JSML (rhymes with dismal). Later we learned that there was some Java thing using those initials, so we quickly picked a replacement name: JSON.

JSON worked really well for communicating between JavaScript and Java. We also used it for interserver communication. We made the first JSON database.

Standardization

We had a difficult time selling the concept of JSON to our customers. They told us that they could not use it because they had already committed to XML. They told us that they could not use it because it was not a standard. I told them it was a standard, it was a subset of ECMA-262. They told us that *that* was not a standard. So I decided to become a standards body.

I bought the domain json.org and set to work formalizing JSON. Up until that time, JSON existed as a gentleman's agreement between Chip, me, and JavaScript. In formulating the standard, I had to make some decisions. My guiding principles were to keep it textual, minimal, and a subset of JavaScript.

The minimal principle was critically important. Standards should be simple and complete. The less we have to agree to, the more easily we can interoperate. The subset of JavaScript principle was very effective in preventing me from adding lots of cute and unnecessary features.

JavaScript allows strings to be quoted with both ' *single quote* and " *double quote*. The minimal principle taught that we did not need both.

I decided to require quotes around property names. I did not want to put the ES3 reserved word list into the standard because it looked really stupid. The inevitable question would be *Why?* and the answer would be *Because JavaScript*. We were trying to convince people to develop their applications in JavaScript, so I did not want the JSON standard to shine a light on JavaScript's bad parts. If we quote all the names, then the issue does not come up. It also simplified the specification because *What is a letter?* had become a very complicated question because of internationalization. So all of those issues are avoided as well. A property name can be any string. Easy. This also made JSON more Python-like, which I thought would help drive adoption.

I added comments because they were allowed by the subset of JavaScript principle and I thought they would be cute. Then I saw some early adopters putting parsing instructions in the comments. That would break interoperability, which was the whole point.

As more JSON codecs were developed for other languages, I noticed that about half of the work in developing a JSON parser was handling the comments. This wasn't because the comments were complicated, but because the rest of JSON was so simple. Comments were slowing down adoption.

Then I was approached by the YAML community. JSON was accidentally similar to a subset of YAML. If we both made some changes, JSON could be a proper subset. Wun of the points of contention was the comments.

JSON was really about connecting programs written in different languages thru the network. Comments are always ignored, so when they are used, they degrade network performance. Comments were superfluous and an attractive nuisance so I removed them.

If you really need comments, there are a couple of ways to do it. Just pipe your commented text thru a minifier like `jsmin`. Unfortunately, this solution is not suitable for coders who lack the skills to script a simple pipe.

The other solution is to formalize the comments and put them in the JSON structure. If the comments are critically important, then they should be given names so they can be properly retained and processed.

I failed in my goal to make JSON a proper subset of JavaScript. Unicode has a pair of invisible control characters, PS *paragraph separator* and LS *line separator* for the benefit of old school word processing systems. JavaScript treats them as line ending characters, just like CR *carriage return* and LF *line feed*. I missed that, so JSON allows them in strings. Fortunately, PS and LS are rarely used. I am not aware of any problems that came from this. ES5 added a built-in JSON parser that handles PS and LS, repairing the incompatibility.

There are some characters in Unicode that Unicode says are not characters. There are Unicode zealots who insist that JSON should not allow the magritte characters. JSON does not care. JSON is a medium, not an enforcer. It is up to the receiver to decide what to do about the characters that are not characters. JSON does not guarantee that everything will be meaningful to every receiver. If a sender and receiver are capable of having a shared understanding, then that shared understanding can be expressed in JSON.

I wanted to make JSON independent of IEEE 754. Java and JavaScript both use IEEE 754 binary floating point, but JSON does not care. JSON can enable communication between languages with different number representations. So binary floating point languages can exchange data with BCD languages, and big decimal floating point languages can interact with languages that have a wacky internal representation in which three digits are packed into 10 bit fields. JSON can survive the obsolescence of IEEE 754.

I excluded `Infinity` and `NaN` because their presence in data indicates an error, and we should not put bad data on the wire. We should not propagate bad data. That is an extremely bad practice.

I included both `e` and `E` as decimal exponent markers, a violation of the minimal principle. I should have excluded `E`. I should have also excluded `+` after the `e`.

I included `null` because computer scientists seem to like it. JSON does not attach a meaning to `null`. That is for the users of JSON to decide. JSON does not specify any behavior. It only specifies a format, a simple grammar for data.

I created a wun page website that described JSON in three ways: A McKeeman Form grammar, railroad diagrams, and informal English. I hoped that a reader would understand at least wun of those.

I did not acquire a trademark for JSON or its logo. I did not put a copyright notice on the page. I wanted to make the JSON standard as free and unencumbered as possible. I did not want to make money off of JSON. I just wanted to be allowed to use it.

I began to get requests to add links to codecs in various languages to the `json.org` site, which I did. Nearly all of them are open and free. I also received donations of translations of the page. Wun benefit of the simplicity of JSON was that the page is easy to translate.

In 2006, I wrote Informational RFC 4627 for IETF for the purpose of assigning a MIME type to JSON. I was hoping to get `text/json` for you, but the best they were willing to give us was `application/json` which was very disappointing.

Given the success of JSON, I think IETF should make `json` a first class media type so that people can register MIME types like `json/geo` and `json/money`.

In 2013, I wrote ECMA-404, which was adopted by ISO as ISO/IEC 21778. JSON had become so important that other standards needed to cite it, and they needed a more formal citation than my web page.

Why JSON Works

JSON was intended to allow programs written in different languages to communicate effectively. This is a difficult problem because the details in the representation of values and data structures in languages can be quite complex. So my approach in designing JSON was to focus on the commonalities.

Languages vary widely in their representations of numbers, but all can agree that a number can be represented as a string of base 10 digits, possibly with a decimal point in it, and possibly with a decimal exponent. Some languages have an integer type, some (like JavaScript) do not. JSON says that we can all make the best sense we can of a string of digits.

Languages have different ideas about strings and character sets. A language might have an internal representation that is UTF-16 (like JavaScript), or UTF-32, or UTF-8 or ASCII or Half ASCII or EBCDIC. JSON does not care. We make the most sense we can from a string of characters from the wire, and turn them into reasonable local representations.

All languages have some data structure that is a linear sequence of values. The details can be wildly different, but all languages, with the aid of a JSON decoder, can make sense of a series of values separated by commas wrapped in brackets. Zero origin languages can exchange data with wun origin languages.

Most languages have some sort of data structure that associates names with values. The details can be wildly different, but all languages, with the aid of a JSON decoder, can make sense of a series of named values separated by commas wrapped in braces.

And that is enough. By finding the intersection of all programming languages, programs written in all of the languages can communicate with each other. The critics said that it could not work. And yet it works.

Influences

I was able to recognize the portability of object literals because of my experience with two other languages. The LISP language has a textual representation called *s-expressions* that is used for both programs and data. The Rebol language also uses the same textual representation for programs and data, but with much richer syntax. It is very natural in Rebol to use that textual representation to serialize data for transmission. I applied that same idea to JavaScript.

I was not the first person to use JavaScript as a data encoding. It was discovered independently by many people, the first as early as 1996. I was the wun who tried to promote it as a standard.

Three languages, JavaScript, Python, and Newtonscript, were all designed about the same time, and all had similar syntax for creating data structures. Next OpenStep Property Lists were created a little earlier with a similar notation.

In the comfort of our Post-XML world, JSON looks like it was inevitable. But as it was unfolding, that was far from certain.

The JSON Object

JavaScript supports JSON with two functions in the JSON object. The functions are called **parse** and **stringify** and that is entirely my fault. I chose **parse** following the bad example of the **Date** function, which we have already seen is deeply flawed. I chose **stringify** because **toString** did not seem right. I should have called the functions **decode** and **encode**.

```
JSON.parse(text, reviver)
```

The **parse** function takes a JSON text and decodes it into JavaScript data. The optional *reviver* function can make transformations. It is given a key and a value, and it returns the desired value for that key.

For example, you might make a *reviver* that turns date strings into date objects. If a key ends with _date or if the value is a string in ISO date format, then replace the value with a **Date** object made from the value. JSON does not formally contain dates, but dates can conveniently be encoded as strings and then turned into date objects on the other side.

```
const rx_iso_date = /
    ^ \d{4} - \d{2} - \d{2}
    (?:
        T \d{2} : \d{2} : \d{2}
        (?:
            \. \d*
        )? Z
    )? $
/;
```

```
const result = JSON.parse(text, function (key, value) {
    return (
        typeof value === "string" && (
            key.endsWith("_date")
            || rx_iso_date.match(value)
        )
        ? new Date(value)
        : value
    );
});
```

JSON.stringify(*value*, *replacer*, *space*)

The **stringify** function takes a *value* and encodes it into a JSON text. The optional *replacer* function can make transformations. It is given a key and a value, and it returns the desired value for that key.

For example, if we want to automatically convert **Date** objects into ISO strings, we could provide a *replacer* function. The result of the *replacer* function is passed to **JSON.stringify** and that result is included in the text.

```
const json_text = JSON.stringify(my_little_object, function (key, value) {
    return (
        value instanceof Date
        ? value.toISOString()
        : value
    );
});
```

(It turns out that we do not need to do this because **Date.prototype.toJSON** already does it automatically. See **toJSON** below.)

The *replacer* argument can also be an array of strings. Only the properties with names in the array are included in the text. This is a whitelist that can filter out properties that are not interesting at the moment. This should have been a separate argument and not an overloading of the *replacer* function.

The JSON format allows whitespace in JSON text to make it more human readable. By default, **JSON.stringify** adds no whitespace so that the text is compact for transmission. If the *space* parameter is used, then line breaks and indentations are inserted. The correct value for *space* is **4**. Obviously. I should have made it a boolean.

toJSON()

Any object is allowed to have a **toJSON** method that is called by **JSON.stringify** when the object is stringified. This is how class free objects can have a JSON representation. A class free object, containing only functions, would ordinarily stringify like an empty object. But if it has a **toJSON** method, then it stringifies as the return value of **toJSON** would.

Date objects inherit a **toJSON** method that encodes date objects as ISO strings.

Security Implications

The first users of JSON used JavaScript's `eval` function (or its equivalent) to decode JSON text. There are inherent dangers in the `eval` function, but in this case the potentially dangerous text was coming from the same server that provided the HTML and all of the scripts, so the security of it was no worse than the web in general.

That changed when the practice of loading JSON from other servers with script tags became popular. Scripts are evaluated by `eval`, and there was no guarantee of any kind that the payload was nice JSON and not an XSS attack. It was convenient and irresponsible.

JSON text should never be built by concatenation because a piece of malicious string could contain quote and backslash characters that could cause misinterpretation of the text. JSON text should always be made with encoders like `JSON.stringify` or similar tools that do not permit those sorts of confusions.

This is why the result of `toJSON` and the result of the *replacer* function are processed by `JSON.stringify`. If the return values of those functions were inserted *as is* into the text, then those functions could be tricked into facilitating string confusions. It would have been better if strings did not start and end with the same character, but they do. That gives us another reason to code wisely.

McKeeman Form

McKeeman Form is a notation for expressing grammars. It was proposed by Bill McKeeman of Dartmouth College. It is a simplified Backus-Naur Form with significant whitespace and minimal use of metacharacters. I like it because it is fully minimally adequate.

We can express the grammar of McKeeman Form in McKeeman Form.

A *grammar* is a list of one or more rules.

> *grammar*
> > *rules*

The Unicode code point U+0020 is used as the *space*. The Unicode code point U+000A is used as the *newline*.

> *space*
> > `'0020'`
>
> *newline*
> > `'000A'`

A *name* is a sequence of letters or _ *underbar*.

> *name*
> > *letter*
> > *letter name*
>
> *letter*
> > `'a' . 'z'`
> > `'A' . 'Z'`
> > `'_'`

An *indentation* is four spaces.

> *indentation*
>> *space space space space*

Each of the *rules* is separated by a *newline*. A *rule* has a *name* on one line, with *alternatives* indented below it.

> *rules*
>> *rule*
>> *rule newline rules*
>
> *rule*
>> *name newline nothing alternatives*

If the first line after the *name* of a *rule* is "", then the *rule* may match *nothing*.

> *nothing*
>> ""
>> *indentation* '"' '"' *newline*

Each *alternative* is indented on its own line. Each *alternative* contains *items* followed by a *newline*.

> *alternatives*
>> *alternative*
>> *alternative alternatives*
>
> *alternative*
>> *indentation items newline*

The *items* are separated by spaces. An *item* is a *literal* or the *name* of a *rule*.

> *items*
>> *item*
>> *item space items*
>
> *item*
>> *literal*
>> *name*
>
> *literal*
>> *singleton*
>> *range exclude*
>> '"' *characters* '"'

Any single Unicode code point except the 32 control codes may be placed within the single quotes. The *hexcode* of any Unicode code point may also be placed within the single quotes. A *hexcode* can contain 4, 5, or 6 hexadecimal digits.

> *singleton*
>> ''' *codepoint* '''
>
> *codepoint*
>> ' ' . '10FFFF'
>> *hexcode*
>
> *hexcode*
>> "10" *hex hex hex hex*
>> *hex hex hex hex hex*
>> *hex hex hex hex*

hex
```
'0' . '9'
'A' . 'F'
```

A *range* is specified as a *singleton*, a . *period*, and another *singleton*. Literal ranges can optionally be followed by - *minus sign* and characters to be excluded.

range
    singleton space '.' *space singleton*

exclude
```
""
```
    space '-' *space singleton exclude*
    space '-' *space range exclude*

A *character* wrapped in " *double quote* can be any of the Unicode code points except the 32 control codes and " *double quote*. The definition of *character* shows an example of a codepoint range and exclude.

characters
    character
    character characters

character
```
' ' . '10FFFF' - '"'
```

JSON Grammar

This is the JSON grammar in McKeeman Form.

json
    element

value
    object
    array
    string
    number
    `"true"`
    `"false"`
    `"null"`

object
    `'{' ws '}'`
    `'{'` *members* `'}'`

members
    member
    member ',' *members*

member
    ws string ws ':' *element*

array
    `'[' ws ']'`
    `'['` *elements* `']'`

elements
    element
    element ',' *elements*

element
    ws value ws

string
    '"' *characters* '"'

characters
    ""

    character characters

character
    '0020' . '10FFFF' - '"' - '\'
    '\' *escape*

escape
    '"'
    '\'
    '/'
    'b'
    'f'
    'n'
    'r'
    't'
    'u' *hex hex hex hex*

hex
    digit
    'A' . 'F'
    'a' . 'f'

number
    integer fraction exponent

integer
    digit
    wunnine digits
    '-' *digit*
    '-' *wunnine digits*

digits
    digit
    digit digits

digit
    '0'
    wunnine

wunnine
    '1' . '9'

fraction
>   " "
>
>   '.' *digits*

exponent
>   " "
>
>   'E' *sign digits*
>   'e' *sign digits*

sign
>   " "
>
>   '+'
>   '-'

ws
>   " "
>
>   '0020' *ws*
>   '000D' *ws*
>   '000A' *ws*
>   '0009' *ws*

Advice To Data Interchange Standard Designers

I did not intend that JSON be the last data interchange standard. JSON was designed for a specific purpose, and it fit that purpose really well. It is now being used successfully for many other purposes. For some purposes, there should be better alternatives. So if you are going to design the next standard, I offer some advice.

0. Please Don't Break JSON.

The best thing I did with JSON was to not give it a version number. If you give something a 1.0, you know there will be a 1.1 and a 1.2, and everything is crap until it is 3.0.

JSON has only wun standard version. There is no way to change JSON without breaking everything. That avoids the versioning hell problems that are the painful and embarrassing side effects of incremental agility and perpetual beta. Every layer in the stack is subject to change except the JSON layer. JSON will always be the way it is right now. It is stable. I can not think of any feature that is more valuable than that.

1. Make It Significantly Better.

I have seen many proposals that want to add wun particular feature to JSON. The problem with that is that there will then be two standards that are mostly but not fully compatible with each other. That creates a Compatibility Tax on the users of both standards that is collected in the form of failures and configuration problems.

Add enough real value to the new standard to compensate for the tax. Do not make trivial or cosmetic changes. Make it substantive and totally worth it.

2. Give It A Better Name.

I have seen a lot of proposals that take the JSON name and stick a letter or digit on the side. Don't do that. Give it a better name. A large part of the job of programming is making up good names for things. Show us what you can do.

The worst thing about JSON is the name. It stands for JavaScript Object Notation.

JS is for JavaScript. The problem with the JS part is that it confuses people. There are people who think that JSON is a JavaScript thing that only works for JavaScript. There are people who think that JSON is defined by the ECMAScript standard, which is wrong because JSON is defined by ECMA-404, the JSON standard. And there is still the old Java ≠ JavaScript confusion.

We included JavaScript in the name because we wanted to give credit to its source. We were not trying to ride on JavaScript's coattails. In 2001, JavaScript was the world's most hated programming language. JavaScript was hated by everywun who liked Java, C#, PHP, Python, Ruby, Perl, C++, and on and on. Not only that, Java-Script was hated by almost everywun who used JavaScript. The Advent of the Gospel of the Good Parts had not yet come to pass.

O is for Object. In JavaScript, an *object* is an informal collection of name : value pairs, and JSON adopted that usage. In other languages, *object* means an instance of a brittle class hierarchy. From that perspective, JSON would be expected to be an object serialization format, which it is not. JSON is a data serialization format. So there is that confusion.

N is for Notation. I don't have a problem with *notation*. If you want to call your format a *notation*, knock yourself out.

## Chapter 23

How Testing Works

● ○ ● ● ●

> Program testing can be used to show the
> presence of bugs, but never to show their
> absence!
>
> *Edsger Dijkstra*

Computer programs are the most complicated things that humans make. Nothing else is made up of as many intricate parts that must all fit together and work together perfectly. A finished program must be perfect in every aspect, for all inputs, for all states, for all conditions, for all time. The contract we have with the computer is that if we give it a program that is not absolutely perfect, then the computer has license to do the worst possible thing at the worst possible time, and it is not the computer's fault. It is your fault.

We have no test for perfection. We can prove that a program contains defects, but there is no test that can prove that a program is free of defects. This failure of testing motivated work on Proofs of Correctness. The idea was that a program would be developed with mathematical proofs of its perfection. This was regarded as the most important outstanding problem in Computer Science, and unfortunately, it was never solved. The proofs were going to be much more complex than the programs they were attempting to prove. The complexity was overwhelming.

Robin Milner and others proposed that type soundness might be a more practical alternative to proofs. Types are more easily integrated into programs than proofs. Milner famously said that well typed programs can not "go wrong". But in languages with good type systems, like Haskell, and languages with terrible type systems, like C++ and Java, programs still go wrong. Maybe someday types will pay off. They haven't yet.

So with the failure of proofs and types, we put programs into production that we know are not perfect, hoping that we will find and correct the errors before anywun finds out. That is crazy. That is the state of the art.

There must be a better way. But if there is, no wun has found it yet.

So that brings us back to testing. Testing, when done well, can identify defects and then give us confidence that the defects were corrected. Even when testing is done well, it still can not prove the absence of bugs. And testing is not always done well.

In the late 1970s and early 1980s, Atari sold more software to more people than any other company on Earth. Most of that software was burned into ROM (read only memory) chips. Errors in ROM could not be corrected. You had to trash them and make new chips. Atari made a home computer that had an operating system in ROM. I was really impressed with that. What amazing confidence they must have in their programming to risk putting that stuff into ROM. How did they do it?

I took a job as a researcher at Atari's corporate lab. This allowed me to find out how Atari did it. This was their secret: They would try the stuff out, and if it seemed to work, they would send it to the factory. They were lucky. Their luck ran out when executives decided that the *E. T.* game did not need more testing. The company did not survive that decision.

Programs at that time were much smaller and simpler. If a program is only a few kilobytes, then careful coding and careful testing could yield good results. Today's programs are enormous. No person can understand it all. How can we be sure that something that is too complex to understand is correct?

Bugs

Bugs were discovered by Thomas Alva Edison. He was developing his phonograph, a device that recorded and reproduced sound with a stylus on a sheet of foil wrapped around a spinning cylinder. His prototype made a chirp on every revolution as the stylus crossed the edge of the foil sheet. Edison mentioned to a reporter that he had been up all night trying to get the *bug* out of the phonograph.

The word stuck. There have been lots of stories over the years about crazy inventors who would strike it rich wunce they got the last bugs out of their inventions.

There is a famous story of a moth that got caught in a relay in the Harvard Mark II. Grace Murray Hopper taped the moth into her log book, with the caption *First actual case of bug being found*. This was not the first bug, but it might have been the first bug caused by an insect. Most of our bugs are still caused by humans, although there is justifiable excitement about the bug making potential of artificial intelligence.

We must try to eliminate as much confusion from our programs as possible. When we expect a program to do wun thing and it then some does something else, that shows that we are confused about the program. We must make our programs as simple and clean as possible to reduce confusion. *Bug* is another word for *confusion*. Eliminating confusion is more productive than testing.

Bloat

Wun of the biggest problems in software development is software obesity, or bloat. Programs are just too big. This can be due to undisciplined feature selection, but it is more often a consequence of bad architecture. Inheritance is a popular code reuse pattern, but it does not work very well, so copy-and-paste is often used instead. There is an overreliance on libraries, platforms, and packages that are all tightly coupled to many other libraries, platforms, and packages. Bloating can be a side effect of agile development practices. Development teams are enlarged to help manage the bloat, but large teams cause even more bloat.

Bloat causes security problems by increasing the attack surface and giving bugs more places to hide. Bloated systems are much more difficult to test adequately.

Caching can mitigate some of the symptoms of bloat in the web browser, but unfortunately, web browsers are not very good at caching. There are tools like lazy loaders and tree shakers that attempt to delay or remove some of the unnecessary code, but by treating the symptoms, they can stimulate more bloating.

The best way to deal with bloat is to not let it happen in the first place. Make software leanness a priority in design and implementation. Avoid adoption of packages that are bloated and tools that encourage bloat. Avoid classes. Employ smaller, better trained development teams. And actively practice code removal. Reserve some development cycles for the removal of unnecessary code and the retiring of problematic packages. Celebrate when the number of lines of code in a project goes down. Adopt *The Principle of Least Big*.

Features have a benefit, but they also have a cost. If we fail to account for the cost, we will pay for it with bloating.

TDD

I like Test Driven Development as a methodology. I hate Test Driven Development as a religion. TDD Zealots have told me that sloppy, error-prone code is allowed, even encouraged under TDD. It is assumed that the tests will find all of the bugs, so there is no need for a disciplined coding style.

This is how a good practice turns into a very bad practice. The truth is that tests can not be depended on to find all of the bugs. We should be investing in bug avoidance. Good coding practices are a cheap investment in quality. My own coding style has changed over the years as I observe the ways that bugs form and the ways I can mitigate that.

I received a bug report for JSLint from a zealot. He included a function that JSLint rejected. He said that JSLint must be wrong because the function passed its unit tests. A casual inspection found that JSLint was correct. JSLint had found a bug in a regular expression that the tests had not found. The tests contained errors. The false negatives always get fixed quickly but the false positives are immortal. Those tests give us false confidence, not quality. What tests the tests?

Unit tests are very effective in low level code. For example, the Big Integer library in Chapter 3 is low level, having little dependence on anything else. I wrote lots of unit tests for it, and those tests were a big help in the development of the library.

Unit tests become less effective as we climb up the pile. As the dependencies increase, the tests become less meaningful. The cost of test making goes up because of the need to develop stubs, mocks, and fakes. (I hear developers wasting time arguing about whether something is a fake or a mock.) And as we ascend, the complexity moves from the components to the connections between the components.

As purity goes down, bugs go up, but unit tests do not test purity. If there is poor modularity, bugs are more likely, but unit tests do not test modularity. As time passes, the code becomes bloated, but unit tests do not test for bloat. At the limit, we are testing the fakes and mocks and not the program. I am not saying that unit tests are bad. I am saying that they are not sufficient. We write more and more tests that find fewer and fewer bugs. In addiction, this effect is called *tolerance*.

It sounds hopeless, but testing is necessary. Good and careful design and coding are critically important, but are not enough. We still have to test effectively. Test we must.

You Shall Not Pass

Most testing libraries support calls like this:

```
assertEquals("add 3 + 4", 7, add(3, 4));
```

It allows me to have a good feeling about having written a test, but is it realistic to think that a single addition is likely to find a subtle error in the **add** function? A great many tests are required over a much greater range of values, but who would want to write all of those tests? Also, this form can not test eventual programs. It can only test functions that are strictly sequential.

That is why I wrote a testing library called JSCheck that was inspired by a Haskell tool called QuickCheck. JSCheck does case generation, automatically producing lots of randomized trials. JSCheck also supports eventual programming for testing server and browser applications.

---

jsc.claim(*name, predicate, signature, classifier*)

The most important function provided by JSCheck is the **claim** function. A claim is an assertion about your program.

The *name* is a descriptive string that is used in reports.

The *predicate* is a function that delivers **true** if the program is working correctly. The *predicate* function takes a *verdict* callback function that is used to deliver the result of each trial. The remaining arguments are determined by the *signature* argument.

The *signature* is an array of generator functions that produces the arguments for the *predicate* function. These generators are easily made with the specifiers provided by JSCheck.

The *classifier* function is optional. It can be used to reject trials that are not valid. It can also classify trials to make patterns easier to evaluate.

---

jsc.check(*configuration*)

You make as many claims as you want, and then you call the **jsc.check** function to check that all of the claims are good.

The **jsc.check** function takes a *configuration* object that can contain any of these properties:

> **time_limit**: in milliseconds. There are three possible outcomes to every trial: PASS, FAIL, and LOST. Any trials that do not deliver a verdict before the time expires are considered LOST. In some situations, getting the right answer too late is indistinguishable from failure.
>
> **on_pass**: a callback for each passing trial.
>
> **on_fail**: a callback for each failing trial.

on_lost: a callback for each trial that failed to deliver a verdict.

on_report: a callback for a report.

on_result: a callback for a summary.

nr_trials: the number of trials that will be performed for each claim.

detail: the level of detail in the report.

  0. There will be no report.
  1. There will be a minimal report, showing the pass score of each claim.
  2. The individual cases that fail will be reported.
  3. The classification summaries will also be reported.
  4. All cases will be reported.

Instead of testing each function in the Big Integer library individually, I designed tests that included several functions working together. For example, the demorgan test used random, mask, xor, or, and, and eq. JSCheck produces random integers that are used to make random big integers that are applied with the DeMorgan Law.

```
jsc.claim(
    "demorgan",
    function (verdict, n) {

// !(a && b) === !a || !b

        let a = big_integer.random(n);
        let b = big_integer.random(n);
        let mask = big_integer.mask(n);
        let left = big_integer.xor(mask, big_integer.and(a, b));
        let right = big_integer.or(
            big_integer.xor(mask, a),
            big_integer.xor(mask, b)
        );
        return verdict(big_integer.eq(left, right));
    },
    [jsc.integer()]
);
```

I made a generator that produced big integers for some of my tests. The specifiers provided by JSCheck are very powerful, but they know nothing of big integers, so I made my own.

```
function bigint(max_nr_bits) {
    return function () {
        let nr_bits = Math.floor(Math.random() * max_nr_bits);
        let result = big_integer.random(nr_bits);
        return (
            Math.random() < 0.5
            ? big_integer.neg(result)
            : result
        );
    }
}
```

I test multiplication and division together. I provide a classifier function to reject trials that would divide by zero.

```
jsc.claim(
    "mul & div",
    function (verdict, a, b) {
        let product = big_integer.mul(a, b);
        return verdict(big_integer.eq(a, big_integer.div(product, b)));
    },
    [bigint(99), bigint(99)],
    function classifier(a, b) {
        if (!big_integer.is_zero(b)) {
            return "";
        }
    }
);
```

I tested multiplication and division together again, but this time incorporating remainders. The classifier emits the signs of the two values, producing the classifications "--", "-+", "+-", and "++". That helped in isolating bugs that were due to sign handling.

```
jsc.claim("div & mul & remainder", function (verdict, a, b) {
    let [quotient, remainder] = big_integer.divrem(a, b);
    return verdict(big_integer.eq(
        a,
        big_integer.add(big_integer.mul(quotient, b), remainder)
    ));
}, [bigint(99), bigint(99)], function classifier(a, b) {
    if (!big_integer.is_zero(b)) {
        return a[0] + b[0];
    }
});
```

I built tests around identities. For example, adding 1 to a string of n 1 bits should have the same result as $2 ** n$.

```
jsc.claim("exp & mask", function (verdict, n) {
    return verdict(
        big_integer.eq(
            big_integer.add(big_integer.mask(n), big_integer.wun),
            big_integer.power(big_integer.two, n)
        )
    );
}, [jsc.integer(100)]);
```

Here is another identity: $(1 << n) - 1$ should be n 1 bits.

```
jsc.claim("mask & shift_up", function (verdict, n) {
    return verdict(big_integer.eq(
        big_integer.sub(
            big_integer.shift_up(big_integer.wun, n),
            big_integer.wun
        ),
        big_integer.mask(n)
    ));
}, [jsc.integer(0, 96)]);
```

I constructed a large set of tests like those. This style of testing gives me much more confidence than I can get from 3 + 4.

JSCheck

This is the implementation of JSCheck. The most interesting parts of it are the specifiers that can produce the test data. Most of them are composable in interesting ways
because the specifiers pass values thru the `resolve` function. The `resolve` function
returns its argument unless the argument is a function.

```
function resolve(value, ...rest) {
```

The `resolve` function takes a value. If that value is a function, then it is called to
produce the return value. Otherwise, the value is the return value.

```
    return (
        typeof value === "function"
        ? value(...rest)
        : value
    );
}
```

You might remember `literal` as `constant` from Chapter 13. It escapes functions, so
that you can have a function passed to all of the trials.

```
function literal(value) {
    return function () {
        return value;
    };
}
```

The `boolean` specifier produces a generator that makes booleans.

```
function boolean(bias = 0.5) {
```

A signature can contain a boolean specification. An optional bias parameter can be
provided. If the bias is 0.25, then approximately a quarter of the booleans produced
will be true.

```
    bias = resolve(bias);
    return function () {
        return Math.random() < bias;
    };
}
```

The `number` specifier, not surprisingly, produces numbers in a range.

```
function number(from = 1, to = 0) {
    from = Number(resolve(from));
    to = Number(resolve(to));
    if (from > to) {
        [from, to] = [to, from];
    }
    const difference = to - from;
    return function () {
        return Math.random() * difference + from;
    };
}
```

The `wun_of` specifier takes an array of values and generators, and returns a generator
that randomly returns those values. The `wun_of` specifier can optionally take an array
of weights that can bias the selection.

```
function wun_of(array, weights) {
```

The `wun_of` specifier has two signatures.

```
//  wun_of(array)
//       Wun element is taken from the array and resolved.
//       The elements are selected randomly with equal probabilities.

//  wun_of(array, weights)
//       The two arguments are both arrays with equal lengths.
//       The larger a weight, the more likely an element will be selected.

    if (
        !Array.isArray(array)
        || array.length < 1
        || (
            weights !== undefined
            && (!Array.isArray(weights) || array.length !== weights.length)
        )
    ) {
        throw new Error("JSCheck wun_of");
    }
    if (weights === undefined) {
        return function () {
            return resolve(array[Math.floor(Math.random() * array.length)]);
        };
    }
    const total = weights.reduce(function (a, b) {
        return a + b;
    });
    let base = 0;
    const list = weights.map(function (value) {
        base += value;
        return base / total;
    });
    return function () {
        let x = Math.random();
        return resolve(array[list.findIndex(function (element) {
            return element >= x;
        })]);
    };
}
```

The `sequence` specifier takes an array of values and generators, and returns a generator that returns those values in order.

```
function sequence(seq) {
    seq = resolve(seq);
    if (!Array.isArray(seq)) {
        throw "JSCheck sequence";
    }
    let element_nr = -1;
    return function () {
        element_nr += 1;
        if (element_nr >= seq.length) {
            element_nr = 0;
        }
        return resolve(seq[element_nr]);
    };
}
```

The `falsy` specifier returns a generator that returns the falsy values.

```
const bottom = [false, null, undefined, "", 0, NaN];

function falsy() {
    return wun_of(bottom);
}
```

The `integer` specifier returns a generator that returns integers in a selected range. If a range is not specified, then it returns a generator that returns random prime numbers under a thousand.

```
const primes = [
    2, 3, 5, 7, 11, 13, 17, 19, 23, 29,
    31, 37, 41, 43, 47, 53, 59, 61, 67, 71,
    73, 79, 83, 89, 97, 101, 103, 107, 109, 113,
    127, 131, 137, 139, 149, 151, 157, 163, 167, 173,
    179, 181, 191, 193, 197, 199, 211, 223, 227, 229,
    233, 239, 241, 251, 257, 263, 269, 271, 277, 281,
    283, 293, 307, 311, 313, 317, 331, 337, 347, 349,
    353, 359, 367, 373, 379, 383, 389, 397, 401, 409,
    419, 421, 431, 433, 439, 443, 449, 457, 461, 463,
    467, 479, 487, 491, 499, 503, 509, 521, 523, 541,
    547, 557, 563, 569, 571, 577, 587, 593, 599, 601,
    607, 613, 617, 619, 631, 641, 643, 647, 653, 659,
    661, 673, 677, 683, 691, 701, 709, 719, 727, 733,
    739, 743, 751, 757, 761, 769, 773, 787, 797, 809,
    811, 821, 823, 827, 829, 839, 853, 857, 859, 863,
    877, 881, 883, 887, 907, 911, 919, 929, 937, 941,
    947, 953, 967, 971, 977, 983, 991, 997
];

function integer_value(value, default_value) {
    value = resolve(value);
    return (
        typeof value === "number"
        ? Math.floor(value)
        : (
            typeof value === "string"
            ? value.charCodeAt(0)
            : default_value
        )
    );
}

function integer(i, j) {
    if (i === undefined) {
        return wun_of(primes);
    }
    i = integer_value(i, 1);
    if (j === undefined) {
        j = i;
        i = 1;
    } else {
        j = integer_value(j, 1);
    }
    if (i > j) {
        [i, j] = [j, i];
```

```
    }
    return function () {
        return Math.floor(Math.random() * (j + 1 - i) + i);
    };
}
```

The `character` specifier returns a generator that returns characters. If it is passed an integer or two, the generator makes characters whose code points are in that range. If it is passed two strings, it returns characters in the range made from the first code point of each string. If it is passed wun string, it returns characters from that string. The default is to return ASCII characters.

```
function character(i, j) {
    if (i === undefined) {
        return character(32, 126);
    }
    if (typeof i === "string") {
        return (
            j === undefined
            ? wun_of(i.split(""))
            : character(i.codePointAt(0), j.codePointAt(0))
        );
    }
    const ji = integer(i, j);
    return function () {
        return String.fromCodePoint(ji());
    };
}
```

The `array` specifier returns a generator that returns arrays.

```
function array(first, value) {
    if (Array.isArray(first)) {
        return function () {
            return first.map(resolve);
        };
    }
    if (first === undefined) {
        first = integer(4);
    }
    if (value === undefined) {
        value = integer();
    }
    return function () {
        const dimension = resolve(first);
        const result = new Array(dimension).fill(value);
        return (
            typeof value === "function"
            ? result.map(resolve)
            : result
        );
    };
}
```

If the argument is an array of values and generators, then the result is an array containing values and the results of the generators.

```
let my_little_array_specifier = jsc.array([
    jsc.integer(),
    jsc.number(100),
    jsc.string(8, jsc.character("A", "Z"))
])
```

```
my_little_array_specifier()        // [179,  21.228644298389554, "TJFJPLQA"]
my_little_array_specifier()        // [797,  57.05485427752137,  "CWQDVXWY"]
my_little_array_specifier()        // [941,  91.98980208020657,  "QVMGNVXK"]
my_little_array_specifier()        // [11, 87.07735128700733,  "GXBSVLKJ"]
```

Otherwise, it produces an array of values. You can supply a dimension or a generator that produces integers. You can also supply a value, or a generator of values. The default is random prime numbers.

```
let my_other_little_array_specifier = jsc.array(4);
```

```
my_other_little_array_specifier()   // [659, 383, 991, 821]
my_other_little_array_specifier()   // [479, 701, 47, 601]
my_other_little_array_specifier()   // [389, 271, 113, 263]
my_other_little_array_specifier()   // [251, 557, 547, 197]
```

The string specifier returns a generator that returns strings. The default is to make strings of ASCII characters.

```
function string(...parameters) {
    const length = parameters.length;

    if (length === 0) {
        return string(integer(10), character());
    }
    return function () {
        let pieces = [];
        let parameter_nr = 0;
        let value;
        while (true) {
            value = resolve(parameters[parameter_nr]);
            parameter_nr += 1;
            if (value === undefined) {
                break;
            }
            if (
                Number.isSafeInteger(value)
                && value >= 0
                && parameters[parameter_nr] !== undefined
            ) {
                pieces = pieces.concat(
                    new Array(value).fill(parameters[parameter_nr]).map(resolve)
                );
                parameter_nr += 1;
            } else {
                pieces.push(String(value));
            }
        }
        return pieces.join("");
    };
}
```

It can also take values and generators and concatenate the results together.

```
let my_little_3_letter_word_specifier = jsc.string(
    jsc.sequence(["c", "d", "f"]),
    jsc.sequence(["a", "o", "i", "e"]),
    jsc.sequence(["t", "g", "n", "s", "l"])
)]);

my_little_3_letter_word_specifier() // "cat"
my_little_3_letter_word_specifier() // "dog"
my_little_3_letter_word_specifier() // "fin"
my_little_3_letter_word_specifier() // "ces"
```

If a parameter produces an integer followed by a string value, it can be used as a length.

```
let my_little_ssn_specifier = jsc.string(
    3, jsc.character("0", "9"),
    "-",
    2, jsc.character("0", "9"),
    "-",
    4, jsc.character("0", "9")
);

my_little_ssn_specifier()                // "231-89-2167"
my_little_ssn_specifier()                // "706-32-0392"
my_little_ssn_specifier()                // "931-89-4315"
my_little_ssn_specifier()                // "636-20-3790"
```

The any specifier returns a generator that returns random values of various types.

```
const misc = [
    true, Infinity, -Infinity, falsy(), Math.PI, Math.E, Number.EPSILON
];

function any() {
    return wun_of([integer(), number(), string(), wun_of(misc)]);
}
```

The object specifier returns a generator that returns objects. The default is to make small objects with random keys and random values.

```
function object(subject, value) {
    if (subject === undefined) {
        subject = integer(1, 4);
    }
    return function () {
        let result = {};
        const keys = resolve(subject);
        if (typeof keys === "number") {
            const text = string();
            const gen = any();
            let i = 0;
            while (i < keys) {
                result[text()] = gen();
                i += 1;
            }
            return result;
        }
        if (value === undefined) {
```

```
            if (keys && typeof keys === "object") {
                Object.keys(subject).forEach(function (key) {
                    result[key] = resolve(keys[key]);
                });
                return result;
            }
        } else {
            const values = resolve(value);
            if (Array.isArray(keys)) {
                keys.forEach(function (key, key_nr) {
                    result[key] = resolve((
                        Array.isArray(values)
                        ? values[key_nr % values.length]
                        : value
                    ), key_nr);
                });
                return result;
            }
        }
    };
}
```

If it is given an array of names and a value, it makes an object using those names as
property names, giving the properties the value. For example, we can supply an array
containing 3 thru 6 names, where the names are 4 lower case letters, and the values
are booleans.

```
let my_little_constructor = jsc.object(
    jsc.array(
        jsc.integer(3, 6),
        jsc.string(4, jsc.character("a", "z"))
    ),
    jsc.boolean()
);

my_little_constructor()
// {"hiyt": false, "rodf": true, "bfxf": false, "ygat": false, "hwqe": false}
my_little_constructor()
// {"hwbh": true, "ndjt": false, "chsn": true, "fdag": true, "hvme": true}
my_little_constructor()
// {"qedx": false, "uoyp": true, "ewes": true}
my_little_constructor()
// {"igko": true, "txem": true, "yadl": false, "avwz": true}
```

If it is given an object, it produces an object having the same property names.

```
let my_little_other_constructor = jsc.object({
    left: jsc.integer(640),
    top: jsc.integer(480),
    color: jsc.wun_of(["black", "white", "red", "blue", "green", "gray"])
});

my_little_other_constructor()    // {"left": 305, "top": 360, "color": "gray"}
my_little_other_constructor()    // {"left": 162, "top": 366, "color": "blue"}
my_little_other_constructor()    // {"left": 110, "top": 5, "color": "blue"}
my_little_other_constructor()    // {"left": 610, "top": 61, "color": "green"}
```

It is possible to compose lots of test data. But if there is some shape of data that is not easily made by composing these specifiers, you can easily make your own. It is just a function that returns a function.

We now get into the workings of JSCheck.

The `crunch` function crunches the numbers and prepares the reports.

```
const ctp = "{name}: {class}{cases} cases tested, {pass} pass{fail}{lost}\n";

function crunch(detail, cases, serials) {
```

Go thru all of the cases. Gather the lost cases. Produce a detailed report and a summary.

```
        let class_fail;
        let class_pass;
        let class_lost;
        let case_nr = 0;
        let lines = "";
        let losses = [];
        let next_case;
        let now_claim;
        let nr_class = 0;
        let nr_fail;
        let nr_lost;
        let nr_pass;
        let report = "";
        let the_case;
        let the_class;
        let total_fail = 0;
        let total_lost = 0;
        let total_pass = 0;

        function generate_line(type, level) {
            if (detail >= level) {
                lines += fulfill(
                    " {type} [{serial}] {classification}{args}\n",
                    {
                        type,
                        serial: the_case.serial,
                        classification: the_case.classification,
                        args: JSON.stringify(
                            the_case.args
                        ).replace(
                            /^\[/,
                            "("
                        ).replace(
                            /\]$/,
                            ")"
                        )
                    }
                );
            }
        }

        function generate_class(key) {
            if (detail >= 3 || class_fail[key] || class_lost[key]) {
```

```
        report += fulfill(
            " {key} pass {pass}{fail}{lost}\n",
            {
                key,
                pass: class_pass[key],
                fail: (
                    class_fail[key]
                    ? " fail " + class_fail[key]
                    : ""
                ),
                lost: (
                    class_lost[key]
                    ? " lost " + class_lost[key]
                    : ""
                )
            }
        );
    }
}

if (cases) {
    while (true) {
        next_case = cases[serials[case_nr]];
        case_nr += 1;
        if (!next_case || (next_case.claim !== now_claim)) {
            if (now_claim) {
                if (detail >= 1) {
                    report += fulfill(
                        ctp,
                        {
                            name: the_case.name,
                            class: (
                                nr_class
                                ? nr_class + " classifications, "
                                : ""
                            ),
                            cases: nr_pass + nr_fail + nr_lost,
                            pass: nr_pass,
                            fail: (
                                nr_fail
                                ? ", " + nr_fail + " fail"
                                : ""
                            ),
                            lost: (
                                nr_lost
                                ? ", " + nr_lost + " lost"
                                : ""
                            )
                        }
                    );
                    if (detail >= 2) {
                        Object.keys(
                            class_pass
                        ).sort().forEach(
                            generate_class
                        );
                        report += lines;
```

```
                    }
                }
                total_fail += nr_fail;
                total_lost += nr_lost;
                total_pass += nr_pass;
            }
            if (!next_case) {
                break;
            }
            nr_class = 0;
            nr_fail = 0;
            nr_lost = 0;
            nr_pass = 0;
            class_pass = {};
            class_fail = {};
            class_lost = {};
            lines = "";
        }
        the_case = next_case;
        now_claim = the_case.claim;
        the_class = the_case.classification;
        if (the_class && typeof class_pass[the_class] !== "number") {
            class_pass[the_class] = 0;
            class_fail[the_class] = 0;
            class_lost[the_class] = 0;
            nr_class += 1;
        }
        if (the_case.pass === true) {
            if (the_class) {
                class_pass[the_class] += 1;
            }
            if (detail >= 4) {
                generate_line("Pass", 4);
            }
            nr_pass += 1;
        } else if (the_case.pass === false) {
            if (the_class) {
                class_fail[the_class] += 1;
            }
            generate_line("FAIL", 2);
            nr_fail += 1;
        } else {
            if (the_class) {
                class_lost[the_class] += 1;
            }
            generate_line("LOST", 2);
            losses[nr_lost] = the_case;
            nr_lost += 1;
        }
    }
    report += fulfill(
        "\nTotal pass {pass}{fail}{lost}\n",
        {
            pass: total_pass,
            fail: (
                total_fail
                ? ", fail " + total_fail
```

```
                    : ""
                ),
                lost: (
                    total_lost
                    ? ", lost " + total_lost
                    : ""
                )
            }
        );
    }
    return {losses, report, summary: {
        pass: total_pass,
        fail: total_fail,
        lost: total_lost,
        total: total_pass + total_fail + total_lost,
        ok: total_lost === 0 && total_fail === 0 && total_pass > 0
    }};
}
```

The module exports a constructor that returns a `jsc` object. A `jsc` object is stateful because it holds the claims to be tested, so every user should get a fresh instance.

The `reject` value is used to identify trials that should be rejected.

```
const reject = Object.freeze({});
```

We export a `jsc_constructor` function. The `check` and `claim` functions are stateful, so they are created in here. I am freezing the constructor because I enjoy freezing things.

```
export default Object.freeze(function jsc_constructor() {
    let all_claims = [];
```

The `check` function is what does the work.

```
    function check(configuration) {
        let the_claims = all_claims;
        all_claims = [];
        let nr_trials = (
            configuration.nr_trials === undefined
            ? 100
            : configuration.nr_trials
        );

        function go(on, report) {
```

Invoke a callback function.

```
            try {
                return configuration[on](report);
            } catch (ignore) {}
        }
```

The check function checks all claims. The results are provided to callback functions.

```
        let cases = {};
        let all_started = false;
        let nr_pending = 0;
        let serials = [];
        let timeout_id;

        function finish() {
```

```
                    if (timeout_id) {
                        clearTimeout(timeout_id);
                    }
                    const {
                        losses,
                        summary,
                        report
                    } = crunch(
                        (
                            configuration.detail === undefined
                            ? 3
                            : configuration.detail
                        ),
                        cases,
                        serials
                    );
                    losses.forEach(function (the_case) {
                        go("on_lost", the_case);
                    });
                    go("on_result", summary);
                    go("on_report", report);
                    cases = undefined;
                }

            function register(serial, value) {
```

This function is used by a claim function to register a new case, and it is used by a case to report a verdict. The two uses are correlated by the serial number.

If the cases object is gone, then all late arriving lost results should be ignored.

```
                    if (cases) {
                        let the_case = cases[serial];
```

If the serial number has not been seen, then register a new case. The case is added to the cases collection. The serial number is added to the serials collection. The number of pending cases is increased.

```
                        if (the_case === undefined) {
                            value.serial = serial;
                            cases[serial] = value;
                            serials.push(serial);
                            nr_pending += 1;
                        } else {
```

An existing case now gets its verdict. If it unexpectedly already has a result, then throw an exception. Each case should have only wun result.

```
                            if (
                                the_case.pass !== undefined
                                || typeof value !== "boolean"
                            ) {
                                throw the_case;
                            }
```

If the result is a boolean, then the case is updated and sent to on_pass or on_fail.

```
                            if (value === true) {
                                the_case.pass = true;
                                go("on_pass", the_case);
```

```
            } else {
                the_case.pass = false;
                go("on_fail", the_case);
            }
```

This case is no longer pending. If all of the cases have been generated and given results, then finish.

```
                nr_pending -= 1;
                if (nr_pending <= 0 && all_started) {
                    finish();
                }
            }
        }
        return value;
    }
    let unique = 0;
```

Process each claim.

```
    the_claims.forEach(function (a_claim) {
        let at_most = nr_trials * 10;
        let case_nr = 0;
        let attempt_nr = 0;
```

Loop over the generation and testing of cases.

```
        while (case_nr < nr_trials && attempt_nr < at_most) {
            if (a_claim(register, unique) !== reject) {
                case_nr += 1;
                unique += 1;
            }
            attempt_nr += 1;
        }
    });
```

All of the case predicates have been called.

```
    all_started = true;
```

If all of the cases have returned verdicts, then generate the report.

```
    if (nr_pending <= 0) {
        finish();
```

Otherwise, start the timer.

```
    } else if (configuration.time_limit !== undefined) {
        timeout_id = setTimeout(finish, configuration.time_limit);
    }
}
```

The **claim** function is used to file each claim. All of the claims are checked at wunce when the **check** function is called. A claim consists of

- A descriptive name that is displayed in the report.
- A predicate function that exercises the claim and returns **true** if the claim holds.
- A function signature array that specifies the types and values for the predicate function.

- An optional classifier function that takes values produced by the signature and that returns a string for classifying the trials, or `undefined` if the predicate should not be given this set of generated arguments.

```
function claim(name, predicate, signature, classifier) {
```

A function is deposited in the set of all claims.

```
    if (!Array.isArray(signature)) {
        signature = [signature];
    }

    function the_claim(register, serial) {
        let args = signature.map(resolve);
        let classification = "";
```

If a classifier function was provided, then use it to obtain a classification. If the classification is not a string, then reject the case.

```
        if (classifier !== undefined) {
            classification = classifier(...args);
            if (typeof classification !== "string") {
                return reject;
            }
        }
```

Create a verdict function that wraps the register function.

```
        let verdict = function (result) {
            return register(serial, result);
        };
```

Register an object that represents this trial.

```
        register(serial, {
            args,
            claim: the_claim,
            classification,
            classifier,
            name,
            predicate,
            serial,
            signature,
            verdict
        });
```

Call the predicate, giving it the verdict function and all of the case arguments. The predicate must use the verdict callback to signal the result of the case.

```
        return predicate(verdict, ...args);
    }
    all_claims.push(the_claim);
}
```

Finally, we construct the instance and return it.

```
return Object.freeze({
```

The Specifiers:

```
        any,
        array,
        boolean,
        character,
        falsy,
        integer,
        literal,
        number,
        object,
        wun_of,
        sequence,
        string,
```

The Main Functions:

```
        check,
        claim
    });
  });
```

Ecomcon

If a file has strong dependencies on other code, I want to put the tests of those
relationships in the same file. The only way to determine that module A plays well
with module B and module C is to run them all together in context.

I developed a simple tool called ecomcon (Enable Comments Conditionally). I can put
testing and metering into the source code in the form of tagged comments.

```
//tag code
```

A tag can be any word, like **test**. It can be followed by some JavaScript code.
Normally, these comments are just comments, so they are ignored. They are removed
by minification. The ecomcon function can enable them, removing the // *slash slash* and
the tag, leaving the JavaScript code that can now be executed.

We can produce a special build with lots of runtime checking and logging and analysis.
It allows access to variables that would ordinarily be hidden in function scopes. It can
monitor values as they flow in and out. It can test the program's integrity, assuring
that critical resources have not been corrupted.

The comments can also act as documentation as they expose and exercise the
internals of the file and its operations.

```
function ecomcon(source_string, tag_array)
```

The *tag_array* contains strings to enable as tags.

The ecomcon function is pretty simple.

```
  const rx_crlf = /
      \n
  |
      \r \n?
  /;

  const rx_ecomcon = /
```

```
                  ^
        V V
        ( [ a-z A-Z 0-9 _ ]+ )
        \u0020?
        ( .* )
        $
/;

// Capturing groups:
//   [1] The enabled comment tag
//   [2] The rest of the line

const rx_tag = /
            ^
    [ a-z A-Z 0-9 _ ]+
    $
/;

export default Object.freeze(function ecomcon(source_string, tag_array) {
    const tag = Object.create(null);
    tag_array.forEach(
        function (string) {
            if (!rx_tag.test(string)) {
                throw new Error("ecomcon: " + string);
            }
            tag[string] = true;
        }
    );
    return source_string.split(rx_crlf).map(
        function (line) {
            const array = line.match(rx_ecomcon);
            return (
                Array.isArray(array)
                ? (
                    tag[array[1]] === true
                    ? array[2] + "\n"
                    : ""
                )
                : line + "\n"
            );
        }
    ).join("");
});
```

## Chapter 24

How Optimizing Works

●●○○○

> More computing sins are committed in the
> name of efficiency (without necessarily
> achieving it) than for any other single
> reason — including blind stupidity.
> *William Wulf*

The first several generations of computers were, by modern standards, quite slow. Since getting a correct answer too late can be indistinguishable from failing to get an answer, performance optimization became a deeply ingrained obsession in programming.

Today's devices are much faster. So it would seem that performance is no longer a concern. And for most applications, it is not. We have more processors than we need, and most of those processors are idle much of the time. We have enormous excess capacity.

Some things still are not fast enough. Sometimes that is because the scale of a problem grows faster than capacity. The big data keeps getting bigger. Even at the scale of human interaction, which is where JavaScript dominates, we can still experience slowness.

When we take too long to deliver responses to people, they get irritated, and then they get frustrated, and then they get angry. If we are trying to create satisfaction and loyalty, then our systems must be responsive.

So it is still necessary to be concerned about performance, but we need to deal with it properly. Optimization can easily make things worse.

It is widely believed that every little optimization helps because all of those saved nanoseconds add up. This is not true. We should only optimize where we can get a significant improvement. Insignificant optimizations are a waste of time. The whole point to optimization is to save time. So we need to optimize our optimizing.

Measurement

Computer programming is also known as *Computer Science* and *Software Engineering*. These are aspirational titles. We do not have enough understanding of this yet to truly do science and engineering. We do not have theory to answer the most important questions in the management of a software project: How many bugs are left, and how long will it take to fix them?

Too much of our art is unquantifiable but we can measure performance. We can execute a program, and observe how much time it took. Those numbers can help us better understand our systems, or they can confuse us.

A very common practice is to take two language features, put them both into loops, and then measure the loops. The faster loop tells us which feature to use. This can be problematic.

The result might be meaningless. Are we testing the performance of the feature, or are we testing the ability of the engine to optimize that feature when you isolate it and run it in a loop a million times? Is this result portable? Will other engines perform the same way? And more importantly, will future engines perform the same way?

The result might be insignificant. In context, in a real program, there might not be an observable difference. So we might be wasting time by basing decisions on meaningless data.

We should instead be choosing the features that gives us programs that are readable and maintainable. It does not help us if it is fast and also broken.

Measure Again

Carpenters have a proverb: **Measure twice, cut wunce.** It looks like it could easily be optimized: Measure wunce and cut. The extra care reduces mistakes, avoiding the wasting of time and materials. It is a big win.

Programmers should use this proverb: **Measure, then cut, then measure again.** Before making an optimization, we should first measure the performance of the code we want to optimize. We do this to establish a baseline and to demonstrate that the code is slowing down the whole program. If the code is not hot, then we should look elsewhere. Then we carefully optimize the code. Then we measure again. If the new code does not perform significantly better than the baseline, then we back out the change. It failed to deliver the expected improvement. We do not check in failures.

Most optimizations add complexity to the code by adding alternate paths and removing generality. This makes the code bigger, harder to maintain, and harder to test adequately. We might consider this to be worth it if we obtain a significant speed up. *If there is not a significant speed up, then we can call the change a bug.* It is causing a reduction in code quality with little or no compensating benefit. Clean code is easier to reason about and maintain. We should be reluctant to give that up.

Most of the code has a negligible impact on performance. It is a waste of time to be optimizing the code that is not slowing the program down.

Time Suck

It is rarely the case that fiddling with code makes it faster because fiddling does not address the underlying cause of the slowness. These are some of the biggest time sucks:

Failure to parallelize: Parseq allows us to take advantage of the inherent parallelism of the universe to make our stuff go faster. If we instead make everything go sequentially, we give that up. At scale, parallel beats sequential.

Violating the Law of Turns: When we block the processing loop, that adds delays to everything that happens in the future until the queue finally becomes empty. The accumulation of delays can prevent the queue from ever becoming empty.

Weak cohesiveness: If our modules do not have high cohesion, then it is likely that they are doing things that we might not need done. Unnecessary work slows things down.

Tight coupling: When modules are tightly coupled, we give up locality. That can lead to excessively chatty protocols that add network latency to every processing step.

Wrong algorithm: A casually constructed $O(n \log n)$ function can easily out-perform a finely crafted, ingeniously optimized $O(n^2)$ function when n is large. When n is small it usually does not matter which is faster.

Thrashing: This used to be a problem in virtual memory systems, and we can still see it in web caches. There is so much junk flowing from the web thru the cache that useful things get flushed out before they can be reused.

Bloat: When the code is big and bloated, it is unlikely that we fully understand what it is doing. It may be doing much more work than necessary. Don't focus on execution speed; focus instead on code size.

Other people's code: Your code probably relies on other packages, libraries, platforms, browsers, servers, and operating systems. I do not know what you have to run with, but I am confident that fiddling with your code will not make their code run any faster. If your code executed in zero time, most web users would not observe much of a difference.

Language

Perhaps the best optimization investment is in the language engine. Optimizations installed there benefit all of the users of the language. That liberates us to focus on writing high quality programs. The engine mechanics will make them fast.

The first JavaScript engines were optimized for time-to-market. Not surprisingly, they were not very fast, which contributed to the story that JavaScript was just a toy language.

Even so, JavaScript was adequately fast for most web applications. Most of the performance problems in the browser were due to misuse of the network, loading assets sequentially instead of pipelining. And there was the DOM API, which was extremely inefficient. The DOM is not part of JavaScript, but JavaScript was blamed for the DOM's performance. And as bad as the DOM was, most web applications ran adequately. The execution speed of JavaScript was rarely a factor.

Since then, the JavaScript engines have gotten quite fast, but it is complicated. All of the easy optimizations have been done. From this point on, things get more and more complicated. There are optimizations that will definitely speed up programs at scale, but that have the cost of increasing start up time. That is wun of those times when people can get irritated, frustrated, and angry.

So they play a very complicated game in which they start fast with slow code, and then optimize in response to the program's behavior. So far they have been very good at playing this game, but it is hard. They can not make everything faster. So it becomes a betting game. They optimize the things they imagine will provide the most benefit to the noisiest developers.

As the language gets more complex, the game gets even harder. The monsters only grow in number. They never diminish. Ultimately, the complexity will be overwhelming and the game will be over. A simpler, cleaner, more regular language would be much easier to optimize.

There is also a nasty feedback loop. The engines make certain features faster. Coders discover that and make heavy use of those features. That establishes a pattern of usage that the mechanics observe and are influenced by. This loop is driving the investments in optimization, but is not necessarily trending in the direction of optimizing good programs.

## Chapter 25

How Transpiling Works

●●○○●

I'm not the wun.

Neo

An increasingly important role for JavaScript is as a compilation target. *Transpiling* is a specialized form of compiling in which wun programming language is transformed into another, often JavaScript. This treats JavaScript as a portable executable format, leveraging JavaScript's universality and stability. JavaScript has become the virtual machine of the web. We had always thought that Java's JVM would be the VM of the web, but it turns out that it's JavaScript. JavaScript is strictly more portable and fast enough to tokenize and parse as minified source.

Sometimes the source language is a JavaScript dialect, sometimes it is another existing language, and sometimes it is an entirely new language that was designed specifically for transpilation.

There are many reasons to build a transpiler.

Experimentation: Transpilers are an ideal way to construct and test experimental languages and features. Ideas can be tested in JavaScript with much less time and effort.

Specialization: Transpilers can be used to implement little languages that are designed for very specific purposes. Such languages can reduce the operational burden of repetitive tasks.

Legacy: Transpilers provide a way of protecting investments in languages that are not popular enough to enjoy JavaScript's reach. By transpiling into JavaScript, old programs could potentially run everywhere. You do not need to understand how JavaScript works in order to use JavaScript. (Not understanding what you are doing is not a good thing.)

Fashion: Coders can be addicted to fashion. Transpiling makes it possible to festoon programs with groovy syntax.

Early access: The rate at which new language features get standardized, implemented, and ubiquitously deployed is slow and uncertain. Transpiling can sometimes make features immediately available by translating next edition JavaScript into current edition JavaScript. Those features are usually fashionable, not critical. But sometimes fashion can not wait.

Security: JavaScript has many inherent security weaknesses. A transpiler can mitigate that by removing problematic features whilst adding runtime checking and indirection to keep potentially malicious programs in check.

Performance: Developments like ASM.js and Web Assembly attempt to gain an execution advantage by removing from JavaScript everything that is good.

Transpilers should never be used in production. I like transpilers for their utility in education and research, but short-sighted concessions to fashion and mode-of-the-past thinking can have big consequences a few years later. My advice is to write excellent JavaScript programs.

Neo

Neo is a transpiled language. In the following chapters, I will show how Neo is implemented in the following stages: Tokenization, Parsing, Code Generation, and Runtime.

Neo is an educational language. It is intended to help transition to the next language by correcting some of JavaScript's biggest mistakes and by removing the features that are most strongly rooted in the old paradigm. In particular, the C syntax is removed. It can be hard to look to the future when you are stuck in the seventies.

Neo is a lot like JavaScript, but is also significantly different. Some of the differences are superficial. Some of the differences are very deep:

- There are no reserved words.
- Names can have spaces. Names can end with a ? *question mark*.
- Comments are made with the # *octothorpe*. A comment ends at the end of a line.
- Neo is semicolon free with meaningful whitespace. Long statements can be broken after (*left paren*, [*left bracket*, { *left brace*, ƒ *florin*.
- Neo has fewer precedence levels. Operator precedence reduces the need for parenthesis, but if there are too many precedence levels, it can be difficult to remember them all, which causes errors. These are the levels, from weakest to strongest:

  0. ? ! *ternary* | | *default*
  1. ∧ *logical and*   ∨ *logical or*
  2. = *equals*   ≠ *not equals*   < *less than*   > *greater than*
     ≤ *less than or equals*   ≥ *greater than or equals*
  3. ~ *concatenate*   ≈ *concatenate with space*
  4. + *add*   − *subtract*   << *minimum*   >> *maximum*
  5. * *multiply*   / *divide*
  6. . *refine*   [ ] *subscript*   ( ) *invoke*

- `null` unifies `null`, `undefined`, and `NaN` into a single object, eliminating the confusion about which to use when. `null` is an empty immutable object. Getting a property from `null` does not fail, it just produces `null`, so path expressions work. Attempts to modify or call `null` will fail.

- There are no prefix operators. Instead there are unary functions. The superficial difference is that functions require parens, whilst parens are optional with operators. Functions are more flexible, so we are eliminating a source of confusion by going exclusively with functions. I am keeping the other operators. If I replace all of the operators with functions, then there is a strong likelihood that I will end up accidentally reinventing LISP. Which would not be a bad thing.

- Neo has wun number type: Big Decimal. That means that decimal arithmetic can be exact. Every number value that JavaScript can represent exactly is also included. Because numbers are big, there is no need for `MIN_VALUE`, `EPSILON`, `MAX_SAFE_INTEGER`, `MAX_VALUE`, nor `Infinity`.

  ```
  0.1 + 0.2 = 0.3     # true at last
  ```

- A sequence of characters is called a *text*.

- Neo has a data type called *record* that unifies JavaScript's objects and weakmaps. We are free now to use the term *object* to include all of the types in the language. A record does not inherit. A record is a container of *fields*. A field has a *key* that can be a text, record, or array. A field has a *value* that can be any value except `null`. Changing the value of a field to `null` deletes the field from the record.

- Arrays are made with array literals and with the `array(`*dimension*`)` function that makes a new array, sets the length, and initializes the elements to `null`. The subscripts are non-negative integers that are less than the *dimension*. Attempting to store outside of that range causes a failure. An array may be appended to with a special form of `let` that also increases the *dimension* by 1.

  ```
  def my little array: array(10)
  let my little array[10]: 666    # FAIL
  let my little array[]: 555

  my little array[0]              # null
  my little array[10]             # 555
  length(my little array)         # 11
  ```

- The `stone` function replaces the `Object.freeze` function, doing a deep freeze. The problem with *freeze* is that it creates an expectation of unfreeze or thaw. There is no coming back from petrification.

- The ternary operator uses ? and !. The condition must be a boolean.

  ```
  call (
      my hero = "monster"
      ? blood curdling scream
      ! (
          my hero = "butterfly" \/ my hero = "unicorn"
          ? do not make a sound
          ! sing like a rainbow
      )
  )()
  ```

- The short-circuiting logical operators are $\wedge$ *solidus reverse solidus* for **and**, and $\vee$ *reverse solidus solidus* for **or**. Logical `not` is a unary function. If $\wedge$, $\vee$, and `not` are given non-boolean values, they fail.

- These unary arithmetic functions are included: `abs`, `fraction`, `integer`, and `neg`. They are unary functions, not operators. Note that – *minus sign* for negation only works with number literals.

- The + *plus sign* operator does addition, not concatenation. The other arithmetic operators are – *minus sign* for subtraction, * *asterisk* for multiplication, / *solidus* for division, >> *greater than greater than* for maximum, << *less than less than* for minimum,

- The ~ *tilde* operator does concatenation. The ≈ *double tilde* operator does concatenation with a separating space.

  ```
  "Hello" ~ "World"    # "HelloWorld"
  "Hello" ≈ "World"    # "Hello World"
  "Hello" ≈ ""         # "Hello"
  "Hello" ≈ null       # null
  ```

  They attempt to coerce their operands into texts.

- The bitwise functions operate on integers of any size: `bit mask`, `bit shift up`, `bit shift down`, `bit and`, `bit or`, and `bit xor`.

- The `typeof` operator is replaced with these predicate functions: `array?`, `boolean?`, `function?`, `number?`, `record?`, `text?`.

- The `Number.isInteger` and `Number.isSafeInteger` functions are replaced with the `integer?` function.

- The `Object.isFrozen` function is replaced with the `stone?` function.

- The `char` function takes a code point and returns a text.

- The `code` function takes a text and returns the first code point.

- The `length` function takes an array or text, and returns the number of elements or characters.

- The `array` function makes an array. How it does that depends on its argument.

  - If the argument is a non-negative integer, then make an array of that dimension. If another argument is provided:

    - If `null`, all of the elements are initialized to `null`.
    - If a function, then the function is called to produce initialization values for the elements.
    - Otherwise it provides the initialization value for the elements.

  - If the argument is an array and the next argument is a function, then map the array.

  - If the argument is an array, then make a shallow copy of the array. Additional arguments can give the starting and ending positions for copying a portion of the array.

  - If the argument is a record, then make an array of the text keys.

  - If the argument is a text and if there is a second argument, then the second argument is used to split the text into an array of texts.

- The `number` function takes a text and returns a number. It can take an optional radix.

- The `record` function makes a record. How it does that depends on its argument.

- If the argument is an array, then use the elements of the array as keys. The values depend on the other argument:
    - If null, all of the values are true. This is sometimes called a *set*.
    - If an array, then its elements are the values. The arrays should have the same length.
    - If a function, then it is used to generate the values.
    - Otherwise, the argument is used as the initial value of all of the fields.
  - If the argument is a record, then make a shallow copy of the record, copying only the text keys. If there is another argument that is an array of keys, then only those keys are copied.
  - If the argument is null, then make an empty record.
- The text function makes a text. How it does that depends on its argument.
    - If a number, it converts to a text. It can take an optional radix.
    - If an array, it concatenates all of the elements together. Another argument can provide separator text.
    - If a text, two additional arguments can specify a subtext. Unfortunately, those arguments specify code units. Ideally, a text should be represented internally as UTF-32. We will have to wait until the next language for that.
- Function objects are made with the ƒ *florin* operator. There are two forms:

  ƒ *parameter list* (*expression*)

  ƒ *parameter list* {
      function body
  }

- A *parameter list* is a , *comma* separated list of names and optional defaults and ... *ellipsis*. Functions are anonymous. To give functions names, use the def statement. Function objects are immutable.
- A function expression returns the value of the expression. A function body must explicitly return a value.
- The default operator is |*expression*|. If the expression or parameter immediately to the left has a value of null, then the *expression* wrapped in vertical bars on the right is evaluated to produce a default value. It is short circuiting.
- The ... *ellipsis* is similar to JavaScript's except that it is always placed after the array term, not before...

  ```
  def continuize: ƒ any (
      ƒ callback, arguments... (callback(any(arguments...)))
  )
  ```

- Using ƒ *florin* as a prefix before an operator produces a *functino*, allowing the use of the operator as an ordinary function. So ƒ+ makes a binary add function that can be passed to a reduce function to make sums. ƒ+(3, 4) returns 7.

$f\wedge$ *and* $f\vee$ *or* $f=$ *equals* $f\neq$ *not equals* $f<$ *less than* $f\geq$ *greater than or equal* $f>$ *greater than* $f\leq$ *less than or equal* $f\sim$ *concatenate* $f\approx$ *concatenate space* $f+$ *add* $f-$ *subtract* $f>>$ *max* $f<<$ *min* $f*$ *multiply* $f/$ *divide* $f[]$ *get* $f()$ *resolve* $f?!$ *ternary* $f||$ *default*

- A function can be called as a method. For example:

```
my little function.method(x, y)
```

does the same thing as

```
my little function("method", [x, y])
```

This simple mechanism makes it possible to use a function as a proxy to a record.

- The `def` statement replaces the `const` statement.
- The `var` statement declares variables.
- The `let` statement can change the value of a variable, or a field of a record, or an element of an array. The `let` statement is the only place where mutation is allowed. There are no assignment operators. I can not eliminate assignment, but I can constrain it.

```
def pi: 3.14159265358979323846264338327950288419716939937510582097494459
var counter: 0
let counter: counter + 1
```

- There is no block scope because there are no blocks. There is function scope.
- The `call` statement allows for calling a function and ignoring its return value.

```
call my little impure side effect causer()
```

- Neo has `if` and `else`. It also has `else` `if` as a replacement for the `switch` statement. If the condition expression does not produce a boolean, then it fails. There are no falsy values.

```
if my hero = "monster"
    call blood curdling scream()
else if my hero = "butterfly" \/ my hero = "unicorn"
    call do not make a sound()
else
    call sing like a rainbow()
```

- The `loop` statement replaces the `do`, `for`, and `while` statements. I want to discourage looping. The `loop` is a simple infinite loop. Use `break` or `return` to exit. Loops can not have labels. Loops may be nested. New functions can not be made in loops.
- Exceptions are replaced with failures. A function can have a failure handler. There is no `try`.

```
def my little function: f x the unknown {
    return risky operation(x the unknown)
failure
    call launch all missiles()
    return null
}
```

- The `fail` statement signals a failure. It does not take an exception object or any other sort of message. If a reason for the failure must be communicated, then log it some other way before the `fail`.

- A module can have several import statements:
  import *name*: *text literal*
- A module can have wun export statement:
  export *expression*

Example

This is the reduce reverse function in Neo. It allows an early exit, and it goes backwards. It takes 3 arguments: array, callback function, and initial value. The callback function is given 4 values: the current value of the reduction, the current array element, the index number of the current element, and an exit function. If the callback function wants to stop early, it returns the result of calling the exit function with the final value.

```
def reduce reverse: ƒ array, callback function, initial value {

# Reduce an array to a single value.

# If an initial value is not provided, then the zeroth element is used
# and the first iteration is skipped.

    var element nr: length(array)
    var reduction: initial value
    if reduction = null
        let element nr: element nr - 1
        let reduction: array[element nr]

# The callback function gets an exit function that it can call
# to stop the operation.

    def exit: ƒ final value {
        let element nr: 0
        return final value
    }

# Loop until the array is exhausted or an early exit is requested.
# On each iteration, call the callback function with the next increment.

    loop
        let element nr: element nr - 1
        if element nr < 0
            break
        let reduction: callback function(
            reduction
            array[element nr]
            element nr
            exit
        )
    return reduction
}
```

The Next Language

Neo is not the next language. It is not even a complete language. It is missing a lot of essential stuff. That is not in itself a serious problem because we know that it is easy to add stuff to a language.

Neo is missing JSON support. No serious 21th Century language can be lacking built-in JSON encoding and decoding.

Neo is missing some form of textual pattern matching. JavaScript uses regular expressions for that purpose. The next language should support context-free languages with a less cryptic notation.

The next language should have better Unicode support. For example, there should be some form of `split` that knows about combining characters, splitting a text into glyphs.

The next language should use UTF-32 as its internal character representation. This might seem wildly extravagant. I remember when 8 bits for a character was considered an extravagance. That was when memories were measured in kilobytes. Today memories are measured in gigabytes. Memories have become so large that the size of a character is in the noise. With UTF-32, the difference between code units and code points vanishes, making it easier to write programs that operate correctly internationally.

The next language should have direct support for blobs. Some data wants to be big and messy and nicely wrapped and mysterious.

The next language should have better support for eventual programming, including a processing loop and a mechanism for message dispatch and ordered delivery.

The next language should have better support for secure networking.

The next language should have support for process management: launching, communicating, and destroying. It should be possible to link processes together into suicide pacts. If wun fails, they all fail, creating an opportunity to start them up again in a fresh state.

The next language should have support for the parallel processing of pure functions. CPUs are not getting faster, but they are more plentiful. Ultimately, the greatest performance improvements come from parallelism.

Neo is not the next language, but it can help us to not be afraid of the next paradigm. Next we build Neo.

Chapter 26

How Tokenizing Works

●●○●○

> Never send a human to do a machine's job.
> *Agent Smith*

The first step in processing a program is to break it into tokens. A token is made from a sequence of characters that form a meaningful feature of the source, such as a name, punctuator, number literal, or text literal. We make a token object for each token in the program.

We use regular expressions to break source text into lines, and to break lines into tokens.

```
const rx_unicode_escapement = /
    \\ u \{ ( [ 0-9 A-F ]{4,6} ) \}
/g;
```

rx_crfl matches linefeed, carriage return, and carriage return linefeed. We are still messing with device codes for mid 20th Century electromechanical teletype machines.

```
const rx_crlf = /
    \n
|
    \r \n?
/;
```

rx_token matches a Neo token: comment, name, number, string, punctuator.

```
const rx_token = /
    ( \u0020+ )
|
    ( # .* )
|
    (
        [ a-z A-Z ]
        (?:
            \u0020 [ a-z A-Z ]
        |
            [ 0-9 a-z A-Z ]
        )*
        \??
    )
|
    (
        -? \d+
```

```
                (?: \. \d+ )?
                (?: e \-? \d+ )?
            )
    |
            (
                "
                (?:
                    [^ " \\ ]
                |
                    \\
                    (?:
                        [ n r " \\ ]
                    |
                        u \{ [ 0-9 A-F ]{4,6} \}
                    )
                )*
                "
            )
    |
            (
                \. (?: \. \.)?
            |
                \/ \\?
            |
                \\ \/?
            |
                > >?
            |
                < <?
            |
                \[ \]?
            |
                \{ \}?
            |
                [ ( ) } \] . , : ? ! ; ~ ≈ = ≠ ≤ ≥ & | + \- * % ƒ $ @ \^ _ ' ` ]
            )
    /y;

//  Capture Group
//      [1]  Whitespace
//      [2]  Comment
//      [3]  Alphameric
//      [4]  Number
//      [5]  String
//      [6]  Punctuator
```

We export a tokenizer factory.

```
export default Object.freeze(function tokenize(source, comment = false) {
```

tokenize takes a source and produces from it an array of token objects. If the source
is not an array, then it is split into lines at the carriage return/linefeed. If comment is
true then comments are included as token objects. The parser does not want to see
comments, but a software tool might.

```
        const lines = (
            Array.isArray(source)
            ? source
```

```
      : source.split(rx_crlf)
);
let line_nr = 0;
let line = lines[0];
rx_token.lastIndex = 0;
```

The factory returns a generator that breaks the lines into token objects. The token objects contain an id, coordinates, and other information. Whitespace is not tokenized.

Each time the token generator is called, it produces the next token.

```
return function token_generator() {
    if (line === undefined) {
        return;
    }
    let column_nr = rx_token.lastIndex;
    if (column_nr >= line.length) {
        rx_token.lastIndex = 0;
        line_nr += 1;
        line = lines[line_nr];
        return (
            line === undefined
            ? undefined
            : token_generator()
        );
    }
    let captives = rx_token.exec(line);
```

Nothing matched.

```
    if (!captives) {
        return {
            id: "(error)",
            line_nr,
            column_nr,
            string: line.slice(column_nr)
        };
    }
```

Whitespace matched.

```
    if (captives[1]) {
        return token_generator();
    }
```

A comment matched.

```
    if (captives[2]) {
        return (
            comment
            ? {
                id: "(comment)",
                comment: captives[2],
                line_nr,
                column_nr,
                column_to: rx_token.lastIndex
            }
            : token_generator()
        );
    }
```

A name matched.

```
if (captives[3]) {
    return {
        id: captives[3],
        alphameric: true,
        line_nr,
        column_nr,
        column_to: rx_token.lastIndex
    };
}
```

A number literal matched.

```
if (captives[4]) {
    return {
        id: "(number)",
        readonly: true,
        number: big_float.normalize(big_float.make(captives[4])),
        text: captives[4],
        line_nr,
        column_nr,
        column_to: rx_token.lastIndex
    };
}
```

A text literal matched.

```
if (captives[5]) {
```

We use `.replace` to convert `\u{xxxxxx}` to a codepoint and `JSON.parse` to process the remaining escapes and remove the quotes.

```
    return {
        id: "(text)",
        readonly: true,
        text: JSON.parse(captives[5].replace(
            rx_unicode_escapement,
            function (ignore, code) {
                return String.fromCodePoint(parseInt(code, 16));
            }
        )),
        line_nr,
        column_nr,
        column_to: rx_token.lastIndex
    };
}
```

A punctuator matched.

```
if (captives[6]) {
    return {
        id: captives[6],
        line_nr,
        column_nr,
        column_to: rx_token.lastIndex
    };
}
    };
});
```

Chapter 27

How Parsing Works

•••○○

> Some believed we lacked the programming
> language to describe your perfect world. But
> I believe that, as a species, human beings
> define their reality thru suffering and
> misery.
>
> *Agent Smith*

In parsing, we weave the stream of token objects into a tree. During the parsing
operation we also look for errors in the source. The token objects are augmented with
new properties. The most important are the `zeroth`, `wunth`, and `twoth` properties. They
give the tree structure. For example, the two operands of an addition are kept in the
`zeroth` and `wunth` properties of a `+` token. An `if` token keeps the condition expression
in `zeroth`, the *then* clause in `wunth`, and the `else` clause in `twoth`. There will be other
properties as well. We will discover them as we go along.

We report errors with the `error` function. We could have it keep a list of errors and
continue, but I want to stop after the first error. When I am in development mode,
I want an error to move my editor's cursor to the next problem. When I am in build
mode, I am looking for a pass or a fail, not a list.

```
let the_error;

function error(zeroth, wunth) {
    the_error = {
        id: "(error)",
        zeroth,
        wunth
    };
    throw "fail";
}
```

The `primordial` object contains the objects that are built into the language. This
includes constants like `true` and functions like `neg`. The `primordial` object is made with
`Object.create(null)` because I do not want the prototype chain polluting the object.
For example, `Object.prototype` contains a `valueOf` method, but I do not want to inherit
it because it could give the appearance of adding a primordial `valueOf` to the language.

```
const primordial = (function (ids) {
    const result = Object.create(null);
    ids.forEach(function (id) {
```

```
      result[id] = Object.freeze({
          id,
          alphameric: true,
          readonly: true
      });
  });
  return Object.freeze(result);
}([
      "abs", "array", "array?", "bit and", "bit mask", "bit or", "bit shift down",
      "bit shift up", "bit xor", "boolean?", "char", "code", "false", "fraction",
      "function?", "integer", "integer?", "length", "neg", "not", "number",
      "number?", "null", "record", "record?", "stone", "stone?", "text", "text?",
      "true"
]));
```

The readonly property blocks the let statement.

Three tokens will always be visible as we advance thru the stream.

The generator function supplies a stream of token objects. Three tokens are visible as prev_token, token, and next_token. The advance function uses the generator to cycle thru all of the token objects, skipping over the comments.

```
let the_token_generator;
let prev_token;
let token;
let next_token;

let now_function;        // The function currently being processed.
let loop;                // An array of loop exit status.

const the_end = Object.freeze({
    id: "(end)",
    precedence: 0,
    column_nr: 0,
    column_to: 0,
    line_nr: 0
});
```

The advance function advances to the next token. Its companion, the prelude function, tries to split the current token into two tokens.

```
function advance(id) {
```

Advance to the next token using the token generator. If an id is supplied, make sure that the current token matches that id.

```
    if (id !== undefined && id !== token.id) {
        return error(token, "expected '" + id + "'");
    }
    prev_token = token;
    token = next_token;
    next_token = the_token_generator() || the_end;
}

function prelude() {
```

If token contains a space, split it, putting the first part in prev_token. Otherwise, advance.

```
    if (token.alphameric) {
        let space_at = token.id.indexOf(" ");
        if (space_at > 0) {
            prev_token = {
                id: token.id.slice(0, space_at),
                alphameric: true,
                line_nr: token.line_nr,
                column_nr: token.column_nr,
                column_to: token.column_nr + space_at
            };
            token.id = token.id.slice(space_at + 1);
            token.column_nr = token.column_nr + space_at + 1;
            return;
        }
    }
    return advance();
}
```

Whitespace is significant in this language. A line break can signal the end of a statement or element. Indentation can signal the end of a clause. These functions help to manage that.

```
let indentation;

function indent() {
    indentation += 4;
}

function outdent() {
    indentation -= 4;
}

function at_indentation() {
    if (token.column_nr !== indentation) {
        return error(token, "expected at " + indentation);
    }
}

function is_line_break() {
    return token.line_nr !== prev_token.line_nr;
}

function same_line() {
    if (is_line_break()) {
        return error(token, "unexpected linebreak");
    }
}

function line_check(open) {
    return (
        open
        ? at_indentation()
        : same_line()
    );
}
```

The `register` function declares a new variable in a function's scope. The `lookup` function finds a variable in the most relevant scope.

```
function register(the_token, readonly = false) {
```

Add a variable to the current scope.

```
    if (now_function.scope[the_token.id] !== undefined) {
        error(the_token, "already defined");
    }
    the_token.readonly = readonly;
    the_token.origin = now_function;
    now_function.scope[the_token.id] = the_token;
}
```

```
function lookup(id) {
```

Look for the definition in the current scope.

```
    let definition = now_function.scope[id];
```

If that fails, search the ancestor scopes.

```
    if (definition === undefined) {
        let parent = now_function.parent;
        while (parent !== undefined) {
            definition = parent.scope[id];
            if (definition !== undefined) {
                break;
            }
            parent = parent.parent;
        }
    }
```

If that fails, search the primordials.

```
    if (definition === undefined) {
        definition = primordial[id];
    }
```

Remember that the current function used this definition.

```
    if (definition !== undefined) {
        now_function.scope[id] = definition;
    }
    }
    return definition;
}
```

The origin property captures the function that created the variable. The scope property holds all of the variables created or used in a function. The parent property points to the function that created this function.

Three objects contain the functions that are used to parse the features of the language: statements, prefixes, and suffixes.

The parse_statement, parse_prefix, and parse_suffix objects contain functions that do the specialized parsing. We are using Object.create(null) to make them because we do not want any of the debris from Object.prototype getting dredged up here.

```
const parse_statement = Object.create(null);
const parse_prefix = Object.create(null);
const parse_suffix = Object.create(null);
```

The expression function (and its helper, argument_expression) is the heart of this parser. An expression can be viewed as having two parts: A left part and an optional right part. The left part is a literal, variable, or prefix thing. The right part is a suffix operator that might be followed by another expression. If there is a suffix on the right and if it has greater precedence, then the left part is passed to the right part's parser, producing a new left part. The right part's parser will probably call expression again itself, possibly with a different precedence.

Expressions can be open or closed. If closed, the expression must fit entirely on the same line. Open expressions should start at the proper indentation and may have a line break before the suffix.

```
function argument_expression(precedence = 0, open = false) {
```

The expression function is the heart of this parser. It uses a technique called Top Down Operator Precedence.

It takes an optional open parameter that allows tolerance of certain line breaks. If open is true, we expect the token to be at the indentation point.

```
    let definition;
    let left;
    let the_token = token;
```

Is the token a number literal or text literal?

```
    if (the_token.id === "(number)" || the_token.id === "(text)") {
        advance();
        left = the_token;
```

Is the token alphameric?

```
    } else if (the_token.alphameric === true) {
        definition = lookup(the_token.id);
        if (definition === undefined) {
            return error(the_token, "expected a variable");
        }
        left = definition;
        advance();
    } else {
```

The token might be a prefix thing: (, [, {, ƒ.

```
        definition = parse_prefix[the_token.id];
        if (definition === undefined) {
            return error(the_token, "expected a variable");
        }
        advance();
        left = definition.parser(the_token);
    }
```

We have the left part. Is there a suffix operator on the right? Does precedence allow consuming that operator? If so, combine the left and right to form a new left.

```
    while (true) {
        the_token = token;
        definition = parse_suffix[the_token.id];
        if (
            token.column_nr < indentation
            || (!open && is_line_break())
            || definition === undefined
            || definition.precedence <= precedence
        ) {
```

```
        break;
    }
    line_check(open && is_line_break());
    advance();
    the_token.class = "suffix";
    left = definition.parser(left, the_token);
}
```

After going zero or more times around the loop, we can return the parse tree of the expression.

```
    return left;
}
```

```
function expression(precedence, open = false) {
```

Expressions do a whitespace check that argument expressions do not need.

```
    line_check(open);
    return argument_expression(precedence, open);
}
```

The `precedence` property determines how the suffix operator is parsed. The `parser` property is a function for parsing a prefix or suffix. The `class` property is `"suffix"`, `"statement"`, or `undefined`.

Let's look at a simple suffix operator. The . *dot* parser is passed the expression on the left and the . *dot* token. It verifies that the left expression is valid. It verifies that the current token is a name. Then it assembles them into the . *dot* token and returns it.

```
function parse_dot(left, the_dot) {
```

The expression on the left must be a variable or an expression that can return an object (excluding object literals).

```
    if (
        !left.alphameric
        && left.id !== "."
        && (left.id !== "[" || left.wunth === undefined)
        && left.id !== "("
    ) {
        return error(token, "expected a variable");
    }
    let the_name = token;
    if (the_name.alphameric !== true) {
        return error(the_name, "expected a field name");
    }
    the_dot.zeroth = left;
    the_dot.wunth = the_name;
    same_line();
    advance();
    return the_dot;
}
```

The [] *subscript* parser is a little more interesting. It is passed the expression on the left and the [*left bracket* token. It verifies that the left expression is valid. It then calls `expression` to get the thing in the brackets. If there was a line break after the [*left bracket* it is an open expression. It advances past the closing] *right bracket*.

```
function parse_subscript(left, the_bracket) {
    if (
        !left.alphameric
        && left.id !== "."
        && (left.id !== "[" || left.wunth === undefined)
        && left.id !== "("
    ) {
        return error(token, "expected a variable");
    }
    the_bracket.zeroth = left;
    if (is_line_break()) {
        indent();
        the_bracket.wunth = expression(0, true);
        outdent();
        at_indentation();
    } else {
        the_bracket.wunth = expression();
        same_line();
    }
    advance("]");
    return the_bracket;
}
```

The `ellipsis` parser is not packaged like the other suffix operators because it is allowed in only three places: Parameter lists, argument lists, and array literals. It is not allowed anywhere else, so we treat it as a special case.

```
function ellipsis(left) {
    if (token.id === "...") {
        const the_ellipsis = token;
        same_line();
        advance("...");
        the_ellipsis.zeroth = left;
        return the_ellipsis;
    }
    return left;
}
```

The `()` *invocation* parser parses function calls. It calls `argument_expression` for each argument. An open form invocation lists the arguments vertically without commas.

```
function parse_invocation(left, the_paren) {

//  function invocation:
//      expression
//      expression...

    const args = [];
    if (token.id === ")") {
        same_line();
    } else {
        const open = is_line_break();
        if (open) {
            indent();
        }
        while (true) {
            line_check(open);
            args.push(ellipsis(argument_expression()));
```

```
                    if (token.id === ")" || token === the_end) {
                        break;
                    }
                    if (!open) {
                        same_line();
                        advance(",");
                    }
                }
                if (open) {
                    outdent();
                    at_indentation();
                } else {
                    same_line();
                }
            }
        advance(")");
        the_paren.zeroth = left;
        the_paren.wunth = args;
        return the_paren;
    }
```

The suffix function builds the parse_suffix array. It takes an operator and a precedence and an optional parser. It can provide a default parser function that works for most of the operators.

```
function suffix(
    id,
    precedence,
    optional_parser = function infix(left, the_token) {
        the_token.zeroth = left;
        the_token.wunth = expression(precedence);
        return the_token;
    }
) {
```

Make an infix or suffix operator.

```
        const the_symbol = Object.create(null);
        the_symbol.id = id;
        the_symbol.precedence = precedence;
        the_symbol.parser = optional_parser;
        parse_suffix[id] = Object.freeze(the_symbol);
    }

    suffix("|", 111, function parse_default(left, the_bar) {
        the_bar.zeroth = left;
        the_bar.wunth = expression(112);
        advance("|");
        return the_bar;
    });
    suffix("?", 111, function then_else(left, the_then) {
        the_then.zeroth = left;
        the_then.wunth = expression();
        advance("!");
        the_then.twoth = expression();
        return the_then;
    });
    suffix("/\\", 222);
```

```
suffix("\\/", 222);
suffix("~", 444);
suffix("≈", 444);
suffix("+", 555);
suffix("-", 555);
suffix("<<", 555);
suffix(">>", 555);
suffix("*", 666);
suffix("/", 666);
suffix(".", 777, parse_dot);
suffix("[", 777, parse_subscript);
suffix("(", 777, parse_invocation);
```

We treat the relational operators a little differently to guard against $a < b \leq c$ errors.

```
const rel_op = Object.create(null);

function relational(operator) {
    rel_op[operator] = true;
    return suffix(operator, 333, function (left, the_token) {
        the_token.zeroth = left;
        the_token.wunth = expression(333);
        if (rel_op[token.id] === true) {
            return error(token, "unexpected relational operator");
        }
        return the_token;
    });
}

relational("=");
relational("≠");
relational("<");
relational(">");
relational("≤");
relational("≥");
```

The **prefix** function builds the **parse_prefix** array. Notice that (*left paren* and [*left bracket* are also in the **parse_suffix** array. That is not a problem. There is no ambiguity. Prefix operators do not need precedence.

```
function prefix(id, parser) {
    const the_symbol = Object.create(null);
    the_symbol.id = id;
    the_symbol.parser = parser;
    parse_prefix[id] = Object.freeze(the_symbol);
}

prefix("(", function (ignore) {
    let result;
    if (is_line_break()) {
        indent();
        result = expression(0, true);
        outdent();
        at_indentation();
    } else {
        result = expression(0);
        same_line();
    }
```

```
        advance(")");
        return result;
    });
```

The array literal parser calls the **expression** function for each element. An element can be any expression, optionally followed by ... *dot dot dot*. There are three ways to write an array literal:

Empty: [*left bracket*] *right bracket*, an array with a length of zero.

Closed: The entire literal on the same line, comma separated.

Open: Line break after [*left bracket*, increase indentation,] *right bracket* restores the previous indentation, expressions separated by , *comma* or ; *semicolon* and/or line break.

The ; *semicolon* makes two dimensional arrays.

```
        [[2, 7, 6], [9, 5, 1], [4, 3, 8]]
```

can be written as

```
        [2, 7, 6; 9, 5, 1; 4, 3, 8]
```

```
  prefix("[", function arrayliteral(the_bracket) {
      let matrix = [];
      let array = [];
      if (!is_line_break()) {
          while (true) {
              array.push(ellipsis(expression()));
              if (token.id === ",") {
                  same_line();
                  advance(",");
              } else if (
                  token.id === ";"
                  && array.length > 0
                  && next_token !== "]"
              ) {
                  same_line();
                  advance(";");
                  matrix.push(array);
                  array = [];
              } else {
                  break;
              }
          }
          same_line();
      } else {
          indent();
          while (true) {
              array.push(ellipsis(expression(0, is_line_break())));
              if (token.id === "]" || token === the_end) {
                  break;
              }
              if (token.id === ";") {
                  if (array.length === 0 || next_token.id === "]") {
                      break;
                  }
                  same_line();
```

```
                    advance(";");
                    matrix.push(array);
                    array = [];
                } else if (token.id === "," || !is_line_break()) {
                    same_line();
                    advance(",");
                }
            }
            outdent();
            if (token.column_nr !== indentation) {
                return error(token, "expected at " + indentation);
            }
        }
        advance("]");
        if (matrix.length > 0) {
            matrix.push(array);
            the_bracket.zeroth = matrix;
        } else {
            the_bracket.zeroth = array;
        }
        return the_bracket;
});

prefix("[]", function emptyarrayliteral(the_brackets) {
    return the_brackets;
});
```

The record literal parser recognizes 4 forms of fields.

- *variable*
- *name*: *expression*
- "*string*": *expression*
- [*expression*]: *expression*

```
prefix("{", function recordliteral(the_brace) {
    const properties = [];
    let key;
    let value;
    const open = the_brace.line_nr !== token.line_nr;
    if (open) {
        indent();
    }
    while (true) {
        line_check(open);
        if (token.id === "[") {
            advance("[");
            key = expression();
            advance("]");
            same_line();
            advance(":");
            value = expression();
        } else {
            key = token;
            advance();
            if (key.alphameric === true) {
                if (token.id === ":") {
```

```
                        same_line();
                        advance(":");
                        value = expression();
                } else {
                        value = lookup(key.id);
                        if (value === undefined) {
                            return error(key, "expected a variable");
                        }
                }
                key = key.id;
            } else if (key.id === "(text)") {
                key = key.text;
                same_line();
                advance(":");
                value = expression();
            } else {
                return error(key, "expected a key");
            }
        }
        properties.push({
            zeroth: key,
            wunth: value
        });
        if (token.column_nr < indentation || token.id === "}") {
            break;
        }
        if (!open) {
            same_line();
            advance(",");
        }
    }
    if (open) {
        outdent();
        at_indentation();
    } else {
        same_line();
    }
    advance("}");
    the_brace.zeroth = properties;
    return the_brace;
});

prefix("{}", function emptyrecordliteral(the_braces) {
    return the_braces;
});
```

The function literal parser makes new functions. It also gives access to *functinos*. The name came to me whilst I was mistyping.

```
const functino = (function make_set(array, value = true) {
    const object = Object.create(null);
    array.forEach(function (element) {
        object[element] = value;
    });
    return Object.freeze(object);
}([
    "?", "|", "/\\", "\\/", "=", "≠", "<", "≥", ">", "≤",
    "~", "≈", "+", "-", ">>", "<<", "*", "/", "[", "(
```

```
    ]));

    prefix("ƒ", function function_literal(the_function) {
```

If the ƒ is followed by a suffix operator, then produce the corresponding functino.

```
        const the_operator = token;
        if (
            functino[token.id] === true
            && (the_operator.id !== "(" || next_token.id === ")")
        ) {
            advance();
            if (the_operator.id === "(") {
                same_line();
                advance(")");
            } else if (the_operator.id === "[") {
                same_line();
                advance("]");
            } else if (the_operator.id === "?") {
                same_line();
                advance("!");
            } else if (the_operator.id === "|") {
                same_line();
                advance("|");
            }
            the_function.zeroth = the_operator.id;
            return the_function;
        }
```

Set up the new function.

```
        if (loop.length > 0) {
            return error(the_function, "Do not make functions in loops.");
        }
        the_function.scope = Object.create(null);
        the_function.parent = now_function;
        now_function = the_function;

    // Function parameters come in 3 forms.
    //      name
    //      name | default |
    //      name...
```

The parameter list can be open or closed.

```
        const parameters = [];
        if (token.alphameric === true) {
            let open = is_line_break();
            if (open) {
                indent();
            }
            while (true) {
                line_check(open);
                let the_parameter = token;
                register(the_parameter);
                advance();
                if (token.id === "...") {
                    parameters.push(ellipsis(the_parameter));
                    break;
```

```
        }
        if (token.id === "|") {
            advance("|");
            parameters.push(parse_suffix["|"](the_parameter, prev_token));
        } else {
            parameters.push(the_parameter);
        }
        if (open) {
            if (token.id === ",") {
                return error(token, "unexpected ','");
            }
            if (token.alphameric !== true) {
                break;
            }
        } else {
            if (token.id !== ",") {
                break;
            }
            same_line();
            advance(",");
            if (token.alphameric !== true) {
                return error(token, "expected another parameter");
            }
        }
    }
    if (open) {
        outdent();
        at_indentation();
    } else {
        same_line();
    }
}
the_function.zeroth = parameters;
```

A function can have a (return expression) or a {function body}.

Parse the return expression.

```
if (token.id === "(") {
    advance("(");
    if (is_line_break()) {
        indent();
        the_function.wunth = expression(0, true);
        outdent();
        at_indentation();
    } else {
        the_function.wunth = expression();
        same_line();
    }
    advance(")");
} else {
```

Parse the function body. The body must contain an explicit **return**. There is no implicit return by falling thru the bottom.

```
    advance("{");
    indent();
    the_function.wunth = statements();
```

```
            if (the_function.wunth.return !== true) {
                return error(prev_token, "missing explicit 'return'");
            }
```

Parse the `failure` handler.

```
            if (token.id === "failure") {
                outdent();
                at_indentation();
                advance("failure");
                indent();
                the_function.twoth = statements();
                if (the_function.twoth.return !== true) {
                    return error(prev_token, "missing explicit 'return'");
                }
            }
            outdent();
            at_indentation();
            advance("}");
        }
        now_function = the_function.parent;
        return the_function;
    });
```

The `statements` function parses statements, returning an array of statement tokens. It uses the `prelude` function to split the verb from the token, if necessary.

```
    function statements() {
        const statement_list = [];
        let the_statement;
        while (true) {
            if (
                token === the_end
                || token.column_nr < indentation
                || token.alphameric !== true
                || token.id.startsWith("export")
            ) {
                break;
            }
            at_indentation();
            prelude();
            let parser = parse_statement[prev_token.id];
            if (parser === undefined) {
                return error(prev_token, "expected a statement");
            }
            prev_token.class = "statement";
            the_statement = parser(prev_token);
            statement_list.push(the_statement);
            if (the_statement.disrupt === true) {
                if (token.column_nr === indentation) {
                    return error(token, "unreachable");
                }
                break;
            }
        }
        if (statement_list.length === 0) {
            if (!token.id.startsWith("export")) {
                return error(token, "expected a statement");
```

```
            }
        } else {
            statement_list.disrupt = the_statement.disrupt;
            statement_list.return = the_statement.return;
        }
        return statement_list;
    }
```

The `disrupt` property marks statements and statement lists that break or return. The `return` property marks statements and statement lists that return.

The `break` statement breaks out of a loop. The parser is passed the `break` token. It sets the exit condition of the current loop.

```
    parse_statement.break = function (the_break) {
        if (loop.length === 0) {
            return error(the_break, "'break' wants to be in a loop.");
        }
        loop[loop.length - 1] = "break";
        the_break.disrupt = true;
        return the_break;
    };
```

The `call` statement calls a function and ignores the return value. This is to identify calls that are happening solely for their side effects.

```
    parse_statement.call = function (the_call) {
        the_call.zeroth = expression();
        if (the_call.zeroth.id !== "(") {
            return error(the_call, "expected a function invocation");
        }
        return the_call;
    };
```

The `def` statement registers read only variables.

```
    parse_statement.def = function (the_def) {
        if (!token.alphameric) {
            return error(token, "expected a name.");
        }
        same_line();
        the_def.zeroth = token;
        register(token, true);
        advance();
        same_line();
        advance(":");
        the_def.wunth = expression();
        return the_def;
    };
```

The `fail` statement is the riskiest experiment in Neo. Exception mechanisms in most languages have been corrupted into communications channels. The `fail` statement attempts to repair that.

```
    parse_statement.fail = function (the_fail) {
        the_fail.disrupt = true;
        return the_fail;
    };
```

The if statement has an optional else clause or else if statement. If both branches disrupt or return, then the if statement itself disrupts or returns.

```
parse_statement.if = function if_statement(the_if) {
    the_if.zeroth = expression();
    indent();
    the_if.wunth = statements();
    outdent();
    if (token.column_nr === indentation) {
        if (token.id === "else") {
            advance("else");
            indent();
            the_if.twoth = statements();
            outdent();
            the_if.disrupt = the_if.wunth.disrupt && the_if.twoth.disrupt;
            the_if.return = the_if.wunth.return && the_if.twoth.return;
        } else if (token.id.startsWith("else if ")) {
            prelude();
            prelude();
            the_if.twoth = if_statement(prev_token);
            the_if.disrupt = the_if.wunth.disrupt && the_if.twoth.disrupt;
            the_if.return = the_if.wunth.return && the_if.twoth.return;
        }
    }
    return the_if;
};
```

The let statement is Neo's assignment statement. The left side is not an ordinary expression. It is a more limited thing called an *lvalue*. An lvalue can be a variable (var not def), or an expression that finds a field or element.

```
parse_statement.let = function (the_let) {
```

The let statement is the only place where mutation is allowed.

The next token must be a name.

```
        same_line();
        const name = token;
        advance();
        const id = name.id;
        let left = lookup(id);
        if (left === undefined) {
            return error(name, "expected a variable");
        }
        let readonly = left.readonly;
```

Now we consider the suffix operators [] . [and {.

```
        while (true) {
            if (token === the_end) {
                break;
            }
            same_line();
```

A [] in this position indicates an array append operation.

```
            if (token.id === "[]") {
                readonly = false;
                token.zeroth = left;
                left = token;
```

```
                same_line();
                advance("[]");
                break;
            }
            if (token.id === ".") {
                readonly = false;
                advance(".");
                left = parse_dot(left, prev_token);
            } else if (token.id === "[") {
                readonly = false;
                advance("[");
                left = parse_subscript(left, prev_token);
            } else if (token.id === "(") {
                readonly = false;
                advance("(");
                left = parse_invocation(left, prev_token);
                if (token.id === ":") {
                    return error(left, "assignment to the result of a function");
                }
            } else {
                break;
            }
        }
        advance(":");
        if (readonly) {
            return error(left, "assignment to a constant");
        }
        the_let.zeroth = left;
        the_let.wunth = expression();
```

A `[]` in this position indicates an array pop operation.

```
        if (token.id === "[]" && left.id !== "[]" && (
            the_let.wunth.alphameric === true
            || the_let.wunth.id === "."
            || the_let.wunth.id === "["
            || the_let.wunth.id === "("
        )) {
            token.zeroth = the_let.wunth;
            the_let.wunth = token;
            same_line();
            advance("[]");
        }
        return the_let;
    };
```

The `loop` statement keeps a stack for dealing with nested loops. The entries in the stack are the exit conditions of the loops. If there is no explicit exit, a stack's status is `"infinite"`. If the only exit is a `return` statement, its status is `"return"`. If the loop exits with a `break` statement, its status is `"break"`. For this purpose, `fail` is not an explicit exit condition.

```
    parse_statement.loop = function (the_loop) {
        indent();
        loop.push("infinite");
        the_loop.zeroth = statements();
        const exit = loop.pop();
        if (exit === "infinite") {
```

```
            return error(the_loop, "A loop wants a 'break'.");
        }
        if (exit === "return") {
            the_loop.disrupt = true;
            the_loop.return = true;
        }
        outdent();
        return the_loop;
    };
```

The return statement changes the status of "infinite" loops to "return";

```
    parse_statement.return = function (the_return) {
        try {
            if (now_function.parent === undefined) {
                return error(the_return, "'return' wants to be in a function.");
            }
            loop.forEach(function (element, element_nr) {
                if (element === "infinite") {
                    loop[element_nr] = "return";
                }
            });
            if (is_line_break()) {
                return error(the_return, "'return' wants a return value.");
            }
            the_return.zeroth = expression();
            if (token === "}") {
                return error(the_return, "Misplaced 'return'.");
            }
            the_return.disrupt = true;
            the_return.return = true;
            return the_return;
        } catch (ignore) {
            return the_error;
        }
    };
```

The var statement declares a variable that can be assigned to with the let statement. If the variable is not explicitly initialized, its initial value is null.

```
    parse_statement.var = function (the_var) {
        if (!token.alphameric) {
            return error(token, "expected a name.");
        }
        same_line();
        the_var.zeroth = token;
        register(token);
        advance();
        if (token.id === ":") {
            same_line();
            advance(":");
            the_var.wunth = expression();
        }
        return the_var;
    };
```

```
Object.freeze(parse_prefix);
Object.freeze(parse_suffix);
Object.freeze(parse_statement);
```

The import and export statements are not included in parse_statement because their placement in the source is restricted. All of the import statements must be placed before any other statements. Only wun export statement is allowed, and it is the last statement.

```
function parse_import(the_import) {
    same_line();
    register(token, true);
    the_import.zeroth = token;
    advance();
    same_line();
    advance(":");
    same_line();
    the_import.wunth = token;
    advance("(text)");
    the_import.class = "statement";
    return the_import;
}

function parse_export(the_export) {
    the_export.zeroth = expression();
    the_export.class = "statement";
    return the_export;
}
```

We export a single parse function. It takes a token generator and returns a tree. We do not need to make a constructor because parse does not retain any state between calls.

```
export default function parse(token_generator) {
    try {
        indentation = 0;
        loop = [];
        the_token_generator = token_generator;
        next_token = the_end;
        const program = {
            id: "",
            scope: Object.create(null)
        };
        now_function = program;
        advance();
        advance();
        let the_statements = [];
        while (token.id.startsWith("import ")) {
            at_indentation();
            prelude();
            the_statements.push(parse_import(prev_token));
        }
        the_statements = the_statements.concat(statements());
        if (token.id.startsWith("export")) {
            at_indentation();
            prelude();
            the_statements.push(parse_export(prev_token));
        }
```

```
        if (token !== the_end) {
            return error(token, "unexpected");
        }
        program.zeroth = the_statements;
        return program;
    } catch (ignore) {
        return the_error;
    }
};
```

Chapter 28

How Code Generation Works

●●●○○

> You have to let it all go, Neo.
> Fear, doubt, and disbelief
> Free your mind.
> *Morpheus*

The next step is to take the tree that the parser wove and transform it into an executable form. This is called *code generation*, but it is really a transformation.

We have many choices of target language. We could produce machine code, or code for a virtual machine, or for another programming language. With a suitable runtime, we could target C, but we are going to target JavaScript.

JavaScript is a surprisingly good target language. It provides excellent (and invisible) memory management, which is often the most difficult aspect in bringing up a new language. Generating code for a real machine can require management of a limited register set. JavaScript allows you to have all of the variables you want. Objects are a very versatile data structure. JavaScript should get more praise for its objects.

We start by making some sets. We need sets of things that produce boolean values, and JavaScript reserved words.

```
function make_set(array, value = true) {
    const object = Object.create(null);
    array.forEach(function (element) {
        object[element] = value;
    });
    return $NEO.stone(object);
}

const boolean_operator = make_set([
    "array?", "boolean?", "function?", "integer?", "not", "number?", "record?",
    "stone?", "text?", "true", "=", "≠", "<", ">", "≤", "≥", "/\\", "\\/"
]);

const reserved = make_set([
    "arguments", "await", "break", "case", "catch", "class", "const",
    "continue", "debugger", "default", "delete", "do", "else", "enum", "eval",
    "export", "extends", "false", "finally", "for", "function", "if",
    "implements", "import", "in", "Infinity", "instanceof", "interface", "let",
    "NaN", "new", "null", "package", "private", "protected", "public", "return",
```

```
        "static", "super", "switch", "this", "throw", "true", "try", "typeof",
        "undefined", "var", "void", "while", "with", "yield"
]);
```

The `primordial` object contains mappings of things from Neo primordial space to JavaScript space. Some go to the Neo run time and some go to JavaScript.

```
const primordial = $NEO.stone({
    "abs": "$NEO.abs",
    "array": "$NEO.array",
    "array?": "Array.isArray",
    "bit and": "$NEO.bitand",
    "bit mask": "$NEO.bitmask",
    "bit or": "$NEO.bitor",
    "bit shift down": "$NEO.bitdown",
    "bit shift up": "$NEO.bitup",
    "bit xor": "$NEO.bitxor",
    "boolean?": "$NEO.boolean_",
    "char": "$NEO.char",
    "code": "$NEO.code",
    "false": "false",
    "fraction": "$NEO.fraction",
    "function?": "$NEO.function_",
    "integer": "$NEO.integer",
    "integer?": "$NEO.integer_",
    "length": "$NEO.length",
    "neg": "$NEO.neg",
    "not": "$NEO.not",
    "null": "undefined",
    "number": "$NEO.make",
    "number?": "$NEO.is_big_float",
    "record": "$NEO.record",
    "record?": "$NEO.record_",
    "stone": "$NEO.stone",
    "stone?": "Object.isFrozen",
    "text": "$NEO.text",
    "text?": "$NEO.text_",
    "true": "true"
});
```

Whitespace is much less important in JavaScript than it is in Neo, so we could produce extremely ugly code and JavaScript would not mind. I think there is too much ugliness in the world. When we have the opportunity to make things better, we should, even if no wun notices.

```
let indentation;

function indent() {
    indentation += 4;
}

function outdent() {
    indentation -= 4;
}

function begin() {
```

At the beginning of each line we emit a line break and padding.

```
        return "\n" + " ".repeat(indentation);
    }

    let front_matter;
    let operator_transform;
    let statement_transform;
    let unique;
```

The naming conventions in Neo and JavaScript are not fully compatible. Neo permits spaces and question marks, and JavaScript does not. So we mangle Neo names if necessary to make them into legal JavaScript names. Neo allows all words, but JavaScript reserves some words. When you use a JavaScript reserved word in Neo, we prepend a dollar sign to the word when we move it to JavaScript space. We convert big decimal floating point numbers into a form that resembles number literals so that programs are more readable.

```
    const rx_space_question = / [ \u0020 ? ]/g;

    function mangle(name) {
```

JavaScript does not allow space or ? in identifiers, so we replace them with _. We give reserved words a $ prefix.

So what me worry? becomes what_me_worry_, and class becomes $class.

```
        return (
            reserved[name] === true
            ? "$" + name
            : name.replace(rx_space_question, "_")
        );
    }

    const rx_minus_point = / [ \- . ] /g;

    function numgle(number) {
```

We make big decimal literals look as natural as possible by making them into constants. A constant name start with $. A - or . is replaced with _.

So, 1 becomes $1, 98.6 becomes $98_6, and -1.011e-5 becomes $_1_011e_5.

```
        const text = big_float.string(number.number);
        const name = "$" + text.replace(rx_minus_point, "_");
        if (unique[name] !== true) {
            unique[name] = true;
            front_matter.push(
                "const " + name + " = $NEO.number(\"" + text + "\");\n"
            );
        }
        return name;
    }
```

Most of our code generator is just some simple functions that convert tokens back into text. They call each other to textualize all of the pieces. We start with op which takes an operator token. It gets the operator's transform. Many of the operators follow a simple pattern, so their transformers are strings. If the token has operands attached, then a function call is composed. For operators that do not fit that pattern, the transform is a function that takes the token and returns a string.

```
function op(thing) {
    const transform = operator_transform[thing.id];
    return (
        typeof transform === "string"
        ? (
            thing.zeroth === undefined
            ? transform
            : transform + "(" + expression(thing.zeroth) + (
                thing.wunth === undefined
                ? ""
                : ", " + expression(thing.wunth)
            ) + ")"
        )
        : transform(thing)
    );

}
```

The `expression` function handles general expression tokens.

```
function expression(thing) {
    if (thing.id === "(number)") {
        return numgle(thing);
    }
    if (thing.id === "(text)") {
        return JSON.stringify(thing.text);
    }
    if (thing.alphameric) {
        return (
            thing.origin === undefined
            ? primordial[thing.id]
            : mangle(thing.id)
        );
    }
    return op(thing);
}
```

This function makes array literals.

```
function array_literal(array) {
    return "[" + array.map(function (element) {
        return (
            Array.isArray(element)
            ? array_literal(element)
            : expression(element)
        );
    }).join(", ") + "]";
}
```

Neo record literals produce objects without prototypes. Empty records are made with `Object.create(null)`. The fields are made by assignment. We wrap the assignments in an immediately invoked function expression. `{[foo bear]: 12.3, two part}` produces

```
(function (o) {
    $NEO.set(o, foo_bear, $12_3);
    o["two part"] = two_part;
}(Object.create(null)))
```

In record literals, variable names are mangled, but field names are not.

```
function record_literal(array) {
    indent();
    const padding = begin();
    const string = "(function (o) {" + array.map(function (element) {
        return padding + (
            typeof element.zeroth === "string"
            ? (
                "o["
                + JSON.stringify(element.zeroth)
                + "] = "
                + expression(element.wunth)
                + ";"
            )
            : (
                "$NEO.set(o, "
                + expression(element.zeroth)
                + ", "
                + expression(element.wunth)
                + ");"
            )
        );
    }).join("") + padding + "return o;";
    outdent();
    return string + begin() + "}(Object.create(null)))";
}
```

Neo is not a boolish language. There are places where it expects to be given boolean values, such as the condition part of an `if` statement. If Neo is given a value that is not a boolean, then it must fail. In order to get this behavior in JavaScript, we may have to wrap such values with the `assert_boolean` function.

```
function assert_boolean(thing) {
    const string = expression(thing);
    return (
        (
            boolean_operator[thing.id] === true
            || (
                thing.zeroth !== undefined
                && thing.zeroth.origin === undefined
                && boolean_operator[thing.zeroth.id]
            )
        )
        ? string
        : "$NEO.assert_boolean(" + string + ")"
    );
}
```

We can stringify arrays of statement tokens and wrap them in blocks.

```
function statements(array) {
    const padding = begin();
    return array.map(function (statement) {
        return padding + statement_transform[statement.id](statement);
    }).join("");
}

function block(array) {
    indent();
```

```
        const string = statements(array);
        outdent();
        return "{" + string + begin() + "}";
}
```

The `statement_transform` object contains the transform functions for all of the statements. Most of the statements are very simple. The `if` statement is complicated because there are 3 forms: no `else`, with `else`, and with `else if`. The `let` statement is the only place where mutation happens. It must deal with the `[]` operator that pushes on the left and pops on the right, and it deals with lvalues.

```
statement_transform = $NEO.stone({
    break: function (ignore) {
        return "break;";
    },
    call: function (thing) {
        return expression(thing.zeroth) + ";";
    },
    def: function (thing) {
        return (
            "var " + expression(thing.zeroth)
            + " = " + expression(thing.wunth) + ";"
        );
    },
    export: function (thing) {
        const exportation = expression(thing.zeroth);
        return "export default " + (
            exportation.startsWith("$NEO.stone(")
            ? exportation
            : "$NEO.stone(" + exportation + ")"
        ) + ";";
    },
    fail: function () {
        return "throw $NEO.fail(\"fail\");";
    },
    if: function if_statement(thing) {
        return (
            "if ("
            + assert_boolean(thing.zeroth)
            + ") "
            + block(thing.wunth)
            + (
                thing.twoth === undefined
                ? ""
                : " else " + (
                    thing.twoth.id === "if"
                    ? if_statement(thing.twoth)
                    : block(thing.twoth)
                )
            )
        );
    },
    import: function (thing) {
        return (
            "import " + expression(thing.zeroth)
            + " from " + expression(thing.wunth) + ";"
        );
```

```
        },
        let: function (thing) {
            const right = (
                thing.wunth.id === "[]"
                ? expression(thing.wunth.zeroth) + ".pop();"
                : expression(thing.wunth)
            );
            if (thing.zeroth.id === "[]") {
                return expression(thing.zeroth.zeroth) + ".push(" + right + ");";
            }
            if (thing.zeroth.id === ".") {
                return (
                    "$NEO.set(" + expression(thing.zeroth.zeroth)
                    + ", " + JSON.stringify(thing.zeroth.wunth.id)
                    + ", " + right + ");"
                );
            }
            if (thing.zeroth.id === "[") {
                return (
                    "$NEO.set(" + expression(thing.zeroth.zeroth)
                    + ", " + expression(thing.zeroth.wunth)
                    + ", " + right + ");"
                );
            }
            return expression(thing.zeroth) + " = " + right + ";";
        },
        loop: function (thing) {
            return "while (true) " + block(thing.zeroth);
        },
        return: function (thing) {
            return "return " + expression(thing.zeroth) + ";";
        },
        var: function (thing) {
            return "var " + expression(thing.zeroth) + (
                thing.wunth === undefined
                ? ";"
                : " = " + expression(thing.wunth) + ";"
            );
        }
    });
```

A *functino* is a built in function that is accessed by putting a ƒ prefix on an operator.

```
    const functino = $NEO.stone({
        "?": "$NEO.ternary",
        "|": "$NEO.default",
        "/\\": "$NEO.and",
        "\\/": "$NEO.or",
        "=": "$NEO.eq",
        "≠": "$NEO.ne",
        "<": "$NEO.lt",
        "≥": "$NEO.ge",
        ">": "$NEO.gt",
        "≤": "$NEO.le",
        "~": "$NEO.cat",
        "≈": "$NEO.cats",
        "+": "$NEO.add",
        "-": "$NEO.sub",
```

```
            ">>": "$NEO.max",
            "<<": "$NEO.min",
            "*": "$NEO.mul",
            "/": "$NEO.div",
            "[": "$NEO.get",
            "(": "$NEO.resolve"
    });
```

The `operator_transform` object contains all of the operator transforms.

```
    operator_transform = $NEO.stone({
        "?": function (thing) {
            indent();
            let padding = begin();
            let string = (
                "(" + padding + assert_boolean(thing.zeroth)
                + padding + "? " + expression(thing.wunth)
                + padding + ": " + expression(thing.twoth)
            );
            outdent();
            return string + begin() + ")";
        },
        "/\\": function (thing) {
            return (
                "(" + assert_boolean(thing.zeroth)
                + " && " + assert_boolean(thing.wunth)
                + ")"
            );
        },
        "\\/": function (thing) {
            return (
                "(" + assert_boolean(thing.zeroth)
                + " || " + assert_boolean(thing.wunth)
                + ")"
            );
        },
        "=": "$NEO.eq",
        "≠": "$NEO.ne",
        "<": "$NEO.lt",
        "≥": "$NEO.ge",
        ">": "$NEO.gt",
        "≤": "$NEO.le",
        "~": "$NEO.cat",
        "≈": "$NEO.cats",
        "+": "$NEO.add",
        "-": "$NEO.sub",
        ">>": "$NEO.max",
        "<<": "$NEO.min",
        "*": "$NEO.mul",
        "/": "$NEO.div",
        "|": function (thing) {
            return (
                "(function (_0) {"
                + "return (_0 === undefined) ? "
                + expression(thing.wunth) + " : _0);}("
                + expression(thing.zeroth) + "))"
            );
        },
```

```
    "...": function (thing) {
        return "..." + expression(thing.zeroth);
    },
    ".": function (thing) {
        return (
            "$NEO.get(" + expression(thing.zeroth)
            + ", \"" + thing.wunth.id + "\")"
        );
    },
    "[": function (thing) {
        if (thing.wunth === undefined) {
            return array_literal(thing.zeroth);
        }
        return (
            "$NEO.get(" + expression(thing.zeroth)
            + ", " + expression(thing.wunth) + ")"
        );
    },
    "{": function (thing) {
        return record_literal(thing.zeroth);
    },
    "(": function (thing) {
        return (
            expression(thing.zeroth) + "("
            + thing.wunth.map(expression).join(", ") + ")"
        );
    },
    "[]": "[]",
    "{}": "Object.create(null)",
    "ƒ": function (thing) {
        if (typeof thing.zeroth === "string") {
            return functino[thing.zeroth];
        }
        return "$NEO.stone(function (" + thing.zeroth.map(function (param) {
            if (param.id === "...") {
                return "..." + mangle(param.zeroth.id);
            }
            if (param.id === "|") {
                return (
                    mangle(param.zeroth.id) + " = " + expression(param.wunth)
                );
            }
            return mangle(param.id);
        }).join(", ") + ") " + (
            Array.isArray(thing.wunth)
            ? block(thing.wunth)
            : "{return " + expression(thing.wunth) + ";}"
        ) + ")";
    }
});
```

It exports a code generator function that takes a tree and returns a JavaScript source program.

```
export default $NEO.stone(function codegen(tree) {
    front_matter = [
        "import $NEO from \"./neo.runtime.js\"\n"
    ];
```

```
        indentation = 0;
        unique = Object.create(null);
        const bulk = statements(tree.zeroth);
        return front_matter.join("") + bulk;
    });
```

Example

This function is similar to the `map` method, but it also works with multiple arrays, scalars, and generators.

```
export ƒ function, arguments... {
    if length(arguments) = 0
        return null
    var index: 0
    def result: []
    var stop: false

    def prepare arguments: ƒ argument {
        def candidate: (
            array?(argument)
            ? argument[index]
            ! (
                function?(argument)
                ? argument(index)
                ! argument
            )
        )
        if candidate = null
            let stop: true
        return candidate
    }

    loop
        var processed: array(arguments, prepare arguments)
        if stop
            break
        let result[]: function(processed...)
        let index: index + 1
    return result
}
```

This is the .js that was produced by `codegen(parse(tokenize(neo_source)))`:

```
import $NEO from "./neo.runtime.js";
const $0 = $NEO.number("0");
const $1 = $NEO.number("1");

export default $NEO.stone(function ($function, ...$arguments) {
    if ($NEO.eq($NEO.length($arguments), $0)) {
        return undefined;
    }
    var index = $0;
    var result = [];
    var stop = false;
    var prepare_arguments = $NEO.stone(function (argument) {
        var candidate = (
            Array.isArray(argument)
```

```
            ? $NEO.get(argument, index)
            : (
                $NEO.function_(argument)
                ? argument(index)
                : argument
            )
        );
        if ($NEO.eq(candidate, undefined)) {
            stop = true;
        }
        return candidate;
    });
    while (true) {
        var processed = $NEO.array($arguments, prepare_arguments);
        if ($NEO.assert_boolean(stop)) {
            break;
        }
        result.push($function(...processed));
        index = $NEO.add(index, $1);
    }
    return result;
});
```

And then...

```
import do: "example/do.neo"

var result: do(f+, [1, 2, 3], [5, 4, 3])
# result is [6, 6, 6]

let result: do(f/, 60, [1, 2, 3, 4, 5, 6])
# result is [60, 30, 20, 15, 12, 10]
```

which transpiles to...

```
import $NEO from "./neo.runtime.js"
const $1 = $NEO.number("1");
const $2 = $NEO.number("2");
const $3 = $NEO.number("3");
const $5 = $NEO.number("5");
const $4 = $NEO.number("4");
const $60 = $NEO.number("60");
const $6 = $NEO.number("6");

import $do from "example/do.neo";
var result = $do($NEO.add, $60, [$1, $2, $3], [$5, $4, $3]);
result = $do($NEO.div, $60, [$1, $2, $3, $4, $5, $6]);
```

## Chapter 29

How Runtimes Work

●●●○●

> I know why you're here, Neo. I know what
> you've been doing... why you hardly sleep,
> why you live alone, and why night after
> night, you sit by your computer.
>
> *Trinity*

A *runtime* is software that supports the execution of programs. Part of JavaScript's popularity as a transcompilation target is due to the the quality of the runtime support it provides. If the semantics of the source language differ from the target, then some specialized runtime support must be added. The form of the Neo-in-JavaScript runtime is an object containing functions that aid in execution.

Neo's two biggest semantic improvements are a better number type and a better object. The number type was developed in Chapter 4. Neo records unify objects and weakmaps. To summarize:

- A key can be a text, a record, or an array. Only the text keys can be enumerated with the `array` function.
- A value of `null` deletes a field.
- Path expressions with missing objects do not fail. They just produce `null`.
- Arrays only accept integers as keys and enforce their bounds.

We start with a centralized `fail` function.

```
function fail(what = "fail") {
    throw new Error(what);
}
```

The only stateful variable in this file is `weakmap_of_weakmaps`. It binds weakmaps to records. Most records will not need weakmaps, but those that do get their weakmaps from `weakmap_of_weakmaps`.

The `get` function retrieves the value of a field from a record or an element from an array. It also implements call-a-function-as-a-method by returning a function. If things go wrong for any reason, the `null` object is returned, which JavaScript knows as `undefined`.

```
let weakmap_of_weakmaps = new WeakMap();

function get(container, key) {
    try {
        if (Array.isArray(container) || typeof container === "string") {
            const element_nr = big_float.number(key);
            return (
                Number.isSafeInteger(element_nr)
                ? container[(
                    element_nr >= 0
                    ? element_nr
                    : container.length + element_nr
                )]
                : undefined
            );
        }
        if (typeof container === "object") {
            if (big_float.is_big_float(key)) {
                key = big_float.string(key);
            }
            return (
                typeof key === "string"
                ? container[key]
                : weakmap_of_weakmaps.get(container).get(key)
            );
        }
        if (typeof container === "function") {
            return function (...rest) {
                return container(key, rest);
            };
        }
    } catch (ignore) {
    }
}
```

The `get` function can be accessed as the ƒ[] functino.

The `set` function is the way to add, update, or delete a field of a record, or update an element of an array. If anything goes wrong, it fails. The `get` function is very forgiving. The `set` function is not.

```
function set(container, key, value) {
    if (Object.isFrozen(container)) {
        return fail("set");
    }
    if (Array.isArray(container)) {
```

Arrays use only big float for keys.

```
        let element_nr = big_float.number(key);
        if (!Number.isSafeInteger(element_nr)) {
            return fail("set");
        }
```

Negative indexes are aliases, so that [-1] sets the last element.

```
        if (element_nr < 0) {
            element_nr = container.length + element_nr;
        }
```

The key must be in the allocated range of the array.

```
        if (element_nr < 0 || element_nr >= container.length) {
            return fail("set");
        }
        container[element_nr] = value;
    } else {
        if (big_float.is_big_float(key)) {
            key = big_float.string(key);
        }
```

If the key is a string, then it is an object update.

```
        if (typeof key === "string") {
            if (value === undefined) {
                delete container[key];
            } else {
                container[key] = value;
            }
        } else {
```

Otherwise, this is a weakmap update. There will be a weakmap associated with each record with object keys. Note that `typeof key !== "object"` is `false` when `key` is an array.

```
            if (typeof key !== "object") {
                return fail("set");
            }
            let weakmap = weakmap_of_weakmaps.get(container);
```

If there is not yet a weakmap associated with this container, then make wun.

```
            if (weakmap === undefined) {
                if (value === undefined) {
                    return;
                }
                weakmap = new WeakMap();
                weakmap_of_weakmaps.set(container, weakmap);
            }
```

Update the weakmap.

```
            if (value === undefined) {
                weakmap.delete(key);
            } else {
                weakmap.set(key, value);
            }
        }
    }
}
```

There is a group of functions that make arrays, numbers, records, and texts.

```
    function array(zeroth, wunth, ...rest) {
```

The `array` function does the work of `new Array`, `array.fill`, `array.slice`, `Object.keys`, `string.split`, and more.

```
        if (big_float.is_big_float(zeroth)) {
            const dimension = big_float.number(zeroth);
            if (!Number.isSafeInteger(dimension) || dimension < 0) {
                return fail("array");
```

```
        }
        let newness = new Array(dimension);
        return (
            (wunth === undefined || dimension === 0)
            ? newness
            : (
                typeof wunth === "function"
                ? newness.map(wunth)
                : newness.fill(wunth)
            )
        );
    }
    if (Array.isArray(zeroth)) {
        if (typeof wunth === "function") {
            return zeroth.map(wunth);
        }
        return zeroth.slice(big_float.number(wunth), big_float.number(rest[0]));
    }
    if (typeof zeroth === "object") {
        return Object.keys(zeroth);
    }
    if (typeof zeroth === "string") {
        return zeroth.split(wunth || "");
    }
    return fail("array");
}

function number(a, b) {
    return (
        typeof a === "string"
        ? big_float.make(a, b)
        : (
            typeof a === "boolean"
            ? big_float.make(Number(a))
            : (
                big_float.is_big_float(a)
                ? a
                : undefined
            )
        )
    );
}

function record(zeroth, wunth) {
    const newness = Object.create(null);
    if (zeroth === undefined) {
        return newness;
    }
    if (Array.isArray(zeroth)) {
        if (wunth === undefined) {
            wunth = true;
        }
        zeroth.forEach(function (element, element_nr) {
            set(
                newness,
                element,
                (
```

```
                        Array.isArray(wunth)
                        ? wunth[element_nr]
                        : (
                            typeof wunth === "function"
                            ? wunth(element)
                            : wunth
                        )
                    )
                );
            });
            return newness;
        }
        if (typeof zeroth === "object") {
            if (wunth === undefined) {
                return Object.assign(newness, zeroth);
            }
            if (typeof wunth === "object") {
                return Object.assign(newness, zeroth, wunth);
            }
            if (Array.isArray(wunth)) {
                wunth.forEach(function (key) {
                    let value = zeroth[key];
                    if (value !== undefined) {
                        newness[key] = value;
                    }
                });
                return newness;
            }
        }
        return fail("record");
    }

    function text(zeroth, wunth, twoth) {
        if (typeof zeroth === "string") {
            return (zeroth.slice(big_float.number(wunth), big_float.number(twoth)));
        }
        if (big_float.is_big_float(zeroth)) {
            return big_float.string(zeroth, wunth);
        }
        if (Array.isArray(zeroth)) {
            let separator = wunth;
            if (typeof wunth !== "string") {
                if (wunth !== undefined) {
                    return fail("string");
                }
                separator = "";
            }
            return zeroth.join(separator);
        }
        if (typeof zeroth === "boolean") {
            return String(zeroth);
        }
    }
```

stone is a deep freeze.

```
function stone(object) {
    if (!Object.isFrozen(object)) {
        object = Object.freeze(object);
        if (typeof object === "object") {
            if (Array.isArray(object)) {
                object.forEach(stone);
            } else {
                Object.keys(object).forEach(function (key) {
                    stone(object[key]);
                });
            }
        }
    }
    return object;
}
```

There is a group of predicate functions that are used to identify the types of things.

```
function boolean_(any) {
    return typeof any === "boolean";
}

function function_(any) {
    return typeof any === "function";
}

function integer_(any) {
    return (
        big_float.is_big_float(any)
        && big_float.normalize(any).exponent === 0
    );
}

function number_(any) {
    return big_float.is_big_float(any);
}

function record_(any) {
    return (
        any !== null
        && typeof any === "object"
        && !big_float.is_big_float(any)
    );
}

function text_(any) {
    return typeof any === "string";
}
```

There is a group of logical functions. These are the functino versions. They are not short-circuiting. Only the operator versions are able to lazily evaluate their operands.

```
function assert_boolean(boolean) {
    return (
        typeof boolean === "boolean"
        ? boolean
        : fail("boolean")
    );
```

```
    }

    function and(zeroth, wunth) {
        return assert_boolean(zeroth) && assert_boolean(wunth);
    }

    function or(zeroth, wunth) {
        return assert_boolean(zeroth) || assert_boolean(wunth);
    }

    function not(boolean) {
        return !assert_boolean(boolean);
    }

    function ternary(zeroth, wunth, twoth) {
        return (
            assert_boolean(zeroth)
            ? wunth
            : twoth
        );
    }

    function default_function(zeroth, wunth) {
        return (
            zeroth === undefined
            ? wunth
            : zeroth
        );
    }
```

There is a group of relational operators.

```
    function eq(zeroth, wunth) {
        return zeroth === wunth || (
            big_float.is_big_float(zeroth)
            && big_float.is_big_float(wunth)
            && big_float.eq(zeroth, wunth)
        );
    }

    function lt(zeroth, wunth) {
        return (
            zeroth === undefined
            ? false
            : (
                wunth === undefined
                ? true
                : (
                    (
                        big_float.is_big_float(zeroth)
                        && big_float.is_big_float(wunth)
                    )
                    ? big_float.lt(zeroth, wunth)
                    : (
                        (typeof zeroth === typeof wunth && (
                            typeof zeroth === "string"
                            || typeof zeroth === "number"
                        ))
```

```
                        ? zeroth < wunth
                        : fail("lt")
                )
            )
        )
    );
}

function ge(zeroth, wunth) {
    return !lt(zeroth, wunth);
}

function gt(zeroth, wunth) {
    return lt(wunth, zeroth);
}

function le(zeroth, wunth) {
    return !lt(wunth, zeroth);
}

function ne(zeroth, wunth) {
    return !eq(wunth, zeroth);
}
```

There is a group of arithmetic operators.

```
function add(a, b) {
    return (
        (big_float.is_big_float(a) && big_float.is_big_float(b))
        ? big_float.add(a, b)
        : undefined
    );
}

function sub(a, b) {
    return (
        (big_float.is_big_float(a) && big_float.is_big_float(b))
        ? big_float.sub(a, b)
        : undefined
    );
}

function mul(a, b) {
    return (
        (big_float.is_big_float(a) && big_float.is_big_float(b))
        ? big_float.mul(a, b)
        : undefined
    );
}

function div(a, b) {
    return (
        (big_float.is_big_float(a) && big_float.is_big_float(b))
        ? big_float.div(a, b)
        : undefined
    );
}
```

```
function max(a, b) {
    return (
        lt(b, a)
        ? a
        : b
    );
}

function min(a, b) {
    return (
        lt(a, b)
        ? a
        : b
    );
}

function abs(a) {
    return (
        big_float.is_big_float(a)
        ? big_float.abs(a)
        : undefined
    );
}

function fraction(a) {
    return (
        big_float.is_big_float(a)
        ? big_float.fraction(a)
        : undefined
    );
}

function integer(a) {
    return (
        big_float.is_big_float(a)
        ? big_float.integer(a)
        : undefined
    );
}

function neg(a) {
    return (
        big_float.is_big_float(a)
        ? big_float.neg(a)
        : undefined
    );
}
```

There is a group of bitwise functions. The work is done by `big_integer`.

```
function bitand(a, b) {
    return big_float.make(
        big_integer.and(
            big_float.integer(a).coefficient,
            big_float.integer(b).coefficient
        ),
        big_integer.wun
    );
```

```
    }

    function bitdown(a, nr_bits) {
        return big_float.make(
            big_integer.shift_down(
                big_float.integer(a).coefficient,
                big_float.number(nr_bits)
            ),
            big_integer.wun
        );
    }

    function bitmask(nr_bits) {
        return big_float.make(big_integer.mask(big_float.number(nr_bits)));
    }

    function bitor(a, b) {
        return big_float.make(
            big_integer.or(
                big_float.integer(a).coefficient,
                big_float.integer(b).coefficient
            ),
            big_integer.wun
        );
    }

    function bitup(a, nr_bits) {
        return big_float.make(
            big_integer.shift_up(
                big_float.integer(a).coefficient,
                big_float.number(nr_bits)
            ),
            big_integer.wun
        );
    }

    function bitxor(a, b) {
        return big_float.make(
            big_integer.xor(
                big_float.integer(a).coefficient,
                big_float.integer(b).coefficient
            ),
            big_integer.wun
        );
    }
```

You might remember the ƒ() functino from JSCheck.

```
    function resolve(value, ...rest) {
        return (
            typeof value === "function"
            ? value(...rest)
            : value
        );
    }
```

There are two concatenation operators. They both return `null` if either argument is null. Otherwise, they attempt to coerce their arguments to texts. The *f≈* functino includes a space separator if both operands are not the empty text.

```
function cat(zeroth, wunth) {
    zeroth = text(zeroth);
    wunth = text(wunth);
    if (typeof zeroth === "string" && typeof wunth === "string") {
        return zeroth + wunth;
    }
}

function cats(zeroth, wunth) {
    zeroth = text(zeroth);
    wunth = text(wunth);
    if (typeof zeroth === "string" && typeof wunth === "string") {
        return (
            zeroth === ""
            ? wunth
            : (
                wunth === ""
                ? zeroth
                : zeroth + " " + wunth
            )
        );
    }
}
```

And then the miscellaneous functions.

```
function char(any) {
    return String.fromCodePoint(big_float.number(any));
}

function code(any) {
    return big_float.make(any.codePointAt(0));
}

function length(linear) {
    return (
        (Array.isArray(linear) || typeof linear === "string")
        ? big_float.make(linear.length)
        : undefined
    );
}
```

All of that goodness is packed into a runtime object.

```
export default stone({
    abs,
    add,
    and,
    array,
    assert_boolean,
    bitand,
    bitdown,
    bitmask,
    bitor,
    bitup,
```

```
    bitxor,
    boolean_,
    cat,
    cats,
    char,
    code,
    default: default_function,
    div,
    eq,
    fail,
    fraction,
    function_,
    ge,
    get,
    gt,
    integer,
    integer_,
    le,
    length,
    max,
    min,
    mul,
    ne,
    neg,
    not,
    number,
    number_,
    or,
    record,
    record_,
    resolve,
    set,
    stone,
    sub,
    ternary,
    text,
    text_
});
```

## Chapter 30

How Wat! Works

●●●●○

> Enough making fun of languages that suck.
> Let's talk about JavaScript.
> *Gary Bernhardt*

On January 12, 2012, at the CodeMash conference in a Sandusky, Ohio indoor water park, Gary Bernhardt presented a lightning talk titled *Wat*.

Bernhardt displayed some of the absurd anomalies in Ruby and JavaScript. After each example he showed a funny picture that was captioned with "WAT". The crowd loved it. It is a classic bit. *Wat* has become *The Aristocrats* of JavaScript.

The video of his brief performance is still accessable somehow on the internet. Many imitators have gone on to produce similar shows. Some simply repeated Bernhardt's material, some have expanded the act, adding new gags. Some were able to get genuine laughter from the audience, as Bernhardt did. Some merely stank up the room.

I have tried in this book to avoid most of the bad parts of JavaScript, but in this chapter we are going to pull the monster's pants down. I am going to show you some of the gags from *Wat* and similar talks and explain how they work. This is not going to be funny or even pleasant.

Many of the jokes are due to the type coercion algorithms behind JavaScript's == *equal sign equal sign* and + *plus sign* operators. The type coercion rules are complex, unmemorable, and in some cases, as you will see, wrong. That is why I recommend against use of == *equal sign equal sign*. It implements ECMAScript's Abstract Equality Comparison Algorithm. It is a can of worms that is not worth opening. Always use === *equal sign equal sign equal sign* instead. Always.

Some people do not like === *equal sign equal sign equal sign* because it looks 50% stupider than == *equal sign equal sign* which is itself twice as stupid as = *equal sign*. Nevertheless, the correct equality operator in JavaScript is === *equal sign equal sign equal sign*. Avoid == *equal sign equal sign*, the incorrect equality operator.

I can not give similar advice about avoiding + *plus sign* because + *plus sign* is the only practical way to add numbers. So enjoy the worms.

```
""  == false        // true
[]  == false        // true
null == false       // false
undefined == false  // false
```

The empty string is a falsy value, so a sloppy equals operator might want to conflate it with false. An empty array is not falsy, yet it also compares to false. And null and undefined *are* falsy values, but neither compares to false.

WAT!

```
[] == []                          // false
[] == ![]                         // true
```

Two empty arrays are not the same object, so they are not equal. But the second line is surprising. It appears that JavaScript is a language in which *x* and *not x* can be equal to each other, which would be a seriously laughable incompetence. This is what is happening:

An empty array is truthy, so ![] is false. The sloppy equals operator wants to compare [] and false as numbers even though neither is a number. The empty array is coerced to empty string which is coerced to zero. And false is also coerced to zero. Zero equals zero, so the answer is true.

WAT!

```
[] + []                           // ""
[] + {}                           // "[object Object]"
{} + {}                           // "[object Object][object Object]"
```

All of these cases should produce NaN. This is what NaN is for. Instead, because the values are not numbers, + *plus sign* wants to concatenate them. First it has to coerce them to strings. The Array.prototype.toString() method converts an empty array to an empty string. It would be better if it acted like JSON.stringify() and returned "[]". The worthless Object.prototype.toString() method renders the objects as "[object Object]". Then those strings get concatenated together.

WAT!

```
9999999999999999                  // 10000000000000000
1e23 + 2e23 === 3e23              // false
```

Most of the integers above Number.MAX_SAFE_INTEGER can not be represented exactly.

WAT!

```
"2" < 5                           // true
5 < "11"                          // true
"11" < "2"                        // true
```

Comparing values of different types should raise an exception. Instead, JavaScript attempts to coerce the values so that a comparison can be made. The coercion rules can break transitivity.

WAT!

```
1 < 2 < 3                         // true
3 > 2 > 1                         // false
```

These cases should have been syntax errors because the language does not want to handle them correctly. In the first case, 1 and 2 are compared, producing true. Then true and 3 are compared. true is coerced to 1. 1 is less than 3, so it is true. So it accidentally gives the right answer. An error that sometimes gives the right answer can easily avoid detection by testing.

In the second case, 3 and 2 are compared, producing `true`. Then `true` and 1 are compared. `true` is coerced to 1. 1 is not less than 1, so it gives `false`.

WAT!

```
"2" + 1                           // "21"
"2" - 1                           // 1
```

The other arithmetic operators also do type coercion, but they use very different rules than + *plus sign* uses. You should manage your types correctly to avoid this sloppiness. Do not do arithmetic on strings. That is what numbers are for.

WAT!

```
Math.min() > Math.max()           // true
```

These functions are sloppy. When passed nothing, they should return `undefined` or `NaN` or perhaps raise an exception. Instead, `Math.min()` returns `Infinity`, and `Math.max()` returns `-Infinity`.

WAT!

```
Math instanceof Math              // throws exception
NaN instanceof NaN                // throws exception
"wat" instanceof String           // false
```

Use of `instanceof` in Java is usually evidence of a failure to understand how to use polymorphism. JavaScript's `instanceof` is not the same as Java's. I do not recommend use of `instanceof` in any language.

WAT!

```
isNaN("this string is not NaN") // true
```

The global `isNaN` and `isFinite` functions are broken. Use `Number.isNaN` and `Number.isFinite` instead.

WAT!

```
((name) => [name])("wat")         // ["wat"]
((name) => {name})("wat")         // undefined
```

The first case shows an example of a fat arrow (or *fart*) function. Farts are an abbreviated way of writing functions. The thing to the left of the fart is a parameter list. The thing to the right of the fart is an expression. The value of the expression is the return value of the function. You do not need to type `function` or `return`. In this case the return value is an array containing the function's argument. This is good.

The second case should reasonably return `{name: "wat"}`, not `undefined`. Unfortunately, JavaScript assumes that a left brace after a fart is a block, not an object literal. This block contains a variable name. Automatic semicolon insertion deposits a semicolon after the name, turning it into a useless expression statement that does nothing. Lacking a `return` statement, the function returns the default return value, `undefined`.

This is why I recommend avoiding farts. They are also easily confused with the comparison operators <= and >=. The small typing convenience is just not worth it.

WAT!

```
function first(w, a, t) {
    return {
        w,
        a,
        t
    };
}
first("wat", "wat", "wat");     // {w: "wat", a: "wat", t: "wat"}

function second(w, a, t) {
    return
        {w, a, t};
}
second("wat", "wat", "wat");    // undefined
```

The first return statement works as expected, returning a new object.

The second return statement differs only in its whitespace, and yet it returns undefined. Automatic semicolon insertion inserted a semicolon after return. The left brace of the object literal is now in statement position where it is treated as a block. The block contains a useless expression statement. In expression position, comma is an operator, not a separator, so this code does not produce a syntax error.

Automatic semicolon insertion is not a feature. It is a hazard. It was added to the language specifically for beginners who might not be sure where to put the semicolon. You should rely on automatic semicolon insertion when you want it to appear that your code was written by a beginner.

WAT!

## Chapter 31

How This Book Works

•••••

> I only ask to be free. The butterflies are
> free.
>
> *Harold Skimpole*

Include

To help put the book together, I made an eventual `include` function. I used it to
assemble the individual chapter files into wun big book file. I used it to insert
the executable JavaScript source code into the chapters. And I used it to assemble
JavaScript code fragments together into the `.js` files that are available at `github.com/`
`douglascrockford`.

---

include(*callback*, *string*, *get_inclusion*, *max_depth*)

The `include` function replaces `@include` expressions in a string with other strings. If
there are no `@include` expressions, then the original string is the result.

Your *callback*(*result*) function is eventually given the processed *result* string.

Your *string* may contain zero or more `@include` expressions.

　　`@include "`*key*`"`

There is a space between the `@include` and the opening `"` *double quote*. Each `@include`
expression is replaced with the inclusion string associated with the *key* if possible. A
key (which could be a filename) is wrapped in parens.

Your *get_inclusion*(*callback*, *key*) function takes a *key* string and eventually passes
the resulting inclusion string to *callback*(*inclusion*). Your *get_inclusion* function
could access a file system, database, source control system, content manager, or JSON
Object. If inclusions are coming from files, and if the environment is Node.js, then
your *get_inclusion* function could look like this:

```
function my_little_get_inclusion(callback, key) {
    return (
        (key[0] >= "a" && key[0] <= "z")
        ? fs.readFile(key, "utf8", function (ignore, data) {
            return callback(data);
        })
}
```

```
            : callback()
    );
}
```

If somehow an `include` package went rogue (as managed packages are known to do), it could not cause much damage with `my_little_get_inclusion`, but it could cause an enormous amount of damage if it had direct access to `fs`.

An inclusion string may contain more `@include` expressions. The *max_depth* argument limits the recursion depth to prevent infinite include loops.

This is the implementation:

```
const rx_include = /
    @include \u0020 " ( [^ " @ ]+ ) "
/;

// Capturing groups:
//   [0] The whole '@include' expression
//   [1] The key

export default Object.freeze(function include(
    callback,
    string,
    get_inclusion,
    max_depth = 4
) {
```

The `include` function does not need direct access to or knowledge of the file system or the database or anything else because that capability is passed in as your `get_inclusion` function. That makes the `include` function versatile and trustworthy.

Nothing is returned. The result is communicated eventually through the `callback`.

```
    let object_of_matching;
    let result = "";
```

The `minion` and its assistants do all of the work. The main `minion` searches for `@include` expressions and calls the `get_inclusion` function with its findings. The `assistant_minion` makes a recursive call to `include` to process the inclusion. The `junior_assistant_minion` appends the processed inclusion to the result.

```
    function minion() {
```

If there is no more string to scan, deliver the result.

```
        if (string === "") {
            return callback(result);
        }
```

Try matching the regular expression against the remaining string.

```
        object_of_matching = rx_include.exec(string);
```

If there is no match, then our work is done.

```
        if (!object_of_matching) {
            return callback(result + string);
        }
```

The characters to the left of the expression are part of the result. Remove that scanned material from the string.

```
    result += string.slice(0, object_of_matching.index);
    string = string.slice(
        object_of_matching.index + object_of_matching[0].length
    );
```

Call the `get_inclusion` function to obtain the replacement string, passing the `assistant_minion` and the key.

```
    return get_inclusion(
        assistant_minion,
        object_of_matching[1]
    );
}
```

```
function junior_assistant_minion(processed_inclusion) {
```

Take the inclusion that was processed by `include` and append it to the result. Then call `minion` to begin the search for the next `@include` expression.

```
    result += processed_inclusion;
    return minion();
}
```

```
function assistant_minion(inclusion) {
```

If `get_inclusion` did not deliver a string, then add the `@include` expression to the result, effectively leaving that part of the string unchanged.

```
    if (typeof inclusion !== "string") {
        result += object_of_matching[0];
        return minion();
    }
```

The inclusion might contain its own `@include` expressions, so we call `include` to process those, passing the `junior_assistant_minion` that adds the processed inclusion to the result. The `max_depth` is reduced to guard against infinte recursion.

```
    return include(
        junior_assistant_minion,
        inclusion,
        get_inclusion,
        max_depth - 1
    );
}
```

Those are the minions. Now back to `include`. If we are out of our depth, then call the `callback`.

```
    if (max_depth <= 0) {
        callback(string);
    } else {
```

The `include` function makes the three minion functions and calls the main `minion`.

```
        minion();
    }
});
```

Colophon

Century Schoolbook is a transitional serif typeface designed by Morris Fuller Benton (1919). It was based on Century Roman by Linn Boyd Benton (1894), his father. New Century Schoolbook was wun of a small handful of typefaces that were included in Apple's LaserWriter Plus. Because of the limited available of typefaces at the time, Century Schoolbook was heavily used. As a result of that overexposure, it was thought to be ordinary, uninteresting, and boring. It is now a century old, and it is still very readable and brilliant.

The section titles use Daley Bold, which I designed for this book. It is based on Susan Kare's Chicago 12, the original Macintosh system font. Those first menu bars and drop downs and buttons and dialogs were set in Chicago 12. It was the most visible part of the introduction of modern user interfaces to the mainstream. To get rid of the bitmap jaggies, I borrowed an idea from ITC Machine, designed by Ronne Bonder and Tom Carnase (1970), using straight lines instead of curves.

The code font is Programma, which I designed for this book. It borrows (steals) ideas from Microgramma by Aldo Novarese and Alessandro Butti (1952), Inconsolata by Raph Levien, and Twentieth Century by Sol Hess (1959).

The Portable Document File that was used to print this book was processed by Prince 12. `www.princexml.com`

The cover was designed by Jim Cokas.

This book is published by Virgule-Solidus. *Virgule* is a latin word meaning *slash*. *Solidus* is a latin word meaning *slash*. // *slash slash* is an important component of the World Wide Web's URLs and is the beginning of a comment in JavaScript and many other languages.

Acknowledgements

I wish to thank Edwin Aoki, Vladimir Bacvanski, Leonardo Bonacci, George Boole, Dennis Cline, Rolando Dimaandal, Bill Franz, Louis Gottlieb, Bob Hablutzel, Grace Murray Hopper, Matthew Johnson, Alan Karp, Gottried Leibniz, Håkon Wium Lie, Linda Merry, Jeff Meyer, Chip Morningstar, Евгений Орехов, Ben Pardo, Claude Shannon, Steve Souders, Tehuti, and most of all, Professor Lisa von Drake.

Post Credits Section

I have experienced these paradigm shifts in my career as a programmer:

- High Level Languages.
- Structured Programming.
- Object Oriented Programming.
- Functional Programming.

The biggest beneficiaries of each of these advances were the programmers who were now able to accomplish more and better work with less effort. The biggest opponents of those advances were those same programmers. They met the new paradigms with suspicion, discomfort, and disbelief. They used their intelligence and experience to craft arguments that felt convincing, but which in hindsight were simply wrong. They were successful using the old paradigm and were unwilling to accept the new wun. It can be very difficult to tell the difference between the new paradigm and a really bad idea.

Each of the shifts took over twenty years to be widely adopted. Functional Programming took twice that. The reason it takes so long is that we do not change minds. We have to wait for a generation of programmers to retire or die before we can get critical mass on the next paradigm.

Max Planck observed a similar thing in Physics, which is now known as Planck's Principle. He wrote:

> A new scientific truth does not triumph by convincing its opponents and making them see the light, but rather because its opponents eventually die, and a new generation grows up that is familiar with it.

He also said it more concisely:

> Science advances wun funeral at a time.

I think it should be obvious by now that the next paradigm is Distributed Eventual Programming. This is not a new idea. It goes back at least to the discovery of the Actor Model (1973). We have made some steps forward since that, but we have also made mistakes with things like remote procedure calls that try to do the distributed thing while holding onto the sequential programming model. I think the reason that JavaScript is interesting is that it was specifically created to do Distributed Eventual Programming. Being developed in ten days, it did not get everything right. It is also a multiparadigm language that encourages retention of the old paradigm. And since its creation, champions of the old paradigm have been trying to drag JavaScript back to its FORTRAN roots.

Wun More Thing

All through this material, you probably noticed the strange spelling of **wun**. It might have distracted you, confused you, or annoyed you. The arguments against the use of that spelling are traditional. It is not what we are used to. It is not how we were taught. It is not what we know. That is all true, but given the conventions of English pronounciation, **wun** should be the correct spelling. It is a bug fix.

Our emotional reaction to **wun** is the same as our emotional reaction to a new paradigm.

The secret to adopting a new paradigm before dying is to experience it. That is easier to do in Programming than in Physics because all you have to do is write good programs. I can talk about making a function that returns a function, and you can understand those words and so think you understand what that is about. But in fact, you can not understand it until you experience it. Write lots of functions that return functions. Write lots of functions that make tail calls. You will get to the point where it stops being unnatural. You can not get there by reading about it or talking about it. If you write well in JavaScript, JavaScript will teach you. If you write badly in JavaScript, JavaScript will punish you. But you already knew that.

Perhaps in my next book we will do something about the spelling of **two**.

Notes

Music is the silence between the notes.
Claude Debussy

Made in the USA
Coppell, TX
21 January 2020